# HOW THE
# IRISH
# BECAME
# WHITE

# HOW THE
# IRISH
# BECAME
# WHITE

Noel Ignatiev

Routledge
New York   London

Published in 1995 by

Routledge
29 West 35th Street
New York, NY 10001

Published in Great Britain by

Routledge
11 New Fetter Lane
London EC4P 4EE

Library of Congress Cataloging-in-Publication Data

Ignatiev, Noel.
    How the Irish became white / Noel Ignatiev.
       p.   cm.
    ISBN 0-415-91384-5
    1. Irish Americans—Cultural assimilation.  2. Irish Americans—Politics
and government.  3. Afro-Americans—Relations with Irish Americans.
I. Title.
E184.I6I36 1995
973'.0491'62—dc20                                                    95–31047
                                                                         CIP

The Irish, who, at home, readily sympathize with the oppressed everywhere, are instantly taught when they step upon our soil to hate and despise the Negro.... Sir, the Irish-American will one day find out his mistake.

> — *Frederick Douglass, May 10, 1853*

Passage to the United States seems to produce the same effect upon the exile of Erin as the eating of the forbidden fruit did upon Adam and Eve. In the morning, they were pure, loving, and innocent; in the evening guilty.

> — *The Liberator, August 11, 1854*

The Irish are the blacks of Europe. So say it loud— I'm black and I'm proud.

> — *The Commitments, 1991*

# CONTENTS

LIST OF ILLUSTRATIONS IX

ACKNOWLEDGMENTS XI

INTRODUCTION 1

I SOMETHING IN THE AIR 6

II WHITE NEGROES AND SMOKED IRISH 34

III THE TRANSUBSTANTIATION OF
AN IRISH REVOLUTIONARY 62

IV THEY SWUNG THEIR PICKS 92

V THE TUMULTUOUS REPUBLIC 124

VI FROM PROTESTANT ASCENDANCY
TO WHITE REPUBLIC 148

AFTERWORD 178

NOTES 189

INDEX 229

# LIST OF ILLUSTRATIONS

Cartoon, Edward W. Clay, lithograph, *American Sympathy
and Irish Blackguardism* (New York, 1843).                    4

Cartoon, "Irish Emigrant" in *Diogenes, Hys Lantern*
August 21, 1852, p. 68.                                       33

Cartoon, "Different Specie-s" in *Diogenes, Hys Lantern*
October 23, 1852, p. 158.                                     61

Broadside, woodcut with letterpress, *Results of
Abolitionism* (n.p., ca. 1835).                              91

Frontispiece illustration to *Life & Adventures of
Charles Anderson Chester* (Philadelphia, 1850).             122

Illustrated title page, *A Full and Complete Account of
the Late Awful Riots* (Philadelphia, 1848).                 147

# ACKNOWLEDGMENTS

Theodore Allen many years ago introduced me to the notion of the white race as a socially constructed category; he also suggested the topic of the book, and commented on the finished manuscript.

Stephan Thernstrom, the advisor to this project when it was a dissertation, extended me the respect of allowing me to proceed at my own pace, even when it must have seemed I was barely moving forward. He served as the critical reader in my mind, forcing me to examine and defend my assumptions. Although we disagree about many things, he never once sought to impose his views on me; his comments were invariably directed toward strengthening my own argument, and his fairmindedness will always be a model to me in my own teaching.

Alan Heimert, David Roediger, Alex Saxton, and Werner Sollors were encouraging and helpful from the beginning. They all read the entire manuscript, and made useful comments.

I was fortunate to have the regular company of people who were interested in what I was doing and who never (well, hardly ever) showed boredom with my monomaniac passion, and instead were always available to discuss it with me and allow me to talk out my ideas. These people, John Garvey, Loren Goldner, Jim Kaplan, Peter Linebaugh, Kate Shea, and Steve Whitman, constituted for me something of a standing committee on the Irish question.

Iver Bernstein, John Bracey, Peter Coclanis, Mary Connaughton, Brenda Coughlin, Emily Cousins, Jeff Ferguson, Ferruccio Gambino, Herbert Hill, Carolyn Karcher, Joel Perlmann, Theresa Perry, Marcus Rediker, Adam Sabra, Ray Sapirstein, Kevin Van Anglen, and Ted Widmer all contributed in various ways, either helping me develop my ideas, reading parts of the work-in-progress, or providing me with criticism, research materials, and other kinds of support as I required. Kerby Miller generously shared with me an unpublished paper he wrote many years ago on the origins of Irish-American attitudes toward the Negro.

Cecelia Cancellaro, editor at Routledge, and Adam Bohannon, editorial and production manager at Routledge, were encouraging and helpful in getting the book to publication.

To any I have omitted, I apologize. I am not sure that having so many friends willing to talk with me about the project helped me get it done more quickly, but I am sure their participation made it a better work. Its errors of fact or judgment, like its profits and labors, are mine.

The staffs of various libraries provided assistance in the patient, generous tradition of their trade. I am particularly indebted to Nat Bunker of the Acquisitions Department at Harvard's Widener Library, and Phil Lapsansky at the Library Company of Philadelphia (without whose help it is difficult to imagine either my own or any of the recent books on nineteenth-century Philadelphia getting written).

During the years I worked on this project, except for the last, I was a graduate instructor in the Program in History and Literature at Harvard. The freedom to develop my own courses of instruction, the friendship of colleagues, and the students who challenged me made it quite simply the best teaching job in the world (except for the money), and I am grateful. To the Whiting Foundation, which provided me with a fellowship that allowed me to take this project over the top, I am grateful as well.

When I was a boy, my father, Irving Ignatin, used to speak to me of Harry Levin (who wrote *The Power of Blackness*). "Do you know how smart he must be," he would ask, "to be a professor of English at Harvard with a name like Harry Levin?" (That was a long time ago.) By the time I got to Harvard, my father no longer had all his wits. Every time I saw him, he would ask what I did for a living. On hearing me explain my duties as a graduate student and teaching fellow, he would invariably ask, "And for this they give you money?" When I think of some of the things I did earlier to earn my bread, his skepticism strikes me as quite reasonable.

My mother, Carrie Ignatin, supported me loyally through my years of labor on this project, as she did on everything I ever undertook. She sent me newspaper clippings and every scrap of material she came across that had to do with relations between Irish- and Afro-Americans, some of which have found their way into the final work.

Both my mother and father died before I finished this book, but their marks are on every page. To their memory it is dedicated. *Lux aeterna.*

# INTRODUCTION

No biologist has ever been able to provide a satisfactory definition of "race"—that is, a definition that includes all members of a given race and excludes all others. Attempts to give the term a biological foundation lead to absurdities: parents and children of different races, or the well-known phenomenon that a white woman can give birth to a black child, but a black woman can never give birth to a white child.[1] The only logical conclusion is that people are members of different races because they have been assigned to them.

Outside these labels and the racial oppression that accompanies them, the only race is the human. I'll be examining connections between concepts of race and acts of oppression. "By considering the notion of 'racial oppression' in terms of the substantive, the operative element, namely 'oppression,' it is possible to avoid the contradictions and howling absurdities that result from attempts to splice genetics and sociology. By examining racial oppression as a particular system of oppression—like gender oppression or class oppression or national oppression—we find further footing for analyzing...the peculiar function of the 'white race'....The hallmark of racial oppression [is the reduction of] all members of the oppressed group to one undifferentiated social status, a status beneath that of any member of any social class" within the dominant group.[2] It follows, therefore, that the white race consists of those who partake of the privileges of the white skin in this society. Its most wretched members share a status higher, in certain respects, than that of the most exalted persons excluded from it.

This book looks at how one group of people became white. Put another way, it asks how the Catholic Irish, an oppressed race in Ireland, became part of an oppressing race in America. It is an attempt to reassess immigrant assimilation and the formation (or non-formation) of an American working class.

The Irish who emigrated to America in the eighteenth and nineteenth centuries were fleeing caste oppression and a system of landlordism that made the material conditions of the Irish peasant comparable to those of an American slave. They came to a society in which color was important in determining social position. It was not a pattern they were familiar with and they bore no responsibility for it; nevertheless, they adapted to it in short order.

When they first began arriving here in large numbers they were, in the words of Mr. Dooley, given a shovel and told to start digging up the place as if they owned it. On the rail beds and canals they labored for low wages under dangerous conditions; in the South they were occasionally employed where it did not make sense to risk the life of a slave. As they came to the cities, they were crowded into districts that became centers of crime, vice, and disease.

There they commonly found themselves thrown together with free Negroes. Irish- and Afro-Americans fought each other and the police, socialized and occasionally intermarried, and developed a common culture of the lowly. They also both suffered the scorn of those better situated. Along with Jim Crow and Jim Dandy, the drunken, belligerent, and foolish Pat and Bridget were stock characters on the early stage. In antebellum America it was speculated that if racial amalgamation was ever to take place it would begin between those two groups.

As we know, things turned out otherwise. The outcome was not the inevitable consequence of blind historic forces, still less of biology, but the result of choices made, by the Irish and others, from among available alternatives. To enter the white race was a strategy to secure an advantage in a competitive society.

What did it mean to the Irish to become white in America? It did not mean that they all became rich, or even "middle-class" (however that is defined); to this day there are plenty of poor Irish. Nor did it mean that they all became the social equals of the Saltonstalls and van Rensselaers; even the marriage of Grace Kelly to the Prince of Monaco and the election of John F. Kennedy as President did not eliminate all barriers to Irish entry into certain exclusive circles. To Irish laborers, to become white meant at first that they could sell themselves piecemeal instead of being sold for life, and later that they could compete for jobs in all spheres instead of being confined to certain work; to Irish entrepreneurs, it meant that they could function outside of a segregated market. To both of these groups it meant that they were citizens of a democratic republic, with the right to elect and be elected, to be tried by a jury of their peers, to live wherever they could afford, and to spend, without racially imposed restrictions, whatever money they managed to acquire. In becoming white the Irish ceased to be Green.

Chapter One frames the study. It looks at the Irish-American response to the 1841 appeal by the "Liberator," Daniel O'Connell, to join with the abolitionists; Chapter Two turns back to the status of Catholics in Ireland and early contacts of Irish emigrants with American race patterns; Chapter Three uses the career of an early Irish immigrant to show how the Party of Jefferson became the Party of Van Buren, and the role it played in making the Irish white; Chapter Four looks at the labor market; Chapter Five examines the effect of anti-Negro rioting by the Irish and others, not on the direct victims but on those doing the rioting; Chapter Six recounts the Irish triumph over nativism, by tracing the career of a Philadelphia politician who played an important, if generally unknown, role in national politics in 1876; and the Afterword is a review of the literature, plus concluding remarks.

In viewing entry into the white race as something the Irish did "on" (though not by) themselves, this book seeks to make them the actors in their own history.

On one occasion many years ago, I was sitting on my front step when my neighbor came out of the house next door carrying her small child, whom she placed in her automobile. She turned away from him for a moment, and as she started to close the car door, I saw that the child had put his hand where it would be crushed when the door was closed. I shouted to the woman to stop. She halted in mid-motion, and when she realized what she had almost done, an amazing thing happened: she began laughing, then broke into tears and began hitting the child. It was the most intense and dramatic display of conflicting emotions I have ever beheld. My attitude toward the subjects of this study accommodates stresses similar to those I witnessed in that mother.

# I

# SOMETHING IN THE AIR

In 1841 sixty thousand Irish issued an Address to their compatriots in America calling upon them to join with the abolitionists in the struggle against slavery. Heading the list of signers was the name of Daniel O'Connell, known throughout Ireland as the Liberator. The Address was the first time Irish-Americans, as a group, were asked to choose between supporting and opposing the color line. Their response marked a turning point in their evolution toward membership in an oppressing race.

To an extent rare in the annals of nations, the history of Ireland between Emmett's Conspiracy of 1803 (aimed at establishing an independent Irish state) and the Great Famine that began in 1845 was the personal story of one man, Daniel O'Connell. He had founded the Catholic Association, the first mass political party in history, which drew its support from low dues collected every week in Catholic churches throughout the country. He had developed the methods of grass roots organizing and the mass meeting which made him the first modern agitator. He had led the campaign for Catholic Emancipation; at a time when Catholics were prohibited from holding public office, an uprising of poor rural voters had elected him to the House of Commons. The campaign succeeded, in 1830, in overturning the last formal restrictions against Catholic participation in public life. He still held his seat in Westminster, where he headed the thirty or so Irish members who constituted something of an Irish party. As a symbol of the esteem his countrymen felt for him, he held the largely honorific post of Lord Mayor of Dublin. O'Connell then led the campaign to repeal the Act of Union of 1800 (which merged the Irish and British Parliments) and restore an Irish parliament under the crown, known as the movement for Home Rule, or Repeal. The Catholic and Irish press, and even general circulation newspapers, in both Ireland and the U.S., frequently reprinted his speeches in parliament and at meetings of the organization he led, the Loyal National Repeal Association. He was the most popular figure in Ireland and among Irish throughout the world.[1]

Ireland had an old antislavery tradition, going back to the Council of Armagh in 1177, which had prohibited Irish trade in English slaves. It was a common boast that in seven centuries no slave had set foot on Irish soil.[2] O'Connell may have been brought to antislavery by the English abolitionist, James Cropper, who argued that Irish textiles could be traded for East Indian sugar, thus dealing at once a blow to Irish poverty and West Indian slavery.[3] In 1830, when O'Connell first entered Parliament, with one other Irish member to support him, a representative of the West India interest approached him, offering the support of their twenty-seven members on Irish issues in return for his silence on the slavery question. He replied, "Gentlemen, God knows I speak for the saddest people the sun sees; but may my right hand forget its cunning, and my tongue cleave to the roof of my mouth, if to save Ireland, even Ireland, I forget the negro one single hour!"[4]

From as early as 1829 O'Connell coupled his denunciations of slavery with attacks on American hypocrisy. "Let America, in the fullness of her pride," he declared, "wave on high her banner of freedom and its blazing stars....In the midst of their laughter and their pride, I point them to the negro children screaming for their mother from whose bosom they have been torn....Let them hoist the flag of liberty, with the whip and rack on one side, and the star of freedom upon the other."[5] It would become a familiar theme of his; he declared that, although he had often wished to visit America, he would not do so while slavery existed there.[6]

O'Connell's declarations aroused resentment in America; he noted in 1835 that "he had given the Americans some severe but merited reproofs, for which they had paid him wages in abuse and scurrility."[7] Among those who expressed their concern were a group of prominent Philadelphia Irish, in a letter to him in February 1838, responding to newspaper reports of a speech he had recently made at an antislavery meeting in London, in which he had reportedly spoken harshly of the

American character. The sentiments attributed to him "had caused no inconsiderable excitement," observed his correspondents. "In the United States," they wrote, "there are hundreds of thousands of our countrymen and countrywomen who have by persecution been driven from the land of their nativity. Here they have been hospitably received and honourably admitted to all the rights, privileges and immunities of native Americans." Noting that "there was not a man [among them] who does not admire and do willing homage to your principles," they went on to remind O'Connell "how jealously and suspiciously we may be looked upon by our native American fellow citizens if the man, whom we have delighted to honour, shall by them believed to have *en masse* deemed them the basest of the base and the vilest of the vile." They asked him to take the appropriate steps to remove from the Irish-Americans "the odium which...had been cast upon them..."[8] In this letter, these spokesmen were giving voice, not for the last time, to the insecurities of an immigrant group whose claim to the "rights, privileges, and immunities of native Americans" was not as secure as they might have wished.

Given O'Connell's record on the slavery question and his influence among Irish everywhere, it was natural that abolitionists in America would wish to make maximum use of his name. On October 20, 1838, Elizur Wright, corresponding secretary of the American Anti-Slavery Society, wrote thanking him for his support: "Severe as your language is, it shall not make you our enemy. While you are dealing death to American slavery you are in truth acting the most friendly part to *genuine* American institutions." Wright continued, "I have been informed that a body of your countrymen in Philadelphia some time since wrote to you for an explanation of language used in one of your Anti-Slavery speeches, and got for answer what it has not suited them to publish! It seems to me that you may do great service to the slave by sending over an address to the Irish portion of our population, giving plainly your views on *slavery*. They will listen to *you*." To make sure O'Connell appreciated the importance and the difficulty of what he would be taking on, Wright added, "In drawing up such an address you will need to bear in mind that, as our parties stand, your countrymen among us hold the balance of power; that three fourths of them at least are democrats and have followed their party to most undemocratic results..."[9]

In January of 1840, James Haughton, Dublin grain merchant and Unitarian, supporter of Repeal, founder of the Hibernian Anti-Slavery Society, and regular correspondent of the leading North American anti-slavery journal of the day, William Lloyd Garrison's *Liberator*, raised with O'Connell the subject of America. "[T]he Irishmen in that country," he wrote, "are such a powerful and influential body that they exercise a paramount influence in the election of the president and in elections of the members of the various legislatures there; but most unfortunately that influence has been given heretofore in favour of slavery....Now with regard to our countrymen in America, the fact stated is most lamentable, your influence over their minds is very great, would you think it wise to address them on this subject one of your powerful appeals?"[10]

The issue came up later that same year at the World Anti-Slavery Convention in London in June, when a Quaker Englishman who had settled in upstate New York, James C. Fuller, asked O'Connell to issue an address to Irish in America. O'Connell replied that he already had such an address in mind.[11] Following the Convention a stream of visitors made their way to Ireland. Among the American abolitionists who toured the country were Garrison, Wendell and Ann Phillips, James G. Birney, and Charles Lenox Remond, who, as a black man, met a particularly enthusiastic response.[12] Remond and his travelling companion John A. Collins, along with Haughton and his fellow Irish abolitionists Richard Allen and Richard Davis Webb, drew up an *Address from the People of Ireland to their Countrymen and Countrywomen in America* in the summer of 1841. By July, fifteen thousand people had signed it, including many Catholic clergymen.[13] Belfast reported that nine thousand signatures were collected during Remond's visit. Estimates of the total number of signers varied, the figure most commonly cited being sixty thousand. O'Connell reportedly was among the last to sign it, and had not known of its existence until asked to sign. Remond brought the Address with him to America when he returned in December, 1841.[14] "Never were my hopes higher, my expectations stronger, or my zeal more ardent, than at present," announced Remond as he prepared to depart from England.[15] Given its importance to the story, the Address is worth quoting at length:

DEAR FRIENDS: You are at a great distance from your native

land! A wide expanse of water separates you from the beloved country of your birth...

The object of this address is to call your attention to the subject of SLAVERY IN AMERICA—that foul blot upon the noble institution and the fair name of your adopted country....

Slavery is the most tremendous invasion of the natural, inalienable rights of man, and of some of the noblest gifts of God, 'life, liberty, and the pursuit of happiness.'...*All who are not for it must be against it.* NONE CAN BE NEUTRAL....

America is cursed by slavery! WE CALL UPON YOU TO UNITE WITH THE ABOLITIONISTS, and never to cease your efforts until perfect liberty be granted to every one of her inhabitants, the black man as well as the white man....

JOIN WITH THE ABOLITIONISTS EVERYWHERE. *They are the only consistent advocates of liberty.* Tell every man that you do not understand liberty for the white man, and *slavery for the black man*; that you are for LIBERTY FOR ALL, of every color, creed, and country....

Irishmen and Irishwomen! *Treat the colored people as your equals, as brethren.* By your memories of Ireland, continue to love liberty—hate slavery—CLING BY THE ABOLITIONISTS— and *in America you will do honor to the name of Ireland.*[16]

The Address was first presented to an American audience on January 28, 1842, at a meeting in Faneuil Hall, Boston. Although the nominal purpose of the meeting was to abolish slavery in the District of Columbia, the abolitionists made special efforts to publicize it among the Irish, including posting handbills around the city and taking out an advertisement in the Boston *Pilot*, the Catholic paper. "I am confident that this address will do much good in this country," Collins wrote.[17]

Garrison chaired the meeting. Phillips introduced several resolutions which were adopted by acclamation, including one supporting Ireland in her struggle against "the fraudulent act of Union." Edmund Quincy drew the parallel between the struggle of Ireland for Repeal and the American

War of Independence. Col. J. P. Miller of Vermont, who claimed Irish descent, declared himself a Repealer, to thunderous applause. George Bradburn of Nantucket, well known in American Catholic circles for his vigorous opposition to nativism, made a special appeal to the Irish as laboring people. "Slavery," he said, "strikes at the interest of every laboring man." Frederick Douglass mimicked the manner of the slaveholders and the Southern clergy, contrasting the hard, horny hands and muscular frames of the laborers, adapted for working, with the slender frames and long, delicate fingers of the masters, matching their brilliant intellects suited to thinking. James C. Fuller, who had stood in the Irish House of Peers when Castlereagh took the bribe for supporting Union, declared that the Irish immigrants to America were republicans by choice, and therefore carried more responsibility to the antislavery cause than the natives. Garrison likened the slaveholder's attitude toward the slave to England's attitude toward Ireland, and then read the Address aloud. Phillips took the floor again, reviewing the history of the Irish commitment to freedom and the longstanding opposition of the Popes to slavery. "Will you ever return to his master the slave who once sets foot on the soil of Massachusetts?" he asked. "No, no, no!" answered the crowd. "Will you ever raise to office or power the man who will not pledge his utmost effort against slavery?" Again the answer was, "No, no, no!" "Then may we not hope well for freedom?" (It was this speech that led O'Connell to declare Phillips superior to himself as an orator).[18] The last speaker was Remond, who contrasted the honor and respect he had received abroad with the indignities to which he had been subjected since his return, and thanked the city authorities for allowing the meeting the use of the hall.

The *Liberator* estimated that no less than four thousand people attended the meeting, including a large number of Irish from Boston and vicinity (whom one observer remarked could be distinguished by their dress as easily as the Negroes).[19] "A more united and enthusiastic meeting was never held in the Old Cradle of Liberty. Its influence will be felt throughout the country," concluded the report.[20]

The next day, Garrison wrote to his wife's father, "We had a great and glorious meeting...everything went off in the most enthusiastic manner. No opposition from any quarter."[21]

Garrison's euphoria was premature. The following day the New York *Herald* printed an account of the meeting from its Boston correspondent. He estimated about twelve hundred Irish present, and reported that the hall rocked with cheers for O'Connell and Repeal, and shouts of "Bloody murther to slavery an' the like iv it." "You will wonder how we could stand by and make no demonstration of disapproval," asked the correspondent for this Northern defender of slavery. "I answer, that the people were taken by surprise. A very few were present but the abolitionists—many just dropt in and then out; but if it were to be repeated, if another meeting were to be held there for the same purpose, viz: to enlist the Irish to join the bloody crusade against the South, by the use and means of a direct, positive foreign influence—but I will not say what....

"The plot thickens indeed," he concluded ominously, "and when it will end, God only knows. Where is Father Hughes?"[22]

Bishop John J. Hughes of New York, the most influential leader in America of the Irish, was not long in responding. He doubted the authenticity of the Address; but if it should prove genuine, it was

> the duty of every naturalized Irishman to resist and repudiate the address with indignation. Not precisely because of the doctrines it contains, but because of their having emanated from a foreign source, and of their tendency to operate on questions of domestic and national policy. I am no friend of slavery, but I am still less friendly to any attempt of foreign origin to abolish.

> The duty of naturalized Irishmen or others, I consider to be in no wise distinct or different from those of native born Americans. And if it be proved an attempt has been made by this address, or any other address, to single them out on any question appertaining to the foreign or domestic policy of the United States, in any other capacity than that of the whole population, then it will be their duty to their country and their conscience, to rebuke such an attempt come from what foreign source it may, in the most decided manner and language that common courtesy will permit.[23]

The first of the Irish newspapers to comment on the Address was the

Boston *Pilot*. Collins, who had persuaded the *Pilot* to accept an advertisement for the Faneuil Hall meeting, had described the paper as "the thermometer of the Irish feeling in this country."[24] In 1839, in an editorial entitled "Abolitionism and 'Popery,'" it had argued that opposition to slavery did not imply approval of abolitionism, which it said was "thronged with bigotted and persecuting religionists; with men who, in their private capacity, desire the extermination of Catholics by fire and sword."[25] Now the thermometer was registering boil. On February 5, 1842, while acknowledging the virtue of O'Connell's sympathy for the slave, the *Pilot* asked how he could reconcile his advocacy of moral force with support for the abolitionists, whose doctrines would "bathe the whole South in blood." It warned against linking the question of Repeal to any other movement, and predicted that the Irish would never be drawn into "the vortex of abolitionism" which threatened the dissolution of the Union.[26] A week later the *Pilot* contributed another argument which would become a standard part of the repertoire of the anti-abolitionist chorus: abolition was a British plot to weaken the United States. "Can the exiled victims of British oppression," it asked, "relinquish the hate they bear the oppressor, and lend their influence for the furtherance of his subtle schemes?"[27]

The Boston *Catholic Diary* did not deny that slavery was unjust, but it declared "infinitely more reprehensible" the "zealots who would madly attempt to eradicate the evil by the destruction of our federal union." The "illustrious Liberator" could afix his signature to any document he pleased, but he had "no right to shackle the opinions of the Irishmen of America....We can tell the abolitionists that we acknowledge no dictation from a foreign source...."[28]

A meeting of Irish miners in Pottsville, Pennsylvania, brought together most of the key arguments. They denounced the Address as a fabrication, and declared they were not willing to look upon colored people as their "brethren." Slavery in America was a legacy of British rule. And they resented those who addressed them from abroad on questions of national policy. "We do not form a distinct class of the community, but consider ourselves in every respect as CITIZENS of this great and glorious republic—that we look upon every attempt to address us, otherwise than as CITIZENS, upon the subject of the abolition of slavery, or any subject whatsoever, as base and iniquitous, no matter from what quarter it may proceed."[29] It was a bit disingenuous for these people, who had come together as Irish and continued to send contributions to the Repeal movement, to object to being addressed as a distinct group. But the irony would hardly appeal to those who accepted without demurral the assurances of a prince of the Church of Rome that he rejected foreign interference in American affairs.[30]

It was this sort of reaction that led Garrison on February 27 to write to his friend Richard Allen in Dublin, "How mortified, how indignant, how astonished you will be to hear that the noble Address to your countrymen in America...is spurned and denounced by the Irish papers in America."[31] On the same day he wrote to Webb, also in Dublin, "[T]he two Irish papers in Boston sneer at the Address, and denounce it and the abolitionists in true pro-slavery style." In his first expression of foreboding, Garrison added, "I fear they will keep the great mass of your countrymen here from uniting with us."[32]

Garrison, the indomitable, was not merely expressing disappointment but calling for assistance, which was soon forthcoming. The Dublin abolitionists passed a resolution vouching for the authenticity of the Address and the signatures, and then went out and collected ten thousand more. All this was duly reported in the abolitionist press.[33]

The abolitionists hoped for their most powerful support from O'Connell, but here the issue got mixed up with the question of Repeal. O'Connell had organized the Loyal National Repeal Association—its name an exact expression of its character—on April 15, 1840, with an initial membership of fifteen. A decade in parliament, during which time the Irish party had on occasion held the balance of power between Whigs and Tories, had failed to win either to embrace self-government for Ireland. Now O'Connell had decided that the time was ripe to launch a campaign for home rule relying on the methods of peaceful agitation that had proved so successful in winning Catholic Emancipation.

The first effort to organize support in the U.S. for Repeal came from Boston.[34] On October 6, 1840, a group of artisans, laborers, and small shopkeepers, including Patrick Donohoe, editor of the *Pilot*, met to plan the formation of a group to aid the cause of Repeal. Some had worked together in the old Hibernian Relief Society. They hired Boyleston Hall and called a public meeting for the following Monday, October 12. Between 1,500 and 2,000 people, for the most part poor Irish, showed up, filling the hall to capacity. A fish packer presided over the meeting; the leading Irish temperance advocate in Boston and a hack driver served as vice presidents; a coal and wood dealer and the assistant editor of the *Pilot* recorded the proceedings. After speeches and resolutions, the meeting launched a Friends of Ireland Society.

The Boston society organized itself and issued an address to sympathizers elsewhere. Within a short time, supporters were recruiting members in thirty-one New England cities and towns.

Until the demise of the Repeal movement, Boston would continue to set the pace. This was partly due to its choice of a president, John W. James, a Yankee, son of a Revolutionary War patriot, and long-time partisan of the Irish cause. Potter suggests that naming a non-Irishmen to head the group reduced the intensity of factional struggles that normally plagued Irish efforts at organization. James was a Democrat in the Federalist-Whig stronghold.

Philadelphia, home of a large Irish population and a United Irishmen tradition, was the next large city to organize, on December 8. Less than a week later, New York followed, although the organization there was soon torn by political discord and personal rivalry.[35]

The movement rapidly built up strength. In the cities, Repeal societies held regular meetings and collected funds. In villages and rural areas, small groups of Irish met and collected money which they forwarded to the nearest Repeal center. Subscriptions were entered on the rolls of the society and published in the Irish press with the name of the donor, the county in Ireland of origin, and the amount. In communities with a Catholic church, the name of the local priest invariably headed the list. Repeal wardens made the rounds to collect dues from those unable to attend the meetings.[36] Laborers on public works gave generously, like the workers building a railroad into western Massachusetts who contributed $145.70 through the section contractor, a man of Irish birth. Soldiers and sailors in the U.S. armed forces held meetings in forts or on ships and sent their donations.

While membership in the societies consisted almost entirely of Catholic Irish, the movement attracted supporters of other backgrounds.

John W. James was, of course, an example, as were William Seward, James Buchanan, Lewis Cass, Horace Greeley, and a number of other public figures, some of whom lent their names for obvious reasons of political expediency.[37] Colonel Richard M. Johnson, Vice President under Jackson, offered, in spite of his age and his shattered arm, to answer the call with arms, if need be. The most important convert, however, was Robert Tyler, the President's son, who joined the movement in Washington and became its national leader. "All I know is that I love Irishmen and hate tyranny in every form," he said in his first speech.

The prominence in the Repeal movement of the son of the slave-holding President was the concentrated expression of the contradiction at the heart of this narrative: the man who hated tyranny in every form and was the leading spokesman in America for the struggle for Irish freedom was at the same time identified with what O'Connell had called the "worst of all aristocracies—that of the human skin," the slaveholders of America, who would find their reward "in the deepest hell, [where] there is a depth still more profound."[38]

Garrison, therefore, had cause for alarm when, in March 1842, he wrote a friend of "a stupendous conspiracy going on in the land. What means," he asked,

> this sudden interest of the slave plunderers in the cause of Irish Repeal?…Again, what means this sudden regard for the sacredness of "Southern institutions" on the part of the leading Irish declaimers at the Repeal meetings of the South, and in other parts of the country? I will tell you. The game is this: "You tickle me, and I will tickle you!" In other words, the bargain obviously is…that the South shall go for Repeal, and the Irish, as a body, shall go for Southern slavery!—Here is a "union," most unnatural and horrible! I most firmly believe that such an agreement has been entered into by the selfish Repeal demagogues at the North, and the mercenary slave-drivers at the South. And will our hard-working, liberty-loving Irish fellow-countrymen allow themselves to be bought for such a purpose, and at such a price? Heaven forbid![39]

A few days later, he repeated his sighting of "a stupendous conspiracy...between the leading Irish demagogues, the leading pseudo democrats, and the Southern slaveholders," the aim of which was to bring the united strength of the Irish to the side of slavery and "if possible, by sending over donations to Ireland, to stop O'Connell's mouth....Now, by the Address, which will cause every toad to start up into a devil as soon as he is touched, we shall be able to probe this matter to the bottom. If O'Connell and our friends in Ireland remain true to us..."

At the same time Garrison proclaimed himself both an Irish and an American Repealer. "I go for the Repeal of the Union between England and Ireland, and for the Repeal of the Union between the North and the South."[40] In the *Liberator* of May 6, 1842, Garrison published an editorial in which he argued that the Constitution was "a covenant with death and an agreement with hell." And beginning with May 13 he printed in boldface capitals at the head of the editorial column of every issue: "A repeal of the union between northern liberty and southern slavery is essential to the abolition of the one, and the preservation of the other." This slogan was not an effort to keep the abolitionists uncontaminated by guilt, as has sometimes been argued, but the expression of a conscious strategy. The abolitionists meant seriously their charge that the north was the true upholder of slavery. By taking the north out of the Union they hoped to remove it from the reach of the fugitive slave law. "No Union with Slaveholders" was a logical outgrowth of the question, asked at every abolitionist rally, Will you send back the fugitive slave who once sets foot here? Phillips more than once declared that if he could establish Massachusetts, or even part of it, as a sanctuary for the fugitive, he could bring slavery down. Nor did the abolitionists depend on constitutional means to achieve their aim, as shown by their efforts in the 1854 Anthony Burns case, when a crowd attacked the Boston courthouse to prevent the return to slavery of a man who had been living in the city and been ruled the property of his former owner. Their opponents regularly charged them with seeking to break up the union, and cited the repeal slogan as evidence.[41]

On February 2 Phillips, Bradburn, and Nathaniel P. Rogers, all men with strong pro-Irish records, attended a meeting of the Boston Repeal Association. Their support for Repeal was received with respect, but when they tried to raise the issue of slavery, they were rebuked from the floor. Phillips characterized the meeting as "low mean politics—demagogical earthly, worldly—pah! the mouth tasted bad for days after...." O'Connell, he said, would have been unable to breathe there.[42]

Meanwhile, in the South, the Repeal Associations were taking pains to stress that their members were "warmly attached to southern institutions."[43] Their assurances did not always satisfy proslavery opinion; following the organizing meeting of the New Orleans Repeal Association, prominent citizens there held a public meeting at which they denounced the Repeal movement, O'Connell, and Garrison.[44]

In the midst of the turmoil stirred up by the Irish Address, the first National Repeal Convention met on Washington's Birthday, in a large hall in the Philadelphia Museum decorated with the flags of Ireland and the U.S., and hung with a full-length portrait of the Liberator. Present were delegations from twenty-six cities and towns. This was no convention of laborers and canal diggers, but of substantial citizens, many of the second and third generation: merchants, traders, shopkeepers, doctors, lawyers, journalists, and contractors with political connections. William Stokes, President of the Philadelphia Repeal Association, welcomed the delegates, and James was elected to preside over the Convention. A committee on resolutions, conscious of the disruptive potential of the Address, made a report confining the resolutions to support for Ireland and Repeal, praise of the U.S. as the exemplary model, and opposition to sectarian divisions in Ireland.

The approach of the resolutions committee was too restrictive for one delegate, Isaac H. Wright, a Democratic politician from Boston, who reported on the recent effort in Boston to associate Repeal with abolition, an attempt "which had fortunately failed." He then moved an explicit resolution stating that "the friends of Ireland in America will not be diverted...by any topics of discord connected with the domestic institutions of the Republic."[45] His motion touched off a passionate debate, not over abolitionism, but over whether to vote on the motion or be satisfied with the approach of the resolutions committee. After spending the remainder of the day in parliamentary wrangling, the Convention referred the question to a committee and adjourned.

The next morning, the convention adopted a resolution, presented by Stokes, reaffirming that the only purpose of the Repeal Association be to help Ireland regain home rule, and denying that there was any "design or desire to interfere...in any matter of religion, politics, or abolition, connected with the social condition or governmental institutions of this country."

A resolution was adopted calling for a boycott of English manufactures, but it ran into trouble when Stokes reminded the Convention that it interfered with U.S. tariff policy and therefore violated the Constitution.[46]

At the end of March, James C. Fuller wrote to O'Connell summarizing the opposition which the Address had provoked in America, and requesting him to speak out directly in his own name.[47] Two days later, Phillips wrote to Richard Allen in Dublin asking him and O'Connell and the Irish antislavery people to "send us a startling, scorching, bitter, unsparing, pointed rebuke...telling the repealers that you don't want the money or voices of slaveholders...laugh, hoot, scorn, hiss, spit at the recreant Irishman."[48]

The abolitionists were asking more from O'Connell than he was willing to deliver. At a meeting of the L.N.R.A. on May 10, he called for the adoption of a conciliatory tone toward proslavery American Repealers.[49] On May 21, two letters were read at the L.N.R.A. meeting. The first, from the Repeal Association of Louisiana, enclosed two hundred pounds along with a note reporting that a Native American Party—"the leaven of what appears to be the old orange party"—had sprung up there, and was accusing the Irish of being enemies of the slaveholders, "who received us among them with a liberality, and extended to us a hospitality which it is fair to presume would not be extended to us in the Eastern States, where prejudice against Irishmen and bigotry against their religion seem indigenous qualities....[O]n behalf of your countrymen in the slaveholding States, I pray you to leave to Americans the control of their own institutions....I assure you," added the correspondent, "that, even in the Northern States...Irishmen have no feelings in common with abolitionists...." The second letter was from the Repeal Association in Albany, New York. After reporting on the efforts of the abolitionists to influence Irish-American opinion, it stated the by-now-familiar arguments about the abolitionists as inciters of violence, the impropriety of addressing the Irish as a distinct class, etc. It then added a new argument: while deprecating the institution of slavery, it noted that the slaves were "not only happier than the emancipated blacks in the free States, but thousands of *nominally* freemen in England and misgoverned Ireland would gladly exchange places with them."

> No petty village magistrate, "dressed in a little brief authority," extorts the little all of misery from the impoverished parent, to leave his offspring to perish from starvation and want....No, Sir, the slaves of America partake of all the necessaries and comforts of life in abundance. They are visited by no periodical famines, too often consequent on the existence of a bloated and voluptuous aristocracy, and their slumbers are uninterrupted by the cries of their famishing children.

At that same meeting, there was another letter read, from the earlier-mentioned Thomas Mooney, also writing from New Orleans, which was also a paean to the condition of the slaves. To that one O'Connell expressed his regret that Mr. Mooney seemed to have "become infected with the atmosphere by which he was surrounded," to believe he could judge the condition of the slave by the quantity of food and clothes he had.[50]

O'Connell's efforts to maneuver in a tight situation led him not to withdraw his opposition to slavery as an institution—that was impossible—but to attempt to place some distance between himself and the abolitionists. He did this by publicly rebuking Garrison for his view of the sabbath—Garrison insisted that every day was sacred—and by insisting that he had not advocated support for any particular abolitionist organization, nor did he countenance breaking the law in any way.[51] The dispute over the sabbath was a replay of an earlier one between Garrison and some associates, who reproached him for burdening the movement with his extreme views on women's rights, antisabbatarianism, etc. Garrison replied that these were his personal views and he was not ascribing them to the abolitionist movement. The conflict came to a head over women speaking publicly before mixed audiences. In response to critics who accused him of dragging the issue of women's rights into the antislavery movement by sponsoring women as speakers, Garrison insisted that he was merely providing a platform to anyone who wished to speak on behalf of antislavery, and that it was those who denied that right to women who were dragging in extraneous issues. The dispute reflected differences in both tactics and principle. It led to a split in antislavery ranks, and the formation of separate organizations with diverging positions on a whole number of questions, including electoral activity and rights for free Negroes. Now, in making Garrison's views an issue, O'Connell was, in effect, siding with Garrison's opponents, Gerrit Smith and Lewis Tappan.[52]

In July an Irish-born Catholic priest who had spent nine years in the South delivered fifty pounds to the L.N.R.A. on behalf of the Mobile (Alabama) Repeal Association, along with a speech in which he alluded to the rejection of the Irish Address and claimed that the slaves were unfit for freedom. In reply O'Connell repeated his opposition to slavery; however, he declared that, in signing the Irish Address, he had not meant to tell anyone in America to become what were known as "abolitionists" in that country, or to join in any movement against property.[53]

The Boston *Pilot*, which had always insisted that it was not proslavery when it opposed the abolitionists, could not have been more pleased. On July 2 it trumpeted O'Connell's announcement that he held "no community of feeling with the fire-brand abolitionists of America, or the no less enthusiastic zealots of his own country." The columnist, Thomas Brady, went on to cite, as a horrible example of the sort of person he was referring to, a speaker at an antislavery convention reporting favorably on the degree of racial amalgamation he had observed in Mexico, the West Indies, and Central America. "Irishmen," asked Mr. Brady, "what think you of that? Are you prepared to amalgamate with the negro, or rather are you not prepared to execrate any wretch, no matter what his own taste may be, who would insult you by such a recommendation?" The Irish in America, he said, had unanimously condemned the Address; nevertheless, it was a slander to call them proslavery.[54]

The abolitionists were furious with O'Connell. Phillips fumed, "He dares not face the demon when it touches *him*. He would be pro-slavery this side of the pond....He won't shake hands with slaveholders, no—but he will shake *their gold*," and added that O'Connell had truly proven himself "The Great Beggarman."[55]

Throughout 1842 the bad feelings simmered, fueled in part by a discussion of whether it was proper to accept contributions from slave-holders. To some extent the issue was a red herring, as most abolitionists did not object to the Repeal movement taking the money, so long as it came without strings, but O'Connell continued to use the issue, as well as Garrison's religious sentiments, to hold them at arm's length. Although the *Liberator* continued to give prominent place to antislavery news from Ireland, in the beginning of July, in a letter to Richard Allen in Dublin, Garrison summed up the situation with regard to the Irish in America.

> It is now quite apparent that they will go *en masse* with Southern men-stealers, and in opposition to the anti-slavery movement. This will not be done intelligently by them, but will be effectually controlled by a crafty priesthood and unprincipled political demagogues. When we had our great meeting in Faneuil Hall, we took all parties by surprise. Our Irish fellow-citizens, who were then present, acted out their natural love of liberty, to the life; for at that time, they had not been instructed how to act by their leaders, and the *Pilot* and *Diary,* and other Irish papers here, had not opened their batteries. Since that time, however, they have kept wholly aloof from us, and it is impracticable to get them to listen to us....

> Let me state one fact, as a sample of many others that might be given. Some time after the Faneuil Hall meeting, we held two public meetings in the Marlboro' Chapel (a central, popular and spacious building), which were extensively advertised in our daily papers, and in large placards that were posted around the city. It was announced, that the Irish Address would be presented on those occasions, for the inspection of all persons, and especially that of our Irish fellow-citizens, in order that all doubts in regard to its genuineness might be put at an end. It was also stated that the speakers would be Wendell Phillips and George Bradburn. Where were our Irish friends? They did not show themselves even in the form of a meagre representation, but avoided our meetings as though the pestilence (instead of the Irish Address) were to be uncovered for the destruction of the city!

And then he added what may be the saddest words ever written about the Irish diaspora: "Even to this hour, not a single Irishman has come forward, either publicly or privately, to express his approval of the Address, or to avow his determination to abide by its sentiments."[56] As if to underscore the gloomy picture Garrison painted, one month later a largely Irish mob in Philadelphia attacked an Afro-American temperance parade.[57]

So the situation remained throughout the year: the abolitionists continuing regularly to publish antislavery resolutions and letters from Ireland, while O'Connell sought to maintain his antislavery connections without antagonizing proslavery forces in America.[58] In the meantime, the Repeal Associations in America continued to carry out their functions. In Philadelphia, for example, the society held meetings throughout 1842, raising funds for Ireland, and began 1843 with a Grand Repeal Ball, attended by Irish militia companies in full uniform.[59]

In September of 1842, the Pennsylvania Anti-Slavery Society had sent a letter to O'Connell and the L.N.R.A. replying in detail to the arguments of the New Orleans and Albany Repealers, in particular refuting the assertions of the happy condition of the slaves, and clarifying the abolitionist attitude toward unjust laws. The letter was read on May 9, 1843, at a meeting of the L.N.R.A. chaired by James Haughton.[60] O'Connell rose and paid tribute to the writers of the letter, declaring that they had opened his eyes to the horrors of slavery. He had never considered the question directly before, but only through those who were trying to maintain good relations with the slaveholders. Now that the state of affairs was clear, he could only cast shame on any man in America who was not antislavery. Answering the charge that the abolitionists were actually holding up the progress of antislavery, he recalled that his opponents had said the same thing when he had begun his campaign for Catholic emancipation. And then he declared, "Over the broad Atlantic I pour forth my voice, saying, Come out of such a land, you Irishmen; or, if you remain, and dare countenance the system of slavery that is supported there, we will recognize you as Irishmen no longer."

They were the strongest words he had yet spoken, and to underscore his seriousness, he added, "I have spoken the sentiments of the Repeal Association. There is not a man amongst the hundreds of thousands that belong to our body, or amongst the millions that will belong to it, who does not concur in what I have stated. We may not get money from America after this declaration; but even if we should not, we do not want blood-stained money. If they make it the condition of our sympathy, or if there be implied any submission to the doctrine of slavery on our part, in receiving their remittance, let them cease sending it at once."[61]

The importance of O'Connell's words can only be appreciated by placing them against the background of events then taking place in Ireland.[62] During 1842 the Repeal movement had lagged and contributions from America had tapered off. Then O'Connell proclaimed 1843 as "Repeal Year," promising that before its end an Irish Parliament would sit at College Green in Dublin, the site of the old Irish Parliament. In February, he made a four-hour speech in the Dublin city government in favor of the right of Ireland to self-government.

He carried the agitation directly to the country, in a series of "monster meetings" at sites enshrined in Irish history. His appearance at Kells, once a famous monastic center, drew audiences as far as the eye could see. Without amplification it was impossible for any but those up front to hear the speaker, but people came, and brought their children, to what they sensed were historic moments. At Tara, the old pagan capital, a million people turned out, according to contemporary estimates. It was, in the words of a contemporary observer, "a triumphal procession such as no Roman emperor ever had."[63]

Sir Robert Peel, the British prime minister, declared his determination not to relinquish the Union and moved troops into Ireland. His response stimulated the movement in America to intense activity; contributions began once more to flow into Dublin. The Boston *Pilot* proclaimed that the crisis had arrived. "The noble, the magnanimous, the fearless strength of the people of Ireland for ten years is about to triumph or perish."

This was the background for O'Connell's speech of May 9, which he must have known would strain relations with his supporters in America. What was he up to?

It is always difficult to identify with certainty the motivations of any public figure, but it may help to review O'Connell's record. As a young man he witnessed the repression that followed the Rising of '98 and the Plot of 1803, which burned into him an absolute horror of revolutionary violence. In later years it was said that O'Connell was the one man in Ireland who could have given the call for armed rebellion, and the one man who would never do so. The Catholic Emancipation Act of 1830, which legalized his election to Parliament, also disenfranchised, with his approval, the forty-shilling voters who made up the bulk of the Catholic peasantry. In Parliament, when Irish peasants rose up in revolt against the forcible collection of tithes for the hated Church of Ireland, he supported the British repression, and settled for a limited, conservative, and unsatisfactory solution of the problem. In the face of Chartism he boasted of his commitment to order, he failed to support the ten-hour day bill, and was always opposed to any Poor Law or any form of aid to the able-bodied. He avoided embarrassing the government on Canada, and was careful never to agitate the Irish question at a time when the English workers were causing trouble. In short, he was the ideal representative of the Catholic middle class who sought freedom to operate without religio-racial restrictions, and who used the discontent of the peasants as a means of exerting pressure on Britain. His class position allied him with the Whig Party, and all his hopes for the realization of his program depended on his ability to gain its cooperation. Now that Party was out of power, and his campaign was embarrassing the Government. He aimed not to overthrow existing power, but to cajole it by skillfully combining loyalty and pressure. In the 1843 letter cited above Engels writes:

> Give me two hundred thousand Irishmen and I will overthrow the entire British monarchy....If O'Connell were really the man of the people, if he had sufficient courage *and were not himself afraid of the people*, i.e., if he were not a double-faced Whig, but an upright, consistent democrat, then the last English soldier would have left Ireland long since, there would no longer be any idle Protestant priest in purely Catholic districts, or any old-Norman baron in his castle. But there is the rub. If the people were to be set free even for a moment, then Daniel O'Connell and his moneyed aristocrats would soon be...left high and dry.[64]

Whatever O'Connell's personal and political contradictions may have been, his antislavery position formed part of the Whig compact, as did his renunciation of insurrectionary methods. It must be remembered that the British government after 1833 was opposed to slavery. This position brought it into conflict with the U.S., around its claimed right to search U.S. ships suspected of carrying slaves, and over Texas. O'Connell had opposed U.S. annexation of Texas in 1837 and had supported Britain's right of search when it raised the specter of war between the two countries. In 1838 he had called for the antislavery movement to focus its attention on America. Now, in thundering his opposition to slavery, O'Connell was in fact reassuring the British government of his loyalty just as he was preparing to undertake a massive campaign to put pressure on it.

The Irish press in the U.S. refused to print O'Connell's May 9 speech. When challenged to do so, the *Pilot* replied, "We never publish such speeches from any source, as we are not specially engaged in the anti-slavery cause."[65] The Repeal Associations of Natchez and Charleston dissolved, the latter with what was perhaps the frankest statement to come out of the whole dispute: "as the alternative has been presented to us by Mr. O'Connell, as we must choose between Ireland and South Carolina, we say South Carolina forever!"[66] The Baltimore Repeal society condemned O'Connell but, as befit its border state position, resolved to continue work for Ireland.[67]

In Philadelphia the speech touched off an intense and protracted struggle. As soon as copies of it arrived in the city, the abolitionists inserted it, as a paid advertisement, in three of the city's leading papers. It attracted wide attention, and crowds came to the office of the Anti-Slavery Society to read the entire correspondence. On June 21 the Repeal Association met to consider what to do about it. A dispute quickly broke out between those who wanted the society explicitly to dissociate itself from the speech and those opposed any discussion of the matter on the floor. At its next meeting, the Association voted "to disclaim all connection and sympathy with every society formed in reference to the politics or domestic institutions of this country." The President of the Association, William Stokes, spoke in support of the resolution, saying that, "It is under the constitution and laws that our Southern fellow-citizens lay claim to the involuntary services of their negro servants. They show the same title to their property which we show to our rights...."[68] At the same meeting, Robert Tyler delivered a long address in which he expressed his difficulty reconciling O'Connell's denunciation of him and other Southerners with the resolution passed scarcely two months earlier commending him for his services to the cause of Repeal. He went so far as to suggest that O'Connell had not made the May 9 speech at all.[69]

The dispute led to the formation of a new group, called Friends of Ireland and of Repeal. Among its first acts was to write to the Dublin Repealers explaining the reasons for the split. Stokes, it charged, had withdrawn from the Repeal movement out of a personal motivation: his wife was a slaveholder. Moreover, the Stokes faction had attacked the Friends of Ireland group for having accepted a contribution from the well-known free Negro, Robert Purvis. O'Connell welcomed the new group and criticized Stokes for being more in love with slavery than with Ireland. Expressing outrage that there could be any objection to a man on the grounds of color, he moved a special resolution of thanks to Purvis.[70]

The old Association continued to contend for the Repeal franchise in Philadelphia. In August it met and recalled the subscription books and records, appointed new Repeal wardens, and warned against the payment of dues to anyone who did not carry its authorization.[71]

Who were the groups and what was their strength? The principal activity of both groups was collecting money and forwarding it to the L.N.R.A. The Repeal Association claimed, after the split, 6,500 members, and an apparatus of 250 Repeal wardens. Alex Diamond served as chairman during Stokes's absence. Joseph Binns was also allied with this faction.[72] The new group was headed by Joseph M. Doran, who was a local judge, and claimed the loyalty of a number of lawyers and other respectable citizens. At one meeting it admitted fifty-four new members; at another it announced eighty-nine new members, including three Catholic priests.[73] It is difficult to determine which of the two groups commanded greater public support; remittances from both were substantial, and both listed the names of prominent Philadelphia Irish among their members.[74] When Col. Johnson visited the city in November, the Friends of Ireland announced he would address its meeting. Instead, he spoke before the Repeal Association, at a meeting chaired by its President, William A. Stokes.[75] Given the absence of any difference between the activities of the two groups after the split, it is possible that the average Irish man or women on the street was unaware of the distinction between them or even of their separate existence. According to one observer, the U.S.-born and the Americanized Irish were for explicitly chastising O'Connell for his interference, while the Irish-born refused to allow any criticism, even indirect, of his leadership.[76] Probably not too much can be made of this distinction, since the dispute was not over slavery directly but over the propriety of rebuking O'Connell for his anti-slavery statements.[77] Moreover, both groups were headed by political leaders and "professional Irish," exactly the sort of people whom Garrison predicted would lead the mass of Irish in the path of the slaveholders.

While the quarrel was unfolding in Philadelphia, it was heating up elsewhere as well. In July the Cincinnati Repeal Association wrote O'Connell complaining about his May 9 speech. Insisting that the future of the American Union depended on the continued existence of slavery, the Cincinnati Repealers resolved to oppose any attempts to abolish it. O'Connell was particularly incensed at this letter, since it largely restated arguments that had already been rebutted, since it came from a free state, and because it was an explicit defense of slavery.[78] Before he could reply to it, though, disaster struck.

O'Connell had announced a "monster meeting" to be held October 8 outside of Dublin, at Clontarf, where Brian Boru had almost a thousand years before stopped the Danish invaders. The meeting was to be the climax of the Repeal campaign. On the day before the meeting was to take place, the British government prohibited it. Soldiers took their places along the roads to Clontarf. Artillery was aimed at the approaches. A British fleet waited in Dublin Bay.

Faced with the likelihood of bloodshed, O'Connell called off the meeting. He sent riders out from Dublin to inform people already on their way of the decision and warn them against even the slightest violent response. Although few knew it at the time, O'Connell's surrender marked the collapse of the Repeal agitation. Later it was said that Irish independence had been won at Clontarf and lost there a thousand years later.

The British authorities, seizing the moment, arrested O'Connell, charging him with conspiracy and inciting to sedition. While he was awaiting trial, he wrote a reply to the Cincinnati Repealers. Issued on October 11, 1843, it represented his most comprehensive treatment of slavery. "It was not in Ireland you learned this cruelty," he declared. "Your mothers were gentle, kind, and humane....How can your souls have become stained with a darkness blacker than the negro's skin?" It went beyond previous addresses of his in that it offered practical suggestions for what Irish in America could do to end slavery: first was never again to volunteer on behalf of the oppressor (this was particularly important in view of the threat of war over the U.S. annexation of Texas); it was followed by injunctions to help educate and secure the franchise for the free Negro, and to support political candidates who worked to abolish the internal slave trade and slavery in the District of Columbia. Let the Irish in America take these steps, he implored, and "never cease [their] efforts, until the crime...of being the worst enemies of the men of color shall be atoned for, and blotted out, and effaced forever."[79]

As before, he accompanied his denunciations of slavery with attacks on certain abolitionists for supposed religious bigotry. Two weeks after the Address, he censured Garrison by name, singled out for praise the moderate antislavery men, Smith and Tappan, and called upon the abolitionists to cooperate with the Catholic and Irish in the spread of Christian charity in America—as Riach points out, the Irish Address in reverse.[80]

The Cincinnati Address came too late to have any effect on the Second National Repeal Convention, which opened in New York in September, 1843. Robert Tyler presided. Alarmed by the British mobilization, the delegates discussed plans to seize Canada with the help of rebellious French Canadians and Irish soldiers in the British army.

After the Convention, when news arrived of the debacle at Clontarf, O'Connell's arrest, and the Cincinnati Address, any antagonism which the latter may have aroused was largely subsumed by concern for events in the old country. The Savannah Repeal Association did dissolve after learning of the Address, but, along with Charleston's, soon reconstituted.[81]

O'Connell's attacks on Garrison did not stop the abolitionists from giving the Address wide publicity. On November 18, they held a meeting in Faneuil Hall on the subject of Irish Repeal and American Slavery.

Many Irish attended. The Address was read, and elicited occasional applause, but not from the Irish in the audience.[82] A Mr. Tucker, who identified himself as vice president of the Repeal Association in Boston, spoke from the gallery, to repeated cheers, pointing out that even if both O'Connell and the Pope were abolitionists, neither spoke for the Irish in America. He was supported by a Mr. O'Brien, who added that, while he was personally opposed to slavery, he regarded it as his duty to uphold American institutions. He, too, received enthusiastic applause. Of those who claimed to be both Irishmen and Repealers, only one person, a Mr. Campbell, took the platform in support of the antislavery movement. When he expressed his disgust for the concern for Ireland pretended by President Tyler and Col. Johnson, and asked his countrymen present in the hall whether such slaveholders could possibly be true friends of Ireland, the response from the hall was "Yes, Yes, Yes!"

"Up to this hour, we believe," commented Garrison, "no other Irishman has ventured publicly to identify himself, in Boston, with the cause of the slave." He was thus reporting a gain of one over his last tally sixteen months earlier.

There is a curious epilogue to this story. O'Connell pursued his course of attempting to demonstrate his loyalty to Britain: as the date for his trial approached, he pointed out that he had always refused the aid of Chartists and French Republicans, and "American sympathy...coloured with the blood of the negro." At the trial itself, he pointed to his attacks on slavery, at a time when large sums of money were coming from America, as evidence of his devotion to principle and British interests.[83] In March of 1845 he assailed the British government's "political cowardice" for backing down before the American "transgressors" and promised that "the throne of Victoria can be made perfectly secure—the honour of the British empire maintained—and the American eagle in its highest point of flight, be brought down. Let them but give us the parliament in College Green, and Oregon shall be theirs, and Texas shall be harmless."[84] A month later, he even departed from his cherished principle of nonviolence to warn that if America attacked England, black regiments from the West Indies would incite slave revolts in the South.[85] He followed this up with an offer to be a "recruiting sergeant for Britain," and praised the valor of Irish troops in the British army.[86]

O'Connell's professions of loyalty did not save him; he was found guilty and sentenced to spend a year in prison. He emerged broken, and died a year later on the way to a pilgrimage to Rome. By then the policy of nonviolence and conciliation of Britain was also dead.

The American Eagle speech had led to the dissolution of the Repeal Associations in Portsmouth and Norfolk, Virginia, and in New Orleans. Robert Tyler, by then President of the Philadelphia Repeal Association, appealed to American Repealers to stay together, declaring that O'Connell's opinions did not represent the feeling of Ireland.[87] The open repudiation of O'Connell in America coincided with the revolt against his leadership in Ireland itself. There the opposition was led by Young Ireland, and its organ, the *Nation*. Rejecting O'Connell's pro-British policy, Young Ireland adopted an ultra-American stance, which led it to abandon agitation of the slavery question.

Some Young Irelanders went further, and openly advocated slavery. The most notorious example was John Mitchel, who after the abortive 1848 revolt emigrated to the U.S., where he published a paper attacking abolitionism and defending slavery. During the Civil War he edited a pro-Confederate newspaper in Richmond; at Fort Sumter his son gave his young life for the cause of slavery.[88]

So it came to pass that events transpired contrary to the way Garrison had hoped; instead of the Irish love of liberty warming America, the winds of republican slavery blew back to Ireland. The Irish had faded from Green to white, bleached by, as O'Connell put it, something in the "atmosphere" of America.

### IRISH EMIGRANT.

*Patrick, (just landing.)* "By my Sowl, you're black, old fellow! How long have ye bin here?"

*N'igger, (imitatng the brogue.)* "Jist three months, my honey!"

*Pat.* "By the powers, I'll go back to Tipperary in a jiffy! I'd not be so black as that fur all the whiskey in Roscrea!"

## II

# WHITE NEGROES
# AND
# SMOKED IRISH

Throughout most of the eighteenth century, Ireland was governed under a series of codes which have become known collectively as the Penal Laws. Under the terms of these Laws, Catholics were not permitted to vote or serve in Parliament or hold public office in any of the municipal corporations, or live within the limits of incorporated towns; they were forbidden to practice law or hold a post in the military or civil service. Catholics were forbidden to open or teach in a school, serve as private tutors, attend university, or educate their sons abroad. They were forbidden to take part in the manufacture or sale of arms, newspapers, or books, or possess or carry arms. No Catholic might own a horse worth more than five pounds. Except in the linen trade, they might take on no more than two apprentices, and Protestants might not take on Catholic apprentices. Catholics might not buy, inherit, or receive gifts of land from Protestants, nor rent land worth more than thirty shillings a year, nor lease land for longer than thirty-one years, nor make a profit from land of more than one-third of the rent paid; no Catholic estate could be entailed but instead had to be divided at death among all the children. By converting to Protestantism a Catholic son could dispossess his father and disinherit all his brothers. A Protestant landowner lost his civil rights if he married a Catholic, a Protestant heiress her inheritance. All bishops of the Catholic Church were ordered to leave the country under penalty of death if they remained or returned; no priest might enter the country from anywhere, and only one priest was permitted per parish, forbidden to set foot outside it without special permission. Like all Irish, Catholics paid taxes to support the Protestant Church of Ireland. Catholic orphans were to be brought up as Protestants. As can be seen, the Penal Laws regulated every aspect of Irish life, civil, domestic, and spiritual. In effect they established Ireland as a country in which Irish Catholics formed an oppressed race.[1]

By the mid-eighteenth century Catholics held only seven percent of Irish land.[2] In the twentieth century African residents of various British colonies in Africa have pointed out that in the beginning the white man had the Bible and the Africans had the land; now the Africans have the Bible and the white man has the land. In Ireland, the transfer of the land from native cultivators to foreign conquerors took place on as large a scale as in any African colony, without even the compensation of the Bible (King James version).

Theodore W. Allen has explained that the distinction between racial and national oppression turns on the composition of the group that enforces elite rule: under a system of national oppression, such as Britain imposed on India or the United States maintains in Puerto Rico, the conquering power implements its dominance by incorporating sections of the elite classes of the subject population (in modern times a portion of the bourgeoisie and state bureaucracy) into the ruling apparatus. Under the system of racial oppression, elite rule rests on the support of the laboring classes of the oppressor group.[3]

Eighteenth-century Ireland presents a classic case of racial oppression. Catholics there were known as native Irish, Celts, or Gaels (as well as "Papists" and other equally derogatory names), and were regarded, and frequently spoke of themselves, as a "race," rather than a nation. The Penal Laws imposed upon them a caste status out of which no Catholic, no matter how wealthy, could escape. The racial and class hierarchy was enforced by the Dissenters, who were mostly Presbyterian farmers, mechanics, and small tradesmen, descendants of soldiers settled by Cromwell and Scots settled later in Ulster. Although the special place accorded the Church of Ireland excluded Dissenters (who made up the majority of non-Catholics) from the ruling group, "the most worthless Protestant," as Lecky observed, "if he had nothing else to boast of, at least found it pleasing to think that he was a member of a dominant race."[4] Under the Protestant Ascendancy the masses of Irish, that is, the Catholics, lived in conditions of misery so severe that they elicited pity and condemnation from Dr. Johnson, Edmund Burke, and a host of others, including the most famous satire in the English language, Jonathan Swift's *A Modest Proposal* (1729); and the poorest among the Dissenters lived under conditions but little removed from those of the Catholic majority.

Swift was a member of the Anglo-Irish propertied class, itself resentful of mercantilist restrictions imposed by the Crown. In the eighteenth century this class began to regard itself as Irish rather than English, and moreover as the true representatives of Ireland, without reference to six-sevenths of the population (counting both Catholics and Dissenters). Seizing on the difficulties Britain was undergoing with the rebellion in the American colonies, the Anglo-Irish landholders launched a movement for free trade and legislative independence, under the leadership of Henry Grattan.

"The champions of the 'colony' against the English government no more thought of themselves as 'Gaels' when they called themselves 'Irish' than Benjamin Franklin or George Washington identified themselves with the Sioux or the Iroquois when they called themselves 'Americans'."[5] Owing, however, to the differences in the relative proportions in the populations of the two countries and the need to mobilize popular support, the Anglo-Irish adopted a more inclusive policy toward Catholics than did the American patriots toward Indians and Africans, calling for the abrogation of the Penal Codes and the extension of the electoral franchise to Catholics. (By contrast, the American patriots went no further than blaming England for imposing slavery on the colonies, while enshrining it in their Constitution, and adopted a more expansionist policy toward Indian lands than that advocated by the Crown.)

During the American War, Britain made a number of economic concessions to Irish demands, but the surrender in America allowed it to withdraw them. The failure of Grattan's parliamentary strategy opened the way for more radical leadership, the Society of United Irishmen, headed by Theobold Wolfe Tone and a group of Dissenting lawyers, centered in Dublin and the north. In 1798 these Irish Jacobins launched their uprising, which was defeated by a military force commanded by General Cornwallis (who had previously lost America). The defeat is ordinarily ascribed to unfavorable winds that kept the promised French aid from arriving on time, but a more important reason is the failure of the United Irish leaders to link their demand for a democratic republic with the struggle of the Catholic peasant for land.

As soon as the uprising was crushed, Britain presented the check: the Act of Union of 1800, engineered by Prime Minister William Pitt and Chief Secretary Lord Castlereagh. In return for giving up the precarious semi-independence represented by their own parliament, the Anglo-Irish landholders gained the security of political merger with their English counterparts; even with this bait, the Act was pushed through the Irish parliament only through bribery on a scale that would become infamous.

The Act, which went into effect in 1801, not only merged the two parliaments, it foreclosed the possibility of an independent Irish economy. Ireland became a supplier of agricultural products to England, and a market for English manufactures, just at the time the Napoleonic Wars closed normal sources of supply to Britain. The increased agricultural prices during the Wars led to a boom in production and brought about some improvement in living conditions in the Irish countryside. The boom also, though, fostered an increase in rents and the rise of a class of middlemen ("rackrenters") who leased land for profit.[6] The fall in agricultural prices at the end of the Wars left many tenants unable to pay their rents, which in turn caused their eviction, destroyed the middlemen, and led to further consolidation of land holdings. The consolidation occurred at the same time that Irish manufactures were being throttled by British competition; the surplus agricultural population, unable to find places in domestic industry, was compelled to emigrate.[7]

The Act of Union also marked a turning point in British colonial policy in Ireland from racial to national oppression, a shift which required sacrificing the Protestant Ascendancy in order to gain the support of the Catholic bourgeoisie. As Allen writes, "The process—from the first exchange of glances to the disestablishment of the Church of Ireland in 1869—occupied a century of vicissitudes. But by 1793 the decision was irrevocable, by 1829 it was affirmed in law, and by 1843 it was defined in practice."[8] Only in Ulster did the old system of race-based oppression prevail. In the final analysis, it probably made little difference to the cottier and agricultural laborer that in many cases the direct enforcers of his misery were his wealthy co-religionists rather than poor and middling Protestant workmen and farmers.

In America, where domestic manufacture had grown as a result of the Napoleonic Wars, there was a shortage of wage laborers. The country scooped up the displaced Irish and made them its unskilled labor force.

From 1815 to the Famine, between 800,000 and one million Irish—about twice the total for the previous two centuries—sailed for North America.[9] Contrary to the popular stereotype, not all were poor, not all were Catholic, and not all even spoke English.

For the first decade-and-a-half after 1815, the majority of Irish immigrants were similar in background to those who had come in the eighteenth century: of those arriving between 1815 and 1819, two-thirds were from Ulster, primarily Presbyterians and Anglicans. Between 1827 and 1832 Ulster still contributed about half of Irish emigrants to North America. It was not until some time in the early 1830s that annual departures by Catholics began to exceed those of Dissenters and Anglicans combined.[10]

Emigrants did not represent the poorest layers of Irish society; in 1820 American port officials recorded that twenty-seven percent of Irish arriving that year were farmers, twenty-two percent artisans, ten percent tradesmen and professionals, while only twenty-one percent were laborers. As the *Dublin Evening Post* lamented in 1818, "Emigration is necessarily restricted to the class immediately above the labouring poor, who cannot raise the money to pay their passage." Even in the years immediately preceding the famine, most Catholic immigrants were not destitute.[11]

Finally, a considerable number of Irish immigrants used Irish, not English, as their primary language. This was most true during the Famine years when desperation broke down the resistance of the traditional Gaelic rural population to emigration. As many as a third of all Famine emigrants—a half-million people—were Irish speakers. Some of these may have known some English as well, since Britain pursued a ruthless policy of imposing the English language in Ireland, although port officials in the 1840s occasionally remarked on the inability of entire shiploads of emigrants to speak English, and missionaries and politicians both stressed the importance of knowing Gaelic if they were to reach Irish-Americans.[12] In 1847 in Philadelphia St. Philip's Catholic Church celebrated mass in Gaelic.[13]

How did this population, varied in social class, religion, and language, become the "Irish" of stereotype? Part of the explanation is to be found in the change in the character of immigration brought about by the Famine. As the historian Kirby Miller notes, the 1.8 million immigrants who came in the decade 1845–1855 were as a rule poorer than those who had come earlier, and the majority of males among them probably worked at least temporarily as canal, railroad, building-construction, or dock laborers.[14]

Part of the explanation for the popular identification of Irish and Catholic lies in the strange story of the so-called Scotch-Irish. As has been stated, the majority of Irish immigrants to America in the eighteenth century and for the first third of the nineteenth were Presbyterians, descendants of Scots who had been settled in Ireland beginning with Cromwell and carrying on through William and Mary. The label "Scotch-Irish" was unknown in Ireland. Many Protestant Ulsterites had intermarried with native Irish women, and their children grew up as simply "Irish." While they were members of a favored "race," they had the same grievances with the Church of England and the British commercial and landholding system as did the Catholics.

From the time they began emigrating to about 1850, Irish Protestants were known in America simply as Irish. As Wittke notes, "The sharp distinction between Irish and Scotch-Irish developed in the United States in the last half of the nineteenth century for reasons that were primarily American. After the great influx of Irish immigrants and the problems created by this sudden boiling over of the melting pot, the Scotch-Irish insisted upon differentiating between the descendants of earlier immigrants from Ireland and more recent arrivals."[15] Thus, as a portion of the Irish diaspora became known as "the Irish," a racial (but not ethnic) line invented in Ireland was recreated as an ethnic (but not racial) line in America.[16]

As for the language issue, it is easy to see that, as Miller points out, "Anglicized middle-class spokesmen were generally unwilling to admit

the existence of linguistic barriers to full acceptance in American society." And so the myth was born that would later be used to explain why
the Irish "made it" more easily than other immigrant groups (a questionable assertion): that they were native English-speakers.

On their arrival in America, the Irish were thrown together with black
people on jobs and in neighborhoods, with predictable results. The
Census of 1850 was the first to include a class it called "mulattoes"; it
enumerated 406,000 nationwide, including 15,000 in Pennsylvania, the
largest number for any free state. There is no closer breakdown, but they
made up a little over a quarter of the state's "colored" population.
Applying that ratio to the 3,000 Negroes living in the heavily Irish
Moyamensing district (whose total population was 24,000) gives a figure
of over eight hundred persons of mixed ancestry, or one out of every
thirty.[17] Even if most of these were the children of slaveholders who
had been manumitted and migrated north, an Irish resident of that
district must have seen on the street constant reminders of the fact and
possibility of sexual union between European-Americans and Negroes.
In general this fact was recorded with disapproval. "Many a husband too
is weeping with his offspring," wrote one Philadelphia missionary, "while
the mother of his little ones is drunk on the streets, or locked up a
vagrant in Moyamensing prison or living with some dirty negro."[18] In 1853
a Philadelphia grand jury issued a report on living conditions in the
Moyamensing district; attached to its report was an article entitled "The
Mysteries and Miseries of Philadelphia," which originally appeared in the
*Evening Bulletin*:

> We will essay a description of a hovel we visited which was kept
> by a hideous looking Irishman, known as Jemmy Quinn. The house
> is a tavern and lodging-house, and is located in Small Street, above
> Fifth. It is a two-story frame of quite a small size, but is neverthe-
> less divided into a numbers of rooms which are about ten feet
> square. The bar room is in front on the ground floor. With the
> exception of this apartment, no other part of the house contained
> a single article of furniture, except some damaged furnaces and
> miserable stoves. The walls were discolored by smoke and filth,

the glass was broken from the windows, chinks in the frame work let in the cold air, and every thing was as wretchedly uncomfortable as it is possible to conceive. Yet in every one of these squalid apartments, including the cellar and the loft, men and women— blacks and whites by dozens—were huddled together promiscuously, squatting or lying upon the bare floors, and keeping themselves from freezing by covering their bodies with such filthy rags as chance threw in their way.[19]

In New York, the majority of cases of "mixed" matings involved Irish women.[20] The same was true of Boston.[21] A list of employees of the Narragansett and National Brick Company in 1850 includes a number described as of Irish nationality who are also listed as "mulatto."[22]

The interaction between Irish- and Afro-Americans was not limited to sexual affairs: in New Orleans Irish moved into the black district, and frequented "Black Rookeries." Irish grocers regularly received stolen sugar and flour brought to them by slaves, and sold them liquor, etc.[23] In one case that came before a Philadelphia court, a white man charged two Negroes with stealing his money. His testimony revealed that the three were friends and had been drinking together at a Fourth Street oyster cellar.[24] Nor did the crossing over always take place under hellish circumstances; heaven had its turn as well: the Twelfth Presbyterian Church in Philadelphia was presided over after 1837 by an Afro-American minister; baptismal records for the next twenty years suggest that one-third of the members were Irish.[25]

The first Congress of the United States voted in 1790 that only "white" persons could be naturalized as citizens. Coming as immigrants rather than as captives or hostages undoubtedly affected the potential racial status of the Irish in America, but it did not settle the issue, since it was by no means obvious who was "white."[26] In the early years Irish were frequently referred to as "niggers turned inside out"; the Negroes, for their part, were sometimes called "smoked Irish," an appellation they must have found no more flattering than it was intended to be. As late as 1864, a forged piece of Democratic campaign propaganda declared, "There is the strongest reason for believing that the first movement toward amalgamation in this country will take place between Irish and

negroes."[27] Part of the reason for its effectiveness among the Irish was
that it hit so close to the truth; as Fanny Kemble noted, the more Irish-
and Afro-Americans were lumped together, the greater the hostility
between them.[28]

"My master is a great tyrant," said a Negro, according to a popular
quip of the day. "He treats me as badly as if I was a *common Irishman*."[29]
The quip points toward the minstrel stage, a place where Irish- and Afro-
Americans came together. Several historians have recently written about
the complex set of attitudes that found expression in minstrelsy; whatever the final assessment of the different vectors, it is surely no coinci-
dence that so many of the pioneers of blackface minstrelsy were of Irish
descent, for the Irish came disproportionately into contact with the
people whose speech, music, and dance furnished the basis, however
distorted, for the minstrel's art.[30] Only a place like New York's notorious
Five Points district, which attracted the "lower million" of both races and
sexes to its saloons, cock pits, dance halls, and theaters (including the
people Frederick Douglass called "the filthy scum of white society"),
could have staged an event like the great 1844 dance contest between the
Irish champion "Master" John Diamond and the Negro William Henry
Lane, known as "Juba."[31]

The ambiguity of the Irish-American situation in the antebellum
period can be seen in the Walnut Street Jail in Philadelphia. Built in
1773, it served from 1790 to 1835 as a state penitentiary and a jail for
Philadelphia County.[32]

As befits a prison founded under Quaker influence, the pillar of the
institution was the system of labor. The inmates worked in sheds in
groups of seven, each under the supervision of an inmate appointed by
the guards. The main occupations were nail, shoe, and rope making, spin-
ning and weaving, carding wool, cutting and chipping logs, and sawing
and polishing marble.

Contrary to early optimistic projections, the maintenance of a labor
regime proved difficult. By 1816 the visiting inspectors discovered the
prisoners working at a "system of trades coextensive with the number
of prisoners...highly destructive to the peace and internal economy of
the Prison, as well as being in direct violation of the *Laws and rules*

governing the institution."[33] The translation of the official complaint is that the inmates, ignoring the jobs assigned them by the prison authorities, had organized their division of labor to provide themselves with articles they wanted. In 1819 the Board reported that "large quantities of flour" were being "pilfered and converted into Bread and Cakes and disposed of by the Convicts."[34] In December 1824, the Board expressed "great astonishment [and] far greater disgust" at what it called a "Christmas Jubilee,"[35] with "almost every shop amply supplied for a winter campaign with provisions and even luxuries, viz. Pork in abundance, Turkies, Fowls, Geese, Fish, butter, lard, pies, eggs, sugar, coffee, tea and spices—the whole, presenting to their view, anything on earth but a prison."[36]

What was disturbing the inspectors' tranquility was not the collapse of order, but the appearance of an alternative order. Inside the prison were two societies: the official society of the Board, which sought to control every moment of the inmates' lives and was enforced (irregularly) by means of starvation, leg irons, and solitary cells; and a counter-society consisting of the autonomous activity of the inmates, who had established, on the foundation of their work and the social relations grown up around it, an authority powerful enough to organize the division of tasks inside the prison, exercise control over the flow of raw materials and finished products through the walls, incorporate lower-level prison officials as accomplices, nullify the hated informer system, and in short, give the Walnut Street Jail the appearance of "anything on earth but a prison." In a report six years later, the inspectors admitted that "any article which the prisoners may be desirous of can be procured with ease owing to the hourly communication with the street by the passing in and out of persons having business with the prison."[37]

In these words the inspectors acknowledged the total breakdown of their plan to isolate the prisoners from society outside the walls. It requires little imagination to envision the brisk trade in prison-made shoes, baked goods, and other staples carried on in the groggeries, brothels, and pawn shops down on the docks less than a mile away, as often as not by the guards. In fact the inmates of the jail were intimately connected with the life of the city around them and their labor was an integral part of the city's economy. Their role in the economy made the inmates not merely prisoners, or convicted criminals, or unfortunate victims of society, but *workers*—in this case unfree workers. Along with slaves, apprentices, and child laborers, as well as the wage-laborers traditionally thought to comprise the working class, they made up part of the capital-labor relation of the time.

On occasion their insubordination compelled prison authorities to summon outside military assistance—to call out the marines. One of these episodes, which prison officials labeled "a general insurrection,"[38] began on the afternoon of March 27, 1820, when forty prisoners attacked a notorious snitch. While he was attempting to flee, one of the convicts crashed in his skull with an iron bar, and another, a man named William McIlhenny, plunged a long knife into him.[39]

The next morning McIlhenny, followed by forty other inmates, attacked the officials. "Down the stairs, in the greatest confusion, tumbled inspectors, keepers, and convicts, black and white, while the upper passages and rooms resounded with shrieks, yells, and groans, and clanging of chains and bars, as the fastenings were torn to pieces with wild fury. In a few moments every door was thrown open, and throughout the whole range the prisoners were released. The force of the rioters was increased by two hundred men, who hastened to the lower hall, and then the entire body of convicts had unlimited sway within the prison. They hurried into the yard to make their escape...."[40] There, the rebelling inmates raised the slogan, "Liberty or Death!"[41]

An alarm spread throughout the city. Armed citizens rushed to the prison, and, from the roofs of the adjoining livery-stable, fired into the crowd in the prison yard, which was trying to batter down the gate with a heavy plank. By this time a company of marines arrived on the scene, and, swarming into the yard with muskets loaded and bayonets fixed, managed to suppress the insurrection.

There were two occasions in 1823 and one in 1825 when prison officials felt sufficiently alarmed by the threat of insurrection to call the marines or other bodies of armed men to help restore their authority in the prison. Thus, by the middle of the decade, Philadelphia's Walnut Street Jail, the "cradle of the penitentiary," had been transformed from a place of confinement into a fortress of revolt.

How important was the prison in the life of the city? In the ten years from 1815 to 1824, 3,308 persons were committed there for felonies.[42] Allowing one-fourth for repeaters gives a figure of almost 2,500 individuals who served time in the Walnut Street Jail during those years.[43] Reducing that figure by one-half to allow for those who died or left the city suggests that there were 1,250 persons living in the city at any one time who had been in the prison. Of these people, more than four-fifths, or 1,000, were male.[44]

The population of metropolitan Philadelphia in 1820, including the Northern Liberties, Southwark, and Moyamensing, was 117,687.[45] Drawing a line horizontally through it gives a figure of 40,000 in the bottom third, the layer from which the prison population was recruited.[46] Since we are dealing only with males here, we may divide this figure by half, and reduce it further by the proportion of children under fourteen, who were excluded from prison. This leaves approximately 12,000 people who constituted what may be called the pool of eligibles for prison. Referring to our earlier figure of 1,000 leads to the conclusion that one out of twelve men in the bottom third of Philadelphia society in the decade of the 1820s had direct personal experience in the Walnut Street Jail, that is, with a regime of perpetual insurrection.[47]

The inmates of the jail were a cross section of the proletariat: laborers, seamen, factory operatives, and service workers.[48] They included a large number of Afro-Americans: of 1,248 men committed between 1818 and 1824, 421, or slightly over one-third, were listed as colored.[49] In addition, there was a significant number of foreigners among them: the Visiting Committee of the Pennsylvania Prison Society reported that of 603 men who were in the prison in 1820, 108 were foreign-born. The report went on to explain, "Penna. joins 3 Slave States and affords an asylum for their Free Blacks and runaway slaves, many of whom, being ignorant (a concomitant of vice) and profligate, soon fall into temptations. This city has been a great landing place for Emigrants from Europe. Some of these linger in the City and after spending their little all, not finding their expectations answered and having no friends, adopt a course of life that brings them to Prison."[50]

The largest single immigrant group in the City was the Irish.[51] Of 520 male prisoners on January 1, 1826, 49 were Irish born.[52] The Irish were also generously represented among the insurgents: Irish surnames appear frequently in the Minutes in connection with various incidents of rebellion in the prison.

One individual, William McIlhenny, was particularly noteworthy in this regard. The first record of him inside the prison was in the Minutes of June 9, 1817, where it was reported that he had been detected preparing poles for an escape and was confined to the cells along with four others thought to be in the plot. Less than a year later, he made another try, which was defeated, and along with two others, he was committed to the cells in irons.[53] On March 11, 1819, McIlhenny, along with five others, managed to get over the wall, but he was taken two weeks later in New York, and brought back to the prison.[54] Later that same year, he is listed, along with Henry Kelly, Barney McCabe, David Miller, John Smith 12th, John Armstrong, John Williams 3rd, James Wall, John Gavin, and Barney Boyle, as a participant in a mass escape attempt.[55] McIlhenny's part in the insurrection of March 1820 has already been recounted. For several years, there is no mention of him in the Minutes, until December 27, 1824, when he was reported as having got over the wall, along with five others, by using a rope ladder with hooks. According to the Inspectors, there was "every reason to believe that McIlhenny was the instigator and prime mover in the whole transaction."[56] In October of the following year he is reported as among those confined to their cells, perhaps as the consequence of the insurrection of July 5 or another escape attempt later that month.[57] His name turns up again in March 1827 as part of a group attempting to scale the walls. "By his account Helmbold, Hale and himself were the originators of the plot and leaders in putting it into execution."[58]

There is no further trace of William McIlhenny in the Minutes. According to the Convict Description Docket of January 1, 1826, he was born in Halifax, Nova Scotia, around 1789.[59] The Sentence Docket describes him as five feet ten inches tall, with light brown hair inclined to bald, medium dark grey eyes, light complexion, "marked on the left arm an anchor on the left hand with India ink." His occupation was given as watchmaker and seaman.[60]

A newspaper account of the 1820 insurrection, written nearly forty years later, said that McIlhenny learned the watchmaker's trade as a youth, left Nova Scotia at the age of eighteen for New York, lived for a while in the West Indies, where he took up burglary as a trade. As an alternative to prison, he served in the British navy and was captured by the French (this would have been during the Napoleonic Wars) and carried to Guadaloupe, whence he was liberated through the interference of the American consul. He spent some time in Charleston, then moved to Baltimore, where he became a sergeant in a cavalry regiment. On release from military service he resumed his extra-legal life in Baltimore, then moved to New York, the scene of his first larceny conviction, for which he was sentenced to four years at hard labor. His first jail stretch in Philadelphia (this would be 1816) was for robbing a jewelry store. The newspaper said he was "not ill-looking, except that his nose, like Mr. Dickens' Monsieur Rigaud, had a tendency to go down as his lip came up, and gave an ugly and sinister expression to his countenance."[61]

No more is known of this man who, around the time of Denmark Vesey and Nat Turner, fought involuntary servitude in the face of the solitary cell, leg irons, "coarse diet," augmented sentences, and hard labor.

One of his fellow conspirators in the 1827 plot, John Hale, born in Ireland, was about thirty-five years old at the time of the escape attempt, and was a laborer, serving a ten-year sentence for larceny.[62] Of the ten named in the Minutes as being implicated in the escape attempt, three were black.

This chapter has looked at prisoner activity as a form of working-class revolt. In the larger society, while Afro-American and Irish-American workers often, and quite militantly, opposed established authority, they rarely collaborated to do so; yet that collaboration was common among the prisoners in the Walnut Street Jail. What accounted for the difference? Put another way, what forces that prevented proletarians in other situations from coming together failed to operate on the prisoners in the Walnut Street Jail?

⁄The issue most relevant for this study is the operation of the color line within the prison. While Negroes were nearly four times as likely as whites to go to prison,[63] the disparity was not so great when allowance is made for social class. Virtually the entire black population fell into those groups from which the prisoners were drawn, compared to one-third of the whites. Of those belonging to what may be called the true proletariat, one out of twelve men, roughly the same proportion among black and white, was putting in his stint in prison, as part of the unfree labor force.

What of the treatment within the prison walls? The record is ambiguous. In 1795, the Board of Inspectors found "confined, in an indiscriminate manner, in the east wing, 26 persons for trial, 15 servants, apprentices and slaves (9 black and 6 white), 8 vagrants, and 5 soldiers." It recommended that the prisoners for trial, sailors, and deserters be confined on the first floor of the east wing, and that the servants, apprentices, and slaves be lodged on the second floor of the east wing, with the vagrants and disorderly persons assigned a third location.[64] Both the failure to mention color as a basis for assignment of lodging and the proposal to house apprentices and slaves together show the prison officials' lack of concern at that time with segregation by color. Two years later, the Board proposed dividing prisoners into four classes, based on seriousness of offense, and assigning each class lodging in a different part of the prison. There was still no mention of color as a basis for classification or assignment.[65] The first director of the prison, Caleb Lownes, noted in 1799 the existence of separate lodging for men and women, with rooms assigned by trade, but made no mention of separation by color.[66] The situation was especially striking to an observer from South Carolina who visited the prison in 1796: "About one-eighth of the number of convicts compose the negroes and mulattoes, between whom and the whites, in this country, are none of those shameful, degrading distinctions you are daily accustomed to in the Southern States. Tried with the same legal solemnities, and by the same tribunals, they have equal privileges with other condemned criminals. At supper, I observed, they were all seated at the same table."[67]

By 1810, though, according to Scharf and Westcott, "at meals the race distinctions were preserved, the whites and blacks eating at different tables."[68] In 1812, when some of the sleeping quarters for youths were integrated in response to overcrowding, the visiting inspectors noted that "this will be an encroachment on the well-directed intention of the Board, in the separation of the black from the white boys, yet as they deem it of the highest importance that the health of the prisoners should be closely attended to, they feel confident this minor innovation will meet the consent of the Board, more especially as it is only intended to have its effect during the night."[69]

It appears that segregation by color at mealtime and in lodging came into existence between 1799 and 1810. If so, why was it noted nowhere in the Minutes of that period? If segregation in lodging was the "well directed intention of the Board," why is there no reference to it in any of the periodic pronouncements that sought to regulate every aspect of prison life from cleanliness to alcohol prohibition to visitors to separation by sex?[70] Was it so unquestioned a part of prison life that they no more bothered to record it than a modern observer would think to note separate toilets for men and women in a government office building? That is not likely in that period when segregation of the races was by no means universal.

At the time they merged the boys' rooms the inspectors spoke of "Black Convict Men's lodging rooms." Each of these rooms, about eighteen feet square, could hold upwards of forty prisoners.[71] In 1820 the Visiting Committee of the Prison Society reported twenty-nine men in solitary cells, including thirteen "refractory" prisoners in irons in consequence of a recent escape attempt, six black men in one cell, three black men each in two cells, and four white men in another cell.[72] Later on, in 1823 and again in 1830, the Minutes referred to escape attempts by black convicts in one or another room; neither reference constitutes conclusive evidence for the existence of segregation, since neither states that the only occupants of the room were Negroes, or that all the Afro-American prisoners were in "black" rooms.[73] Moreover, "black" and "white" rooms could be located side by side within a wing of the prison.[74]

An anonymous writer around 1820, describing the Prune Street apartment, reported that it housed "a motley crew composed of counterfeiters, horse thieves, highway robbers, murderers, pickpockets, etc. Here are white, black, mulatto and very little distinction made as to colour or crime." He also noted, however, that "the whites eat first, and then the blacks."[75] The Acting Committee of the Prison Society described the place as a "common receptacle of all grades before trial also for vagrants, apprentice boys and girls disobedient to their masters, deserters from the army and runaway slaves. For this motley group (save the separation of the sexes) there is no means of classification."[76] About ten years later, a grand jury looking into conditions in the Arch Street prison, which had been opened in 1817 to relieve overcrowding at Walnut Street, reported that in the section assigned to debtors, "white and black were found in one hall together."[77]

Why did Vaux, the Prison Society, and the Board all fail to mention color segregation in any of their writings on the prison, including the Minutes of the Board of Inspectors, although they repeatedly stressed the need for separation by sex, age, and type of offense? Many individuals were named in the Minutes; their color was often not specified. The omission reveals much about official attitudes. More significant is that in some cases where it has been possible to identify individuals through court records, the omission was found to occur in the case of Negro as well as white prisoners.

It is difficult to determine the extent or consistency of the color line within the prison, or who was responsible for it, not because of the lack of evidence, but because there was no single, true picture. While practice on race segregation during meal times and at night varied, black and white prisoners were normally thrown together in the workshops and yard. Official society in the North was working out its stance toward the free Negro, and the indeterminacy within the prison was an expression of the contradictory aspects of the process.

During the entire period from 1815 to 1830, there was not a single battle in the Walnut Street Jail between black and white prisoners, as such. This stands out in sharp contrast to the picture in the city outside the walls.

The incident which came closest to aligning whites against Negroes generally in the prison was in July 1819, in which a number of prisoners helped the guards thwart an escape attempt. None of the ten men named as part of the attempt were identified by race; of the six whose race it has been possible to establish, all were white. Among the prisoners who took the side of the guards were four Negroes and five whites. One of the whites was stabbed three days later "by some person at present unknown, it is believed in consequence of the part he took in quelling the riot."[78]

In America at that date no conflict involving Afro-Americans and whites would have been free of racial overtones. But even if all those attempting to escape were white and a disproportionate number of the prisoners who opposed them were black, two things demonstrate that the sides were not determined by color: first, the men trying to get out were equal opportunity stabbers; second the prisoners themselves interpreted it not as a race conflict but a break for freedom.

It will be recalled that the insurrection of March 1820, began as a fight between a Negro and a white. Prison observers were aware of its essentially nonracial character: the Visiting Committee of the Prison Society reported that it was "occasioned by a dislike the coloured men took to a Blackman" but that it "was not confined to the blacks; the whites took considerable part in it."[79]

The experience of the prison in those years shows not the absence of color awareness on the part of prison officials or prisoners, or perfect harmony among prisoners of different backgrounds, but the weakness of "race" as a social definition within the prison. The absence of fixed, institutional distinctions between black and white led prisoners of European descent, particularly the Irish who are the subjects of this study, to view themselves, and act, more as people trying to get out of jail than as whites.

Thomas Branagan personifies some of the ambiguities of the Irish stance toward Afro-Americans in the early period. He was born in Dublin on December 28, 1774, of a prosperous, respectable Catholic family. As a child he was so affected by the beggars who stood in front of a church that he vowed to devote half his earnings to the poor forever. When he was thirteen he went to sea, with his father's consent, first on short voyages across the English channel, then to Seville, and later to Russia, Denmark, and Poland. Mistreated on one of these voyages, he jumped ship and made his way back to Dublin. The captain, however, was a friend of his father's, who reprimanded Thomas for not giving notice. A few days later he left Dublin for Liverpool, now on his own.[80]

In 1790 he sailed from Liverpool on a slave ship, arriving on the west coast of Africa after a frequently stormy voyage of two or three months. The ship stayed in Africa for about six months, while the crew traded with the natives, bought slaves, and explored. Once, following a quarrel with the chief mate, Thomas deserted the ship for several weeks and lived with Africans, who treated him like "a dear friend or relative."

After completing its cargo, the ship sailed for Grenada, "with such a number of slaves on board that there was not room for the sailors below." Paid off in Grenada, Thomas stayed on in the West Indies, sailing to many of the islands on English and Dutch ships. He also made a trip to Savannah, "escaping many alarming dangers of the American coast." Upon being defrauded of his wages for a voyage, he signed on an English privateer, but he decided to "relinquish the wages of iniquity" and left it without receiving a penny of the loot. After a few more voyages, he settled in Antigua, where he served as an overseer on a plantation.

Twenty years old when he began in Antigua, he remained there for four years. Sometime during his stay he took up religion, converting to Protestantism. Part of his conversion was awakening to a realization of the evils of slavery. He vowed

> I would not have a slave to till my ground—
> To carry me—to fan me while I sleep,
> And tremble when I wake—for all the wealth
> That sinews bought and sold have ever earn'd:
> No;—dear as freedom is, and in my heart's
> Just estimation prized above all price,
> I had much rather be myself the slave,
> And wear the bonds, than fasten them on him.[81]

The evening prior to his departure from Antigua, he exhorted and prayed with the slaves. He returned to Dublin, after an absence of eight years, to settle his father's estate. At first he was received warmly, but when his relatives learned he had "forsaken the church of Rome, they persecuted [him] as a heretic, and defrauded [him] of [his] rights with impunity."

And so, like many of his countrymen in those years, he set off for Philadelphia, arriving in 1799 after being cast away at the Capes of Delaware, and being robbed of everything but his clothes by one of the passengers. There he began to preach the gospel to the "poor and needy, the halt, the maimed and the blind." He also began to write.

Branagan's first work to see print was the *Preliminary Essay on the Oppression of the Exiled Sons of Africa*, published in Philadelphia in 1804. It was 278 pages long and contained sections on the beauty and fertility of Africa and the noble character of its inhabitants, the cruelties of slavery, a survey of the ancient world, a comparison of conditions in the British, Dutch, and French colonies based on personal observation, an appeal to the Christian world, reminding it of the price Babylon had paid for its crimes, and appeals to the British Houses of Parliament and the legislature of South Carolina. He appended to it a letter to Napoleon he had written in 1801.

Branagan's *Preliminary Essay* was a wholehearted denunciation of slavery, based on an unequivocal defense of the natural equality of all men. He put forward a Lamarckian theory of evolution, explaining differences of color and other physical characteristics as adaptations to climate, and gave numerous proofs of the intelligence of Africans. "Do not the Africans," he asked,

> possess the same specific nature, the same faculties and powers, corporal and mental, the same attachments and aversions, sensations and feelings, with the inhabitants of Asia, Europe, and America? Is it not a prevailing sentiment among all the nations of mankind, that all men, as they come into the world, are equal? Does not this equality comprehend Adam's family from his first born, to his youngest son, with all his countless intermediate children? Are not all subsequent distinctions adventitious and accidental? Are not the innumerable millions of mankind, members of one family and children of one father? Was it ever known, was it ever heard, that one child of a family had a right to enslave another?[82]

His solution was unconditional and complete abolition of slavery, and until that was effected, legislation to reduce its harshness. In his 1839 memoir, Branagan recalled that Thomas Jefferson had admired the *Preliminary Essay*, and had written to George Logan, senator from Pennsylvania, who from that time became Branagan's "most generous patron."[83]

Early in 1805 Branagan published *Avenia: A Tragical Poem on the Oppression of the Human Species, and Infringement on the Rights of Man*, a 308-page epic poem in frank imitation of the *Iliad*, probably begun before the *Preliminary Essay*.

Awake my muse, the sweet Columbian strain,

Depict the wars on Afric's crimson plain.
Sing how the poor, unhappy sable dames
Are violated at their rural games;
How Afric's sons surrounded with alarms,
Die in the cause of liberty, in arms;
How with their bloody scourge the Christians go
To Africa, dread ministers of woe;
How big with war their tilting dungeons ride,
Like floating castles o'er the yielding tide.
What pen can half their villainies record?
What tongue can count the slaughters of their sword?[84]

The poem tells of the African princess Avenia, her lover the faithful Angola, her noble brother Louverture (!), the horrors perpetrated by Christian slave traders, the wars between the Africans and the marauders, the triumph of superior weaponry, and the carrying of Avenia off to a plantation in the West Indies, where she is ravished by her master and commits suicide by flinging herself into the sea.

Later that same year he published *The Penitential Tyrant; or, Slave Trader Reformed*, another epic poem recounting the rural happiness of the Africans and the cruelties of slavery. It may have been an earlier version of *Avenia*.[85]

The year 1805 saw the appearance of a new work, *Serious Remonstrances Addressed to the Citizens of the Northern States, and Their Representatives*, also published in Philadelphia. It marked quite a turn for Branagan. While certainly antislavery, the work no longer rested its argument on the humanity of the Africans, but appealed to the self-interest of white people in the free states. "The tyrants of the South," he wrote, referring to the three-fifths clause, "gain an ascendancy over the citizens of the North…accordingly as they enslave and subjugate the inoffensive, the exiled sons of Africa" (xiii).

The most harmful consequence of the slave system was the production of free Negroes, "the refuse and off scouring of the citizenry of the South" (xiii). Free Negroes were a dangerous class, because it would be "impossible for the blacks in the North ever to be reconciled to the whites while hundreds of thousands of their countrymen are groaning, bleeding, and dying…in the South" (39). "If a certain family used my father and his family (myself excepted) as the Christians do the exiled Africans, could I forget it" (43)? Aside from harboring natural desires for revenge, the free Negroes brought with them "all the accumulated depravity which they have been long accustomed to: such as lying, pilfering, stealing, swearing, deceit, and a thousand meaner vices, the fruits of slavery" (68). Among their most offensive characteristics was an excessive fondness for white women (and an exaggerated appeal for them). He complained of "white women married to, and deluded through the arts of seduction by negroes" (71). The greatest centers for these alliances were "gentlemen's houses, where the maid servants are generally white, and the men servants black" (74). There were "more bound and hired white girls in such men's houses, deluded by black men, than anywhere else" (102). The result was a growing mass of "mungrels and mulattoes," with the inevitable consequence that "in the course of a few years…half the inhabitants of the city will be people of Colour" (80). Along with the revulsion at such matings came appeals on behalf of immigrants from Europe:

> The hardy Irish, and industrious Germans, flying from European bondage and settling among us is vastly advantageous, and should be greatly encouraged….But how must it damp their spirits when they come and have to associate with negroes, take them for companions, and what is much worse, be thrown out of work and precluded from getting employ to keep vacancies for blacks." (79)

He admitted that the best plan would be to gradually emancipate the slaves, and educate them for citizenship (38). Unfortunately that would produce "unpleasant effects" (39) under the actual circumstances; therefore, he called for the federal government to "appropriate a few hundred thousand acres of land, at some distant part of the nation" (22) for free Negroes. It would be wrong, however, to extend citizenship to them, even in a separate territory: "the naturalization of the blacks is unavoidably connected with the degradation of the whites" (124). They must be maintained as wards of the state.

What explains Branagan's transformation from abolitionist to proto-colonizationist? What would lead a man to rail against "mungrels and mulattoes" when but a year earlier he had neutrally offered the fertility of the offspring of sexual union of Africans and Europeans as proof of the common humanity of the people of all nations? How could a man who had written of all men as children of one father now speak of two families, one injuring the other? Gary Nash offers a partial explanation: on July 4, 1805, several hundred Afro-Americans assembled in the Southwark district and marched in military formation, armed with bludgeons and swords, treating roughly whites who crossed their path and entering the house of a hostile white, pummeling him and his friends. The next evening, they gathered again, "damning the whites and saying they would shew them St. Domingo."[86]

There is another explanation, and the reference to St. Domingo is key; for it was in 1804 that Dessalines, the successor to Toussaint L'Ouverture, tore the white stripe out of the flag of Haiti and launched his campaign to exterminate the whites of that country. Sure enough, *Serious Remonstrances* contains one long disquisition and several passing remarks on "the tragical scene acted in Hispaniola" (49–53, 67, 71). The man who had given the name of Louverture to the hero of his epic poem now shrunk from the reality of servile insurrection. The man who had exhorted and prayed with Africans on the eve of his departure from Antigua now saw himself a potential victim of their struggle for freedom.[87]

Branagan poured out a mighty flood of literary works over his lifetime, dealing with patriotism, true religion, the rights of women, physiognomy, geography, ancient and modern history, and other subjects. In one of them, *The Charms of Benevolence* (Philadelphia, 1813), he included a long passage on the injustices suffered by Ireland, as an indictment of monarchy. He traveled the east coast, preaching in every town between Maine and Philadelphia. On one occasion he felt it his duty to address the students at Princeton on true Christian divinity:

> I therefore posted my bill on the market-house, and rode up the street till I was nearly opposite the college, when with palpitating heart, quivering voice, and eyes fast closed, I sung a hymn, still on horseback—a crowd of colegians and others soon gathered, and some began to laugh an geer [sic], when I began my discourse, but soon were all attention, and continued so till I ended it.[88]

What audacity, what dedication he must have had to attempt to preach religion to Princeton students, and what power, to gain and hold their attention!

In 1839 Branagan published in New York *The Guardian Genius of the Federal Union*, consisting mostly of selections from his earlier works. In it he returned to the subject of slavery, perhaps moved by efforts to annex Texas and reintroduce slavery there. Slavery, he declared, was "the greatest evil and the sum-total of all evils under the sun" (25), and "to sanction and support slavery in Texas is a national crime that would have disgraced Sodom and Gomorrah" (66). His attitude toward the Negro was now ambiguous: quoting Jefferson's proposal for gradual emancipation and resettlement, he adds:

> What place can possibly be more cheap, convenient, and proper, than their own native soil of America? To suppose that the country will be so liberal as to declare them free, transport, and settle them in colonies, and lose all their valuable labour, is to presuppose a liberality adequate to colonize them at home; that is, make them free citizens where they now are, and save the immense expense and risk of removal, and secure their services to the country. (46)

It is not clear whether he is still talking about colonization, differing only in the proposed location of the colony, or if he means to make the Negroes "free citizens where they are now." In the same work he quoted O'Connell, "I have often longed to go to America, but as long as that country is tarnished by slavery, I will never pollute my feet by treading on its shores" (90).

Thomas Branagan, born Dublin 1774, died Philadelphia 1843, with his fervent heart, his devotion to learning, his hatred of injustice, and his retreat from the consequences of his own vision, carried within himself the divided soul of the Irish in America.

Recently a literary historian asked about Mark Twain's character Huck Finn, "Was Huck Black?"[89] Through a comparison of Afro-American speech patterns with Huck's speech, and through the discovery of a ten-year-old Negro boy who may have served Twain as a model for Huck, she concluded that yes, Huck Finn was part black. Her question prompts another: Was Huck Irish?

The evidence is suggestive, in the first place the surname Twain gave him, Irish if ever there was. Beyond the name, there are the facts of Huck's life: son of the town drunk, Huck has run away from Widow Douglas, Miss Watson, his father, and the entire community of St. Petersburg. He meets Jim, a slave of Miss Watson, who has also run off, and they set off together on a raft down the Mississippi, intending to turn north at Cairo, up the Ohio River to freedom. On the journey they have adventures and swap tales. From Jim he learns about omens and charms. It is a very "Irish" story.

There is evidence that Twain himself saw Huck as Irish. In a May 7, 1884, letter, Twain wrote, "I returned the book-back [book cover for *The Adventures of Huckleberry Finn*]. All right and good, and will answer, although the boy's mouth is a trifle more Irishy than necessary."[90] But even if Huck's Irishness is pure fancy, it suggests a profound truth about America, that the national character, embodied in the country's most beloved literary figure, is part Irish as well as part Negro.

The climax of *Huck Finn*—and perhaps the most intense moment in all of American literature—comes when Huck is forced to choose between doing what respectable society expects of him, writing the letter that will return Jim to his rightful owner, and following another part of his mind. He writes the letter, but before he can send it his mind turns to their trip down the river: "Somehow I couldn't seem to strike no places to harden me against him, but only the other kind."

...and then I happened to see that paper.

It was a close place. I took it up, and held it in my hand. I was a-trembling, because I'd got to decide, forever, betwixt two things, and I knowed it. I studied a minute, sort of holding my breath, and then says to myself:

"All right, then, I'll go to hell"—and tore it up.

It was awful thoughts and awful words, but they was said. And I let them stay said; and never thought no more about reforming. I shoved the whole thing out of my head, and said I would take up wickedness again, which was in my line, being brung up to it, and the other warn't. And for a starter I would go to work and steal Jim out of slavery again; and if I could think up anything worse, I would do that, too; because as long as I was in, and in for good, I might as well go the whole hog.

As we know, the Irish in America chose not to go the whole hog, but opted instead for the privileges and burdens of whiteness. The outcome was not a foregone conclusion. In this chapter I have tried to suggest that, while the white skin made the Irish eligible for membership in the white race, it did not guarantee their admission; they had to earn it. The following chapters will examine how they did so.

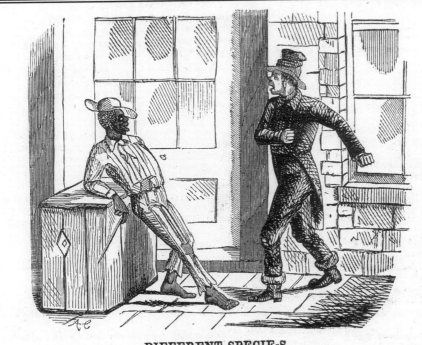

**DIFFERENT SPECIE-S.**

*Native American Voter, just Naturalized.* "GIT OUT O' THE WAY WID YOU! DON'T YOU SEE I'M ONE OV THE SOVERIN PEOPLE, BAD LUCK TO YOU?"

*Independent Ethiopian.* "IS YA? S'POSIN YOU ARE, AIN'T I ONE OB DE GUINEA PEOPLE? YAH! YAH!"

# III

# THE
# TRANSUBSTANTIATION
## OF AN
# IRISH REVOLUTIONARY

In 1838, as Daniel O'Connell was loudly proclaiming his opposition to threatened U.S. annexation of Texas, a group of prominent Philadelphia Irish wrote him regarding some remarks he was reported to have made in which he spoke harshly of the American character. "The natives of Ireland," they pointed out, "bear true allegiance to the country that has adopted them and are ever ready to serve her." O'Connell's remarks, they wrote, would cause them to be looked upon "jealously and suspiciously...by our native American citizens." They therefore requested an explanation "in order to remove from the natives of Ireland...the odium which...had been cast upon them." One of the signers of the letter was John Binns, at the time a Philadelphia alderman.[1]

Binns was a representative figure. He was born in Dublin in 1772, of mixed Anglican and Dissenter stock. His mother was widowed when he was two years old. Although lacking a regular education, he early developed a reading habit. When he was fourteen, he was apprenticed to a soap-boiler.[2]

His grand-uncle was a representative on the Dublin Common Council, "and a speaker of fearless ability on the liberal political side." Binns was personally acquainted with James Napper Tandy and Archibald Hamilton Rowan, both prominent figures in the movement for Irish independence led by Henry Grattan, and as a youth took part in maneuvers of the Irish volunteers.[3]

"It seems scarcely possible for the people of the present century," wrote Binns in his memoirs, "to form a correct idea of the enthusiastic rejoicings and powerful sympathy of a large portion of the human family on the outbreak of the French Revolution of 1789....The people and the press emulated each other in their congratulations, and in their praises and glorifications of France and of the French people. Spirited and expensive scenic representations of the 'Destruction of the Bastille,' were performed at all the theatres and circuses, not only in London, but in all the cities and large towns in Great Britain and Ireland. In them were introduced, sung, and danced, the popular French airs, *Ca Ira, Carmagnole,* etc."[4]

In Britain, one of the fruits of that enthusiasm was the London Corresponding Society, organized in 1791 by Thomas Hardy, a shoemaker. The Society has been called the world's first working-class organization.[5] According to Binns, it "occupied the public mind, and the attention of the Government, more than any other popular political association, save only the Whig Club." Many of its active members were Irish residing in England. Its avowed object was parliamentary reform based on universal suffrage, but "the wishes and hopes of many of its influential members carried them to the overthrow of the monarchy and the establishment of a republic."[6]

In 1791, as part of its efforts to suppress rising popular discontent in England, the British government declared war on France. The Society soon found itself in trouble. In 1794, Thomas Hardy and other members were tried for high treason, but were acquitted. That same year, Binns moved to London, where he became a traveling deputy for the Society. The following year he chaired a demonstration in London against starvation called by the Society, which was attended by as many as 150,000. Three days later a London crowd attacked King George III's carriage, hissing and shouting, "No War," "Down with Pitt," and "No King."[7]

In 1796 Binns was appointed the Society's delegate to Birmingham. Hardly had he begun his duties when he was arrested, charged with having delivered "seditious and inflammatory lectures."[8]

Between his arrest and trial, there took place the naval mutinies at Spithead and the Nore, which, as Melville later wrote, "jeopardized the very existence of the British navy."[9] For a week the mutineers blockaded the Thames, and there was talk among them of sailing the fleet to France. 11,500 Irish sailors and 4,000 Irish marines contributed to the insurrectionary mood. Some of the sailors were in contact with the Society.

According to E. P. Thompson, it is likely that the Society during that period developed an underground section, and that Binns was a member. The illegal organization was strong among the Irish coal-heavers on the Thames, and was also alleged to have considerable strength in Liverpool and Manchester.[10]

Binns was brought to trial in August of 1797, and acquitted.[11] He was then twenty-four years old. In that dawn when "bliss was it to be alive, but to be young was very heaven," it was not easy to persuade a British jury to convict someone for delivering seditious and inflammatory lectures.

The following year the Irish, encouraged by promises of French support, broke out in rebellion. Sympathy for the rebellion was widespread. The Society called upon English soldiers in Ireland to refuse to act as "Agents of enslaving Ireland." The British government rounded up those Society leaders it could get its hands on.[12]

Binns himself was arrested on his return from a trip he made to the coast to arrange for the smuggling of arms to Ireland. He was first charged with attempting to leave Britain without a valid passport, was released and then rearrested on a charge of high treason. Examined by the Privy Council, including Pitt, he was sent first to the Tower of London, and then to Maidstone prison, to await trial. On the 24th of May, 1798, he was once again acquitted by a jury. On his return to London, he learned of another warrant for his arrest, and so he retreated to the countryside, "where [he] had many friends," and lived for a while "very agreeably" under his mother's maiden name. Five months later, he returned to London.[13]

In March of 1799 a secret committee of the House of Commons reported attempts to form a Society of United Englishmen (modeled on the Society of United Irishmen that had initiated the rebellion of 1798), and named Binns as one of the conspirators. It cited a "seditious paper" from the London Corresponding Society—the 1798 tract encouraging rebellion among English troops in Ireland. (Binns, in his memoirs, claimed authorship.) Once more arrested and charged with high treason, Binns was again hauled before the Privy Council, and then transferred to Gloucester prison, where he spent the next two years.[14]

While in prison, Binns wrote to the Duke of Portland, home secretary, declaring the charge against him false. "If I am a traitor," he proclaimed, "let me be proven so! Let the sanguinary sentence of the law be executed—let my panting heart be flung in my face—let my streaming head be held up as a terror to evil-doers—let my limbs be left to bleach in the winds of heaven..." He demanded to be brought immediately to trial, or released on bail. "Let me be perfectly understood," he wrote, "I will give bail for my appearance, to answer whatever charges may be exhibited against me. But *I will not* give bail for what the law terms good behavior. I am, in common with every member of society, bound by its general laws, and subject to their penalties. I will not tacitly acknowledge guilt by imposing peculiar restrictions upon myself."[15]

In March 1801 he was released from prison without a trial. By that time, the revolutionary tide had receded, and the London Corresponding Society had been broken up. On the first of July, 1801, John Binns set off from Liverpool for Pennsylvania.[16]

Binns was following in the wake of the 30,000 Irish who arrived in Philadelphia during the decade of the 1790s.[17] Many of them, especially those who arrived after 1795, were influenced by the radical currents circulating in Ireland at the time. One publicist warned that 1,500 assassins organized by the Society of United Irishmen were conspiring to carry out an insurrection, with French aid, in Philadelphia.[18] While such fears were unwarranted, the majority of Irish immigrants did gravitate toward the Republican party (as Jefferson's supporters were known).[19]

The Federalists were alarmed by the threat to their power represented by the influx of voters sympathetic to the opposition, and on July 1, 1797, Harrison Gray Otis, Federalist Congressman from Boston, delivered a speech on the floor of Congress in which he declared he did "not wish to invite hoards of wild Irishmen, nor the turbulent and disorderly of all parts of the world, to come here with a view to disturb our tranquility, after having succeeded in the overthrow of their own governments." Out of this fear arose the Alien and Sedition Acts of 1798, which restricted naturalization, and hence voting rights, of immigrants. Some Federalists even sought to restrict the political rights of foreign-born citizens: Otis moved that they be barred from holding office, and Representative Samuel Sewall, also of Massachusetts, called attention to the danger of allowing Irish to hold seats in the government even after a residence of five years, owing to "the present distracted state of the country from whence they have emigrated." The Federalists' special concern with the Irish was logical, on quantitative as well as qualitative grounds: Irish made up fifty-five percent of all those naturalized in Philadelphia between 1789 and 1800.[20]

Otis's speech and the Federalists' suspicion of immigrants brought about the very result they wished to prevent. Pennsylvania Federalists attributed their defeat in the gubernatorial election of 1799 to a statewide coalition of Irish and German voters; in Southwark, Philadelphia, an Irish stronghold, the Jeffersonian party received seventy-three percent of the votes.[21]

Binns arrived in Baltimore, then a major port for southeastern Pennsylvania, on September 1, 1801, after a sea voyage of nine weeks. Kept away from the city by reports of yellow fever, the passengers stopped at a hotel a mile out of town. Binns later recalled, "What with bull-frogs, common frogs, tidetids, etc. etc., and negro huts, in which there was much shouting, screaming, and clapping of hands, my ears never before had been assailed by such a multitude of confused, unusual, and unmusical sounds....At the hotel where we stopped, for the first time I ate cakes made of that delicious vegetable, Indian corn." The next day, he set off on foot, accompanied by three wagons loaded with supplies he had brought with him. On his arrival in Harrisburg he hired a boat to carry him and his supplies to Northumberland, a lively commercial town on the Susquehanna River, about one hundred miles northwest of Philadelphia.[22]

Although he had never before tasted Indian corn, Binns quickly found his place in the party politics of the young Republic. He made contact with two Englishmen who had held seats in the French Convention of 1793 and who were now living in Northumberland: Dr. Joseph Priestly, the famous chemist and philosopher, and Thomas Cooper, who later became president of the University of South Carolina.

Binns had the support of William Duane, fellow Irishman and editor of the Philadelphia *Aurora*, the most influential Jeffersonian paper in the state.[23] In 1802, Duane offered him the editorship of a Republican newspaper about to be established in Washington, or, if he should prefer to live in Philadelphia, editorial charge of the *Aurora*. Binns chose to remain in Northumberland for the time being, and set about canvassing subscribers for a paper there. Early the next year, the first issue of the *Republican Argus* came out under his editorship.[24]

The Republican Party was dedicated to preserving national unity through conciliation of the slaveholding South. While the merchant-landlord coalition on which it was based remained intact, it functioned effectively—so effectively that Federalism virtually ceased to exist as a distinct party. "We are all Republicans, we are all Federalists," proclaimed Jefferson. However, the growth of market culture in the North, together with the rise of cotton in the South, produced new strains. The crisis of 1819–1820 over whether to admit Missouri as a slave state revealed a regional split in the governing coalition, and led to the collapse of Jefferson's Party.

Speaking of the solid block of Northern congressmen who voted against Missouri, John Quincy Adams commented, "Here was a new party ready formed…terrible to the whole Union, but portentously terrible to the South—threatening in its progress the emancipation of all their slaves, threatening in its immediate effect that Southern domination which has swayed the Union for the last twenty years…."[25]

Jefferson showed that he was aware of the danger, when he noted that the "wholesome" "party divisions of whig and tory" served to "keep out those of a more dangerous character."[26] His famous "firebell in the night" remark, then, wherein he warned that "a geographical line, coinciding with a marked principle, moral and political, once conceived and held up to the angry passions of men, will never be obliterated," was as much, if not more, a reiteration of his opposition to placing the slave question on the national agenda as it was a meditation on the immorality of slavery.

Missouri showed the slaveholders the need for a new party to secure their domination over the Union. The person who gave it to them was Martin Van Buren, and his instrument was Andrew Jackson. Van Buren's accomplishment is shown in the continuous rule of the Democratic consensus from 1828 to 1860, even through two nominally Whig administrations.

The Democratic Party Van Buren built was the first political party based on popular constituencies instead of parliamentary caucuses. It represented, as he wrote, a "political combination...between the planters of the South and the plain Republicans of the North."[27] At first sight its constituent elements would appear to have had little in common. They were held together by white supremacy, which yoked the Party's popular Northern base to the most infamous of all aristocracies. White supremacy was not a flaw in American democracy but part of its definition, and the development of democracy in the Jacksonian period cannot be understood without reference to white supremacy. As it became the pillar of the Democratic Party, Jeffersonian reservations over slavery and willingness to entertain notions of natural human equality (expressed in his *Notes on Virginia*) gave way to militant racial ideology. Little wonder, then, that an 1833 traveler remarked that he had never met a Negro who was not "an anti-Jackson man."[28]

The United States of North America, after the electoral reforms of the Jacksonian period, was perhaps the most truly democratic republic the world had ever seen up to that time, and arguably more democratic than any it has seen since. That assertion is based, first, on the lack of significant property restrictions on the franchise among the free population, and, second, on the weakness of the state, that is, the relative absence of administrative organs and bodies of armed men, differentiated from the general population and therefore insulated from politics, charged with maintaining order. Karl Marx was probably thinking of this situation when he referred to the U.S. workingmen as "the true political power of the North." The present writer, certainly not alone, read those words on numerous occasions without stopping to think about what they meant, passing over them as hyperbolae prompted by the occasion on which they were written (an address of the International Workingmen's Association to Abraham Lincoln toward the end of the Civil War). Only since undertaking to write this chapter have I understood their import; the entire passage reads:

> While the workingmen, the true political power of the North,
> allowed slavery to defile their own republic; while before the
> Negro, mastered and sold without his concurrence, they boasted it

the highest prerogative of the white-skinned laborer to sell himself and choose his own master; they were unable to attain the true freedom of labor or to support their European brethren in the struggle for emancipation, but this barrier to progress has been swept off by the red sea of civil war.[29]

In a certain sense, this study may be understood as a meditation on how the Irish, an important contingent of "the true political power of the North," came to boast the white skin as their highest prerogative.

Slaveholder ideologists understood full well the importance of gaining the support of Northern laborers, and made special appeals to them. Francis W. Pickens, a Calhoun lieutenant, declared in the House of Representatives in 1837 that Southern planters stood in relation to Northern capital "precisely in the same situation as the laborer of the North," declaring them the "only class of capitalists…which, as a class, are identified with the laborers of the country." And the affection was reciprocal. During Calhoun's presidential drive between 1842 and 1844, laborite historian Fitzwilliam Birdsall wrote him that "the radical portion of the Democratic Party here…is the very portion most favorable to you." Later on, when James H. Hammond of South Carolina, another Calhoun lieutenant, lashed out in a famous speech against "wage slavery," he received many letters from Northern workers thanking him for exposing their conditions.[30]

In the combination of Southern planters and the "plain Republicans" of the North, the Irish were to become a key element. The truth is not, as some historians would have it, that slavery made it possible to extend to the Irish the privileges of citizenship, by providing another group for them to stand on, but the reverse, that the assimilation of the Irish into the white race made it possible to maintain slavery. The need to gain the loyalty of the Irish explains why the Democratic Party, on the whole, rejected nativism. It also explains why not merely slavery but the color line became so important to it. To trace, therefore, the movement from the Republican Party that carried out the "civil revolution of 1801" to the Democratic Party that served as the center of parliamentary opposition to the civil revolution of 1854–1877 (counting from the first shots fired in Kansas to the withdrawal of the last federal troops from the South) is to explain the link between the Jacobin, agitator, conspirator, gunrunner, and jailbird who left Ireland in 1801 and the alderman who swore his allegiance to the Constitution and slavery in 1838. It is also to answer the question, how did the Irish become white in America?

If this were a work of fiction, the character John Binns would, along with other radicals, jump on the Jackson bandwagon when it made its first appearance in 1822, and be rewarded by a government post through which he dispensed public works jobs to working-class Irish while upholding the slave system and helping to subjugate the free black people of the North. While that is essentially what happened, the facts are considerably messier than that simple tale (one of the reasons why art is often truer than life), and since the rules of the historian's craft differ from those of the novelist's, the writer will have to extract the essential truth from a series of complicated and bewildering events.[31]

In 1805, Binns backed an insurgent candidate for Pennsylvania governor against the incumbent Republican, who had allied with the Federalists. Although his candidate was defeated, the campaign expanded Binns's influence in the state.[32]

Binns's near-success in 1805 persuaded him to move to Philadelphia from Northumberland to establish a new paper. The first issue of the *Democratic Press* appeared on March 27, 1807, with the motto, "The Tyrant's Foe; the People's Friend." As Binns noted in his memoirs, "It was the *first* paper published in the Union, or anywhere else, under the title of DEMOCRATIC...." Binns published the paper until 1829, and during those years he was a major political power in the state. John Quincy Adams noted, "Pennsylvania has been for about twenty years governed by two newspapers in succession...the *Aurora*...and...the *Democratic Press*."[33] Both, it may be noted, were published by "wild Irishmen."

In 1808 Binns's candidate was elected governor, and for the next nine years Binns "enjoyed a very large portion of [the governor's] confidence, and greatly influenced his judgement and his appointments."[34]

When a new governor was elected in 1817, with Binns's backing, it appeared that Binns's position was secure, but surprisingly the governor, under pressure from other factional allies, denied him the alderman's post he had expected, removed him as one of the directors of the

Pennsylvania Bank, and then, worst of all, shifted the government printing contract from the *Democratic Press* to the newly established *Franklin
Gazette*. As Binns said, he "could not have been in a worse situation if a
federal governor had been elected."[35]

Binns retaliated by launching a campaign to impeach the new governor. The campaign failed, and the legislative committee of inquiry issued
a report denouncing "mercenary parties, whose sole object is the emol-
ument or factitious consequences of office." The report amounted to a
rebuke of Binns.[36]

Binns was in a tough spot, with nowhere to turn but to the camp of
the despised Federalists. As he recounted in his memoirs, "I cannot but
smile at the awkwardness of my political position....The members of the
party with whom I had now to act...desired the influence of my paper,
and did not feel under any obligation to give me pecuniary assistance."
When he pressed the desperation of his situation, they responded by
offering him a mortgage on his house.[37] However, in 1820 the state elected
a new governor, and in 1822 he appointed Binns as an alderman of the
city of Philadelphia.

A city alderman was the face of the state, such as it was in that
period. He heard criminal cases, granted tavern licences, and decided
small claims. The alderman's office "was a community center in every
ward, the point of origin for all court business as well as the headquarters of a prominent neighborhood politician...." All day long, ward residents streamed in and out of the alderman's office, bringing him a variety of civil and criminal business from marriage to murder. Constables
attached to the alderman waited for an opportunity to serve a summons
or an arrest warrant. Bail bondsmen loitered about looking for business. Notorious lawyers, "the vermin of the profession," also frequented
the offices in pursuit of clients. On a typical day in 1848, one alderman
heard six assault-and-battery cases, three larceny cases, three breach of
ordinance cases, one firecracker case, one fast-driving case, and one case
of throwing torpedoes on the stage of the Arch Street Theatre. He
committed three boys to the House of Refuge; issued two landlord's
warrants of eviction, two private notices, and eight summonses; and had
one man examined for life insurance and one operated on for opthalmia.
In addition, he conducted one marriage ceremony. An alderman also

granted tavern licences, and worked on piece-work, an arrangement which, as can be imagined, allowed for a wide latitude of interpretation.[38]

Binns opened an office to discharge his duties, and was gradually able to recover his losses.[39] In the course of his years in office, he compiled two handbooks, *Binns' Justice* and *Binns' Daily Companion*, which became the standard reference works for aldermen and justices throughout Pennsylvania.[40]

In 1822 the Congressional Republican caucus nominated for president William Crawford of Georgia. Hoping to restore his standing in the party, Binns supported him against Clay, Adams, Jackson, and Calhoun. As part of his strenuous exertions on Crawford's behalf, Binns produced a handbill depicting Jackson as the executioner during the War of 1812 of six militia men who had left the service when their term of duty expired, without the express permission of the General.[41] Although Pennsylvania went overwhelmingly for Jackson in 1824 (indeed, it was the state that launched his candidacy), no candidate received a majority of electoral votes, and Adams was chosen as president by the House of Representatives.

The "coffin handbill" gained a great deal of notoriety; on election night a mob of Jackson supporters tried to force its way into Binns's house, with the aim of putting him in a coffin and parading him around town. It also had a lasting effect on Binns's political career. He had burned his bridges to the General. "At the next presidential election," he wrote in his memoirs, "General Jackson was the candidate of the Democratic Party. If I had not so entirely committed myself by what I had previously published against General Jackson,...*now* was the time for me to return to my first love...I have sometimes thought that if my aid had not been so anxiously sought and myself thought purchasable, it is not altogether improbable that I should have fallen into the ranks with my old friends...."[42]

For a while he "was thrown, head and heels, newspaper and all, into the Federal ranks," but that alliance could not endure. A year after Jackson's election, Binns ceased publication of the *Democratic Press*.

Even after he surrendered his newspaper, Binns remained a power in local politics. His continued presence was made possible by the peculiar conditions that prevailed in Pennsylvania, which resisted the formation of national, or even statewide, parties longer than any other state in the northeast. Richard P. McCormick notes that, in Pennsylvania, "the forces that shaped party loyalty in state contests were frequently in conflict with powerful counterforces that became operative in presidential elections, with disastrous consequences to party cohesion. The manifestations of instability persisted until 1840....One receives the impression that from an early date the 'better element' in the state exercised little political influence, with the result that politics became the business of men who were interested in the tangible rewards of jobs and money. There was considerable corruption, fraud, and even violence in the conduct of elections, and political management was oligarchic rather than democratic. Campaigns were more commonly focused on scandals, personalities, or local concerns than on broad issues of public policy."[43]

Binns held onto his aldermanic position until 1844, when he was ousted by the Nativist party. (The aldermanic post had been made elective in 1840.)[44] Some idea of what kept him in office can be gained from the following description, left by one of the "better element":

> We had a stormy meeting last night. It is a curious fact that altho at the polls we have double the number of votes that the two united factions of old school men, and Binnites did at the last two elections; yet at the ward meetings, and at Town meetings they can manage to bring forward such a number of the canail more than we can, that they have often beaten us at those places....Binns, Harper & and a few others have in addition great influence with a number of newcomers from Ireland, who are admitted at Ward and Town meetings, altho they have no votes at an election.[45]

The "canail" followed Binns because he was loyal to their racial interests, if no other. He opposed capital punishment in a series of articles in the *Democratic Press* that ran from 1808 to 1811. He called for humane treatment of persons convicted of crime, and denounced criminal law "concocted and enacted to protect the property of the wealthy...."[46] In 1810 he delivered a Fourth of July oration in which he depicted the country as divided between "aristocrats" and "democrats," and vowed to maintain the principle that "Persons, not Property" should form the basis of representation.[47]

For him society broke down along Jacksonian lines, based on estates, or the division between "producers" and "parasites," rather than social classes defined by relation to the production process. In 1814 he complained that "all the trades, callings, and professions in all the villages, towns, and cities in Pennsylvania, are meeting, combining, incorporating and resolving and fixing the rates at which they will buy and sell work." In 1836 he dedicated a popular treatise, *An Exposition of the Law*, to the apprentices of Pennsylvania. In the dedication he admonished them to acknowledge the mutuality of interest between them and their masters, to be obedient always, and to abjure "grumblings or complainings," bad language, and "winebibbing."[48]

Consistent with his Jacksonianism, he excluded Afro-Americans from the category of citizen. Addressing the need to mobilize labor for the War of 1812, he described the free black people of Philadelphia as a "very numerous and useless" class, which "could be better spared [for the war] than any other."[49] When the Missouri Crisis broke out, the *Democratic Press* published an article denying the right of Congress to prohibit slavery anywhere.[50] Sensitive to charges that he was a "zealous, active abolitionist," in his memoirs Binns defended himself by boasting that, soon after Denmark Vesey's slave insurrection of 1822, the governor of South Carolina visited him and thanked him for his editorial support. The *Democratic Press*, according to the governor, "was the only newspaper north of Mason and Dixon's line, which ever published a sentence in defence of the conduct of the authorities of the State and City during that alarming period."[51] Quite a distinction! In 1834, following a riot in which a mob, largely composed of Irish laborers, destroyed homes throughout the section of Philadelphia they shared with black people, the mayor appointed an investigating commission. The commission's report identified as a principal cause of the riot the belief that some employers were hiring black people over whites, and that as a result, many white laborers were out of work. This matter the commission recommended "for correction, to the consideration and action of individuals." The reporter for the commission was John Binns, alderman.[52]

Four years later, in 1838, he wrote the letter to O'Connell quoted at the beginning of this chapter. Five years after that, he again took up his pen against O'Connell, this time in response to O'Connell's Cincinnati Address, in which the Liberator had threatened to recognize as "Irish no longer" those of his countrymen and countrywomen in America who continued to uphold slavery. On that occasion Binns wrote

> Our lips would curl with scorn and contempt at the puerile conceit which must inflate the man who should undertake to expatriate and disown, forever, a million of his country people because they did not violate their consciences and their oaths, and walk in the path which their supercilious contemner has chalked out for them....If you do thus cast reproach, you will sink, in our estimation, where fathom line can never reach.

Introducing this letter in his memoirs, Binns showed a flash of the old revolutionary of '98, attacking O'Connell for remarks the latter had made against the United Irishmen.[53]

Whether he called himself Federalist or Democrat, whether he backed Crawford or Adams, Binns remained a Jacksonian. Writing his memoirs at the age of eighty-two, he expressed regret that, whereas forty years earlier there were only four Federalist representatives in the state legislature, "now Pennsylvania has elected a Federal governor, and a Federal majority in the House of Representatives, and in Congress."[54] The "Federal majority" he was deploring were the Whigs, among whom were some of the future leaders of the Republican Party.

The fact of Irish attachment to the Democratic Party has been well established. By 1844, the Irish were the most solid voting bloc in the country, except for the free Negroes (who cast their ballots in the opposite direction from the Irish), and it was widely believed that Irish votes provided Polk's margin of victory in that year.[55] The special relationship between the Irish and the Democratic Party was not an automatic attachment, nor a simple legacy of the "civil revolution" of 1800, but a bond renewed in the Jacksonian upsurge, and continuously thereafter.

The Philadelphia branch of the Tammany Society was established in 1795, with a charter from the parent Society in New York. It replaced the Democratic Club which had disbanded following the Whiskey Rebellion. From its inception it admitted aliens. The Jeffersonians became the champions of the immigrants, supporting a law in 1804 that made naturalization easier, incidentally expanding their base of support. As one contemporary Federalist commentator put it, "It was not now necessary to be an American to become a son of Tammany, for the magic spell of wiskinky, so savage was it, could convert the sons of Erin into Aborigines of the American wilds."[56] The Democratic-Republicans continued this policy in the 1820s, by reducing property and residential qualifications for voting.

The Irish did not vote Democratic-Republican and then Democratic out of sentimental attachment to those who gave them the vote. The Democratic Party eased their assimilation as whites, and more than any other institution, it taught them the meaning of whiteness. Key to this was the Party's rejection of nativism.

Strong tendencies existed in antebellum America to consign the Irish, if not to the black race, then to an intermediate race located socially between black and white. Nativism expressed this tendency, and nativism appealed to many artisans who were resentful of immigrants coming into the country. Many craftsmen of the time, and some historians subsequently, have spoken of "low-paid" immigrant (like "cheap" black) labor, as if cheapness were some quality in the labor itself. "American Mechanics" opposed the "great influx of pauper and convict immigration upon our shores."[57] If, therefore, the Democratic Party decided, after some vacillation, to reject nativism, the decision had far-reaching consequences. Nativism lost out not to the vision of a nonracial society, but to a society polarized between white and black. Part of the project of defeating nativism was to establish an acceptable standard for "white" behavior. Jean Baker has shown how the Democratic Party created the "white vote," even in areas with few or no black people.[58]

Everywhere, the movement that expanded the franchise for whites curtailed it for persons of color. The New York Constitutional Convention of 1821, which broadened the franchise, also introduced, for the first time, an explicit property qualification for black voters, and five years later, when the last serious barriers to white manhood suffrage were lifted, the discriminatory property qualification was retained. In Pennsylvania, neither the 1776 nor the 1790 state constitutions had barred Negroes from voting. In 1822 it was noted that "notwithstanding the laws of Pennsylvania do not forbid it, no blacks vote at elections, at least in the eastern part of the state."[59] In 1837 and 1838 the disparity between the legal situation and the reality in the state was rectified, as persons of color were formally disenfranchised.[60] During the discussion of the constitutional issues a largely Irish mob expressed its view by burning the abolitionist hall in Philadelphia. At the 1846 New York state constitutional convention, one delegate denounced a proposal to give black men equal suffrage with whites, on the grounds that such a proposal would condemn white immigrants to Negro rule for five years.[61]

The Irish were by no means passively obedient to the official Democratic Party, but even in those cases where Irish and other white radical movements stretched the Jacksonian consensus, they did not challenge, and often reinforced, the white solidarity that underlay it. The prominent New York City politician Mike Walsh is representative of this tendency.[62] Walsh was born in Ireland in 1810, the son of a veteran of the uprising of 1798. When he was a child, his family emigrated to New York. After starting an appenticeship with an engraver, Walsh traveled to New Orleans, supporting himself by common labor, returning to New York in 1839, where he began work as a correspondent for the New York *Aurora* (edited for a time, as historian Sean Wilentz notes, by "another footloose artisan, Walt Whitman").

Like many aspiring politicians, Walsh was a volunteer fireman. In 1840, he and a group of friends organized the Spartan Association, which Wilentz describes as "a rough amalgam of an Irish secret society, a political gang, and a workingman's club." An anti-Tammany Democrat, Walsh ran for Congress in 1841 on Bishop Hughes's ticket, drawing enough votes away from the regular nominee to elect the Whig. In 1843, Walsh and his friend George Wilkes started a newspaper, the *Subterranean*.[63] On one occasion the Spartans temporarily took control of a Tammany gathering in City Hall Park, and named their own slate of candidates for office, headed by Walsh. Although the party regulars succeeded on that occasion in restoring their control, the pressure continued to build, and in 1846 Tammany gave in and nominated Walsh for the state assembly. There he served three terms, "advocate of no political party—the tool of no corrupt clique," as he described himself.

Walsh was extreme among New York Democrats for his denunciations not just of wealth, but of the capitalist system, and his adoption of a labor theory of value. "What is capital," he asked, "but that all-grasping power which has been wrung, by fraud, avarice, and malice from the labor of this and all ages past?" In an 1845 column in the *Subterranean* he wrote,

> Demagogues tell you that you are freemen. They lie—you are slaves, and none are better aware of the fact than the heathenish dogs who call you freemen. No man devoid of all other means of support but that which his labor affords him can be a freeman, under the present state of society. He must be a humble slave of capital, created by the labor of the poor men who have toiled, suffered, and died before him.

"No man," he declared, "can be a good political democrat without he's a good social democrat."

Walsh supported the antirent movement in upstate New York and was for a time allied with George Henry Evans, leading land reformer and editor of the *Working Man's Advocate*.[64] After attending a labor reform convention in Boston, he addressed striking Lowell female textile operatives, and toured the Fourierite community at Brook Farm.[65]

What did Walsh and the Spartans stand for? According to Ernst, they opposed convict labor, whipping in public institutions, imprisonment for debt, contracting of labor on public works, monopolies, and the concentration of wealth; they favored rotation in office, and fought to limit the working day and regulate conditions of apprentices and minors in industry. In 1846, Walsh boasted of their accomplishments:

> We broke up the market, or meat monopoly—we brought the land question, or freedom of the soil, before the people—we destroyed the infamous pilot monopoly—we prevented honest pedlars from being outlawed by rich store keepers—the Erie Rail Road from monopolizing the emigrant passenger business....Singly and alone we advocated the Annexation of Texas long before Tammany Hall or any of its organs dared touch the question.

The reference to Texas is crucial. In 1842, in his capacity as Washington correspondent for the *Aurora*, Walsh had met President Tyler, and established a connection with him. In 1843, Walsh, physically protected by the Spartans, had proposed a toast to Calhoun at a Van Buren rally. Thus he early in his career linked his radicalism to the Southern wing of the Democracy.

Walsh was elected to Congress in 1852, as part of a general Democratic victory that placed Pierce in the Presidency. Once there he wasted no time in making clear where his allegiances lay. He denounced free-soilers (who opposed the extension of slavery into the territories) as a

> mean, despicable, and hollow-hearted set of hungry traitors who, at a pepper-and-salt convention, held in Buffalo in 1848, fraternized...with disappointed and disloyal Whigs, rampant Abolitionists, and long-heeled Negroes, pampered by the traitorous artifices of demagogues....

During the debate on the fate of Kansas, Walsh delivered a long speech on slavery, in which he once again expressed his opposition to abolition. The only difference between the black slave in the South and the white wage-slave of the North, he said, was that "the one has a master without asking for him, and the other has to beg for the privilege of becoming a slave. The one is the slave of an individual; the other is the slave of an inexorable class."

Thus did Walsh's radicalism lead him into alliance with the most powerful class of exploiters in the country. This strange marriage was characteristic of the white labor radicalism of the day. For example, in an 1840 article, "The Laboring Classes," Orestes Brownson compared the systems of slave and free labor. "Of the two," he wrote,

> the first is, in our judgement, except so far as the feelings are concerned, decidedly the least oppressive. If the slave has never been a free man, we think, as a general rule, his sufferings are less than those of the free laborer at wages. As to actual freedom one has just about as much as the other. The laborer at wages has all the disadvantages of freedom and none of its blessings, while the slave, if denied the blessings, is freed from the disadvantages.[66]

The comparison between free and slave labor in favor of the latter was more than a rhetorical flourish; it was a guide to action for the movement of white laborers. This was explicitly stated by George Evans, follower of Robert Owen and Fanny Wright, activist in the New York Working Men's party after 1829, and editor of the *Working Man's Advocate*. Evans attained his greatest prominence as a proponent of free land in the West (a program which found white supremacist form in the Free Soil and Republican parties). In a letter to the antislavery leader Gerrit Smith, Evans wrote

> I was formerly, like yourself, sir, a very warm advocate of the abolition of slavery. This was before I saw that there was white slavery. Since I saw this, I have materially changed my views as to the means of abolishing negro slavery. I now see, clearly, I think, that to give the landless black the privilege of changing masters now possessed by the landless white, would hardly be a benefit to him....

In response to the argument that he justified slavery by saying it was not as bad as the situation of the free laborer, Evans insisted that he opposed slavery, but added, "there is more real suffering among the landless whites of the North, than among the blacks of the South," and that the abolitionists "err[ed] in wishing to transfer the black from the one form of slavery to the other and worse one."[67]

Evans was not alone. The American Fourierists criticized the abolitionists for thinking slavery was the only social evil to be extirpated, and warned of the dangerous consequences of their view. "Negro slavery in the South," they explained, "was one only of many forms of slavery that existed on the earth....Consequently [the Associationists] did not contemplate the removal of this one evil alone and direct their exertions wholly against it; they wished to abolish all evil and all forms of slavery."

The point must be underscored: in every case, these arguments comparing unprosperous whites with blacks aimed not at broadening the abolitionist vision but at deflecting it. The abolitionists had a ready reply:

> Before we can settle the relations of man to society, we must know who and what is man....Anti-slavery then underlies all other reforms, for it asserts the natural equality of all men, without regard to colour or condition. Until this principle is recognized as

practically true, there can be no universal reform. There can be even no partial reform...for the evils of Slavery...permeate the relations of every individual in the land."[68]

Involved in this exchange were fundamental issues of direction for free labor radicalism. The story of one labor activist, Seth Luther, shows where the choices led. Luther was born in Rhode Island in 1795, the son of a Revolutionary War veteran. He grew up in poverty, and had only a few years of common-school education, but did manage to learn carpentry. As a young man he took off on a tour of the West and South. Returning to New England, he did a stint in the cotton mills, which he left for a career as an itinerant labor agitator. A circular he wrote for a strike of Boston carpenters sparked the 1835 Philadelphia general strike. In 1832 he made his *Address to the Working Men of New England*, which he delivered on numerous occasions and which was printed the following year in a New York edition on George Evans's presses and went through several editions afterwards.[⁴] In that address, Luther angrily denounced the factory system at length for its cruelties. He repeatedly compared its victims to Southern slaves, usually to the disadvantage of the free laborer. For example, he pointed out that six-year old children in the U.S. worked longer hours in the mills than slaves in the West Indies, whose work day was limited to nine hours. He noted that "the wives and daughters of the rich manufacturers would no more associate with a 'factory girl' than they would with a negro slave." He pointed out that the women who labored their life away in the mills "have not even the assurance of the most wretched cornfield negro in Virginia, who, when his stiffened limbs can no longer bend to the lash, must be supported by his owner." And he noted that "the slaves in the South enjoy privileges which are not enjoyed in some of our cotton mills.ᵞAt Dover, N.H., we understand, no operative is allowed to keep a pig or a cow." [ᵏ]

What are we to make of this rhetoric? In the first place, Luther was not exaggerating the evils of the factory system (although, of course, he was omitting from the comparison with chattel slavery the degradation of being *property*, which no wage laborer suffered). In the second place, Luther was personally sympathetic to the plight of the slave; in another address he told of his travels in the South and his conversations with slaves, which taught him to respect their intelligence and pity their condition. But he could not see slavery as part of the labor problem.[69] Not only slavery but race discrimination, South and North, was absent from his calculations, as we shall see.

In the state of Rhode Island a high property qualification for suffrage kept about two-thirds of the state's white male adults from voting. A major portion of these were Irish laborers, concentrated in the Hardscrabble and Olney areas of Providence, and in the mill towns of the Pawtucket valley. As early as 1824, they had made their presence felt in the Hardscrabble antiblack riot.[70] As part of the popular upsurge of the period, a movement developed aimed at striking down the restrictions. It gained quite a bit of support, particularly among working men, and Luther became involved, with an *Address on the Right of Free Suffrage*, which he delivered in 1833 in Providence. In 1840 Providence mechanics and working men formed the Rhode Island Suffrage Association, which renewed agitation for the franchise. The leader of the movement, Thomas Dorr, was a descendant of an old Yankee family, graduate of Phillips Exeter and Harvard; in the past he had supported abolitionist causes.

What to do when the group legally empowered to broaden the franchise refuses to do so? The Suffrage Association decided to call a People's Convention to draft a new state constitution.

At first black people took part in Suffrage meetings and voted in Association elections. The issue of their role came up explicitly in September of 1841 when a black Providence barber, Alfred Niger, was proposed as treasurer of the local suffrage association. His nomination was defeated, and conflicting resolutions on the subject were brought to the People's Convention, which met in October. A number of leading abolitionists, including Frederick Douglass and Abby Kelley, visited Rhode Island, agitating to strike the word "white" from the proposed constitution. The Convention, after debate, refused, thus answering the question, what is a man? At the convention Dorr argued in favor of black suffrage. When his plea was rejected, he nevertheless chose to remain with the Suffragists. Garrison expressed disappointed abolitionist sentiment when he wrote, "It is not for me to espouse the cause of any politician, especially one like Thos. W. Dorr...."[71]

The October Convention, naming Dorr as its candidate for governor, resolved to hold elections in April of the following year, based on universal white manhood suffrage. In the fall of 1841, the Law and Order Party was on the defensive as the Suffragists mobilized people to vote in the spring. The only active opposition came from the abolitionists, who denounced the attempt by "pseudo friends of political reform, to make the rights of a man dependent on the hue of his skin."[72] Mobs of Suffragists broke up their meetings, made proslavery speeches, and denounced the Law and Order party as the "nigger party."[73] Dorr was present on one occasion while a mob broke up an abolition meeting, and watched silently.[74]

The Suffrage Association went ahead with its election in April 1842. Announcing that it represented a majority of voters, it declared Dorr governor. Rhode Island was now presented with a classic situation of dual power—two administrations, each claiming to be the legal government of the state. It was an unstable situation, and everyone knew it.

Each side rallied its forces; Walsh and about twenty Spartans made an effort to join the Dorrites. In a clever maneuver, the Law and Order Party offered to grant the vote to black men on the same terms as to whites (on the basis of a somewhat broadened electorate), in return for their support against the Dorrites. On the night of May 18, the Dorrites attempted to capture the arsenal. The attempt failed. Black men serving in militia units guarded vital points in Providence and played a key role in defeating the Dorrite assault. Following the failure of the arsenal assault, black volunteers helped suppress Dorrite resistance throughout the state.[75]

In the aftermath of the rebellion, the Law and Order Party granted voting rights to Rhode Island black men on the same basis as to native-born whites. A freehold requirement was passed for foreign-born voters, which required that they own land to vote. As one historian has put it, "The Law and Order party simultaneously picked up an ally and made it difficult for their antagonists, the Irish, to vote."[76]

What of Seth Luther? He fought valiantly in the assault on the arsenal, and served as organizational secretary in the Dorrite encampment, but was captured and imprisoned. Held after other prisoners were released (perhaps because he refused to renounce the suffrage cause, instead denouncing cowards and turncoats), he was put on trial for treason. Convicted and sentenced to jail, he attempted to escape, failed, was discharged from prison, immediately rearrested, and was finally released in March of 1843. He at once embarked on a tour of the West, where he sought to enlist support for Dorr. From Illinois he wrote, "Thousands are ready, able and willing to march on Rhode Island equipped and provisioned to the rescue of Governor Dorr...." Among them was Mike Walsh; as late as 1845, he threatened to lead five hundred of his followers to Providence to flatten the Rhode Island state house and pillage the city.

Luther sought to enlist the support of Calhoun, who refused it, on the grounds that if he came out in support of suffrage for propertyless whites in Rhode Island, John Quincy Adams would be sure to introduce a resolution supporting the right of the slaves to form a constitution. Returning to the East, Luther volunteered to serve in the army for the Mexican War. Some have called his gesture a striking departure and attributed it to a mental breakdown, but, like the overture to Calhoun, it was consistent with his Democratic politics. Nothing came of his offer (he was forty-seven years old), and the next heard of him was an unsuccessful attempt to rob a bank in Cambridge, Massachusetts. He was committed to a lunatic asylum, shifted around among institutions, and died in an asylum in Brattleboro, Vermont, on April 29, 1863—barely two months before the outbreak of the New York City Draft Riots, which revealed the depth of white-labor opposition to abolition.

On April 28, 1844, Philadelphia diarist Sidney George Fisher recorded:

The union of the country is factitious, and is becoming less real every day. Every day the difference between the North and South is becoming more prominent and apparent. The difference exists in everything which forms the life of a people—in institutions, laws, opinions, manners, feelings, education, pursuits, climate and soil. Edinburgh and Paris are not more dissimilar than Boston and New Orleans. A Union not founded on congeniality—moral and intellectual—a Union between two people who, in fact, in all important characteristics are broadly contrasted, must be a weak one, liable at once to be broken when at all strained....Such a Union is one of interest merely, a paper bond, to be torn asunder by a burst of passion or to be deliberately undone whenever interest demands it—local sectional interest, the interest of the hour, or, as things go here, the interest of a party. In this case interest and passion may speedily both combine to produce a separation.[77]

In *Walden* (begun 1846) Thoreau wrote, "We are in great haste to construct a magnetic telegraph from Maine to Texas; but Maine and Texas, it may be, have nothing to communicate." He was expressing no more than sober judgement based on the day's events.

When David Wilmot rose on the floor of Congress to offer his famous rider to Texas annexation—that slavery be barred from the new territories seized from Mexico—it shattered the governing consensus. Wilmot's Proviso, and the Free Soil movement that followed it, marked the emergence into the light of day of the inner tensions of Jacksonianism. The hunger of the free Northern population for land in the West collided with the demand of the slaveocracy for more territory. The collision would lead to a new system of political parties and eventually to Civil War. If the European uprisings of 1848 marked the breakup of the Third Estate, the U.S. election of 1848 marked the breakup of its American counterpart, Jacksonianism.[78]

"I plead the cause of the rights of the white freeman," said Wilmot. "I would preserve for white labor a fair country, a rich inheritance, where the sons of toil, of my own race and own color, can live without the disgrace which association with negro slavery brings upon free labor."[79] Free Soil was not "soft" abolitionism; it was the antagonist of abolitionism.[80] Walt Whitman grasped the distinction quite clearly: "The whole matter of slavery," he wrote, "...will be a conflict between the totality of White Labor, on the one side, and on the other, the interference and competition of Black labor, or of bringing in colored persons on *any* terms."[81] Hence it was perfectly consistent for the Free Soil Party to name as its presidential candidate in 1848 none other than Martin Van Buren, "a Locofoco [the name applied to radical Democrats], a Dorrite who has done more for slavery than any other Northern man."[82]

While Free Soil (for whites only) appealed to many Northern workingmen, who eventually came to identify with the Republican Party, it never made any headway among the Irish. Even after other sectors of the laboring class broke with the Democratic Party, the Irish remained faithful to it. Why was this so?

The Irish were less attracted than any other group to the promise of land in the West. "The Irish immigrant was primarily a phenomenon of the development of urban life in the United States. The number who took up farming as a means of livelihood always remained low," writes Wittke. "The body of urban floating labor, the hod carriers, the draymen, the diggers of foundations and the like...remained unbudged," summarized Potter.[83]

For early immigrants, who came largely from the depressed industrial areas of England and Ireland, part of the explanation may be found in the warning "To Emmigrants," which appeared in the *Mechanic's Free Press* (Philadelphia), July 28, 1828. The paper advised those from England and Ireland "brought up in the Mechanical business" not to be tempted by cheap land in the West. Those "whose former habits in life neither qualify or fit them for labours in the field" would find that farming in America was "arduous beyond description."[84]

While the difficulties of farming may have discouraged Irish immigrants from artisan and industrial backgrounds, it would not explain the reluctance of later arrivals, who were mainly displaced peasants and agricultural laborers, to take up work on the land. A partial explanation may be found in the attitude of Bishop Hughes. There was one well-publicized project which sought to rally the support of the Irish community and the Church behind Western colonization. Hughes opposed it, and gave several reasons for doing so: he was suspicious of the promoters, in particular Thomas D'Arcy McGee, whom he resented for earlier criticisms McGee had made of the role of the Church in the failed uprising of 1848; he questioned the financial soundness of the venture, and did not wish to involve the Catholic clergy as "recruiting sergeants" for it; he doubted the capacity of the Irish to succeed as farmers; he opposed all separate settlements along religious or ethnic lines. In addition he may have feared the loss of Catholic authority over Irish scattered among Protestant populations in the West, and may not have wished to disperse his power base. Whatever his reasons, his opposition undoubtedly played a part in dooming the colonization project.[85]

Hughes's opposition to colonization cannot be a sufficient explanation for the general failure of the Irish to take up farming. There still remains the question, why did the ordinary Irish heed him, particularly since other prominent Catholic clergymen supported colonization, and Hughes himself claimed not to oppose individual settlement.

The ordinary Irish were undoubtedly reluctant to abandon the community ties they had established in the Eastern cities, which helped them survive in a hostile Protestant world. However, the most important reason so few of them them took up farming was likely to have been that they simply could not afford it.

Free Soil did not imply free soil.[86] Taking into account the costs of land purchase, clearing and fencing, implements, seed, and livestock, as well as travel costs and the cash needed to survive until the first crop was brought in and sold, a minimum of $1,000 was required to equip a family farm in the West—a sum so far beyond the reach of the savings possible on a laborer's wage that the available land for settlement might as well have been located on the moon. Representative Orlando B. Ficklin of Illinois, arguing in 1852 in favor of the Homestead Bill, predicted that if the bill were passed, the actual settlers "will be generally of the middle, or rather not of the very poorest class, and…the number will not be so large by a great deal as is anticipated by some gentlemen."[87]

Whatever the reason, "free soil, free labor, and free men" held little appeal for the Catholic Irish population. Unable or unwilling to avail themselves of the white-skin privilege of setting themselves up as independent farmers, the vast majority clung to the Democratic Party, which continued to protect them from the nativists and guarantee them a favored position over those whom they regarded as the principal threat to their position, the free black people of the North (the only group as "free" of either property or marketable skills as the Irish).

Although when war broke out, large numbers of Irish in the North volunteered to fight for the Union, Irish loyalty to the Democratic Party persisted even after it began to skate along the border of treason to the Union. "The Irish know," wrote an 1860 correspondent in the New York *Evening Day Book*, "that the Republicans would give the nigger preference over them—witness Massachusetts, the nigger is elevated, the Irishman is degraded."[88] As the needs of war pushed the Union toward emancipation, the Irish expressed growing disillusion. One soldier in the field wrote back:

> It has turned out to be an abolition war, and ninety-nine soldiers out of one hundred say that if the abolitionists are going to have to carry on this war, they will have to get a new army. They say they came out here to fight for the Union, and not for a pack of —— niggers.[89]

Get a new army, of course, is precisely what Lincoln did, with his decision to recruit black troops. Shortly after the first Afro-Americans appeared in uniform, verses began to circulate under the name "Private Miles O'Reilly"

> Some tell us 'tis a burnin' shame
>> To make the naygurs fight;
> And that the thrade of bein' kilt
>> Belongs but to the white:
> But as for my, upon my sowl!
>> So liberal are we here,
> I'll let Sambo be murthered instead of myself,
>> On every day in the year.[90]

The verse had little effect, because the Irish, like everyone else in the country, knew that the enlistment of black soldiers would inevitably lead to the emancipation of the slaves. The Irish were rejecting not the rigors but the aims of the War. On February 28, 1863, the *Metropolitan Record*, newspaper of the Catholic archdiocese of New York, suggested that "*since fight we must, may it not be necessary yet to fight for the liberty of the white man rather than the freedom of the Negro?*"[91]

This sentiment found expression in the New York City riots of July of 1863.[92] Misnamed "draft riots," they were an insurrection against the government that was waging the war, at a moment when the military forces of the enemy were a hundred-odd miles from the City. The number of Irish who took part in the riots was not less than the number who wore the blue uniform. Given that every rioter was a volunteer against official policy and all respectable opinion, it is likely that the riots expressed Irish attitudes at least as much as Irish service in the Union army.

The Irish had two aims in the war: to establish their claim to citizenship, and to define the sort of republic they would be citizens of. Whether in the Army or on the barricades, they took up arms for the White Republic, and their place in it. As we shall see, their stance was rooted in the desire to escape their miserable conditions.

# IV

# THEY SWUNG THEIR PICKS

In an episode in a nineteenth-century Irish-American novel, a character named James O'Rourke lands in New York in the 1850s after a journey that began in Queenstown, County Cork. Knowing no one in the city, O'Rourke walks up Broadway gazing at the buildings, the street lined with wagons and drays, and the sidewalk crowded with people. Approaching a stranger, he asks where he may find employment. The stranger leads him through narrow streets to a man seated behind a desk, who takes all his money and sends him off with directions to a drygoods shop. The drygoods shop does not exist, and nightfall finds the greenhorn by the East River, footsore, weary, and dejected. He meets a sympathetic countryman, Terence McManus, to whom he tells his story. Expressing rage at the swindlers, McManus puts him up for the night in a third-floor room where he lives with his wife and baby. The next morning McManus, who is a longshoreman, takes O'Rourke with him to start work on the docks.[1]

Although the story may seem ordinary, McManus's willingness to help O'Rourke find employment is not so natural as might at first appear. Why should he bring another jobseeker, perhaps not even from the same county, to the docks? Even granting his wish to help a countryman, how did McManus, a lowly docker, acquire the power to dispose of even one job?

The Irish tradition of labor organization goes back to the Defenders of 1641, the earliest known example of a secret society in Ireland. In the eighteenth century there appeared the Whiteboys, so called because its members wore white shirts over their clothes as a disguise. Other names were Molly Maguires, Levellers, and Right Boys. Usually locally based and springing up in hard times, the secret societies defended the peasants against enclosure, eviction, and rent increases, using whatever means were available, including violence against landlords and their agents and destruction of fences, crops, and livestock. They were not confined to Catholics: aside from the Orangemen, Peep O'Day Boys, and other Protestant secret societies with sectarian aims, there also existed the Oak Boys, an organization of Protestant tenants in Armagh, which fought against the system of forced labor on the public highways. The most powerful secret society in the nineteenth century was the Ribbonmen, which flourished in three periods of large-scale activity, 1814–16, 1821–23, and 1831–34, each tied to a fall in grain prices. A Ribbon password of 1833 suggests a presence in America:

Q: How long is your stick?

A: Long enough to reach my enemies.

Q: To what trunk does the wood belong?

A: To a French trunk that blooms in America and whose leaves shall shelter the sons of Erin.[2]

Among the first flowers of the Ribbon societies in America was the 1834 outbreak near Williamsport, Maryland, along the Chesapeake and Ohio Canal, where 1,800 Irish immigrants were employed by agents under contract with the company.[3] Laborers from Cork had organized to establish job control along the canal. On January 16, the Corkonians fatally beat a laborer from County Longford. Work along the line halted as both sides prepared for war. On January 24, 700 Longford men routed 300 Corkonians, killing at least five and wounding an unknown number. Thirty-four were arrested and order was restored by the local militia with the help of two voluntary companies and U.S. troops from Fort McHenry. Delegates from the two groups of laborers met and signed a truce, each pledging not to interfere with the other's right of employment.[4]

In November 1834, the discharge of workers led to the beating and then killing of the offending superintendent. Again the military restored order. Three hundred Irish were arrested; one man was sentenced to death and two others to prison for eighteen years. One of the contractors who testified at the trial was later compelled to resign under threat of death.[5]

In February 1835, laborers on a section of the canal struck for higher wages. In January 1836, another clash occurred between two groups of Irish. In April 1836, Irish workers struck again, attacking a group of "Dutch and country borns" who refused to join the strike, dispersing them and halting work along that section. The strike spread through the whole line after one of the contractors fired all the strikers and contracted slaves in their place. In May and June 1837, Irish strikers drove off forty English immigrant workers who had been brought in by one of the contractors. In the Spring of 1838 Irish burned shanties of German laborers "whose presence threatened to reduce the jobs for the Irish and force down wages." In May 1838, the withholding of wages by contractors led workers to seize the stocks of blasting powder with the aim of destroying the work they had done. On several of these occasions military force was required to suppress the disorders. Canal officials attributed the disturbances to "a regularly organized society [with] branches in all the States where internal improvements are in progress."[6]

On August 11, 1839, the canal erupted again, as one hundred Irish laborers, armed with guns and clubs, assaulted two sections where German workers were employed. On August 27, more than two weeks after the initial outbreak, the Maryland militia restored order, in the course of which they shot at least eight laborers, seized 120 weapons, tore down shanties, and took twenty-six prisoners, of whom fourteen were sent to the penitentiary for terms from five to eighteen years.[7]

The story of construction labor unrest elsewhere is similar to that on the C&O Canal. Commons estimates that two-thirds of the "riots" of that time were in fact unorganized strikes.[8] In 1829, laborers on the Pennsylvania canal struck for a wage increase and refused to allow others to take their place. They were quelled by the local police and militia, including cavalry. A Catholic priest, Reverend Father Curran, used "his personal influence over the rioters [to] induce them to submit to civil authority."[9] The same year on the Baltimore and Ohio Railroad, one man was killed and several wounded, a home was destroyed and railroad tracks were torn up before the militia arrived. Two years later laborers on the same project tore up the tracks when a contractor absconded with their wages. In 1835 they did so again, provoked by the same cause. In April 1834, workers on the Boston and Providence Railroad "rioted" for higher wages. In the fall of the same year, Irish laborers were said to have murdered several contractors on the Washington Railroad.[10] In the building of the Troy and Schenectady Railroad, laborers from different Irish provinces battled over jobs. One 1841 outbreak spread down the line for ten miles, and it took a sheriff's posse to subdue the workers, who were armed with scythes, clubs, and muskets. The following year, one thousand Irish workers rioted on the Welland Canal (connecting Lake Erie to Lake Ontario), where contractors had lured them with false promises of employment. On discovering that no work was to be had, they assembled with banners and proceeded to help themselves to goods from several stores and flour from a local mill, even boarding a ship and seizing the pork it was carrying. It took three British military companies to suppress them.[11]

One of the means the laborers employed was to send a warning notice to the offending contractor; if the notice was ignored, they followed it up by destroying equipment.[12] Although investigators some-times saw the hand of a centrally organized conspiracy, the outbreaks were in fact responses of groups of workers to their conditions, drawing upon a tradition of secret organization, using whatever means were at hand, and passing along their experience as they followed the work on the canals and railroad projects—in short, strikes, waged without bureau-crats, treasuries, or the other tokens of formal organization available to workers more favorably situated.[13] More than anything else, they resem-bled the strikes or rebellions of plantation slaves (which might have been occurring simultaneously nearby).[14]

As often as not, these early labor rebellions were organized along county or regional lines.[15] The participants showed little awareness that being white, or immigrant, or Catholic, or even Irish, formed a basis for solidarity. When Irish workers encountered Afro-Americans, they fought with them, it is true, but they also fought with immigrants of other nationalities, with each other, and with whomever else they were thrown up against in the marketplace. For example, in 1825 Irish cartmen in New York attacked their Connecticut counterparts for carrying larger loads than the New Yorkers. A similar incident occurred the following year at a construction project at Dandy Point, in New York.[16] In New York City, where the Irish dominated cartage, the cartmen on the east side of Manhattan were rivals of the westsiders, and the dockers vied with the coal cartmen. When a new immigrant first entered a factory, he remained suspect until he revealed from what part of Ireland he had come. Clashes between Irish and Germans were frequent. In 1846, some five hundred Irish laborers at the Atlantic Dock in Brooklyn went on strike for a wage increase and a reduction of the working day from thirteen hours to ten. The contractors brought in freshly landed Germans to break the strike, ordering the Irish to leave the premises. The strikers responded militantly, occupying the shanties where they had been living and driving the Germans off, until the sheriff sent in the militia.[17]

To the extent color consciousness existed among newly arrived immigrants from Ireland, it was one among several ways they had of identifying themselves.'To become white they had to learn to subordinate county, religious, or national animosities, not to mention any natural sympathies they may have felt for their fellow creatures, to a new solidarity based on color—a bond which, it must be remembered, was contradicted by their experience in Ireland.＼

America was well set up to teach new arrivals the overriding value of the white skin. Throughout the eighteenth century, the range of dependent labor relations had blurred the distinction between freedom and slavery. The Revolution led to the decline of apprenticeship, indenture, and imprisonment for debt. These changes, together with the growth of slavery as the basis of Southern society, reinforced the tendency to equate freedom with whiteness and slavery with blackness. At the same time, the spread of wage labor made white laborers anxious about losing the precarious independence they had gained from the Revolution. In response, they sought refuge in whiteness. Republican ideology became more explicitly racial than it had been during the Revolutionary era. The result was a new definition of citizenship, what Alexander Saxton has labeled the "White Republic." Blackness was the badge of the slave, and in a perfect inversion of cause and effect, the status of the Afro-Americans was seen as a function of their color rather than of their servile condition.[18] The Connecticut Colonization Society summarized the situation in 1828:

> In every part of the United States, there is a broad and impassible line of demarcation between every man who has one drop of African blood in his veins, and every other class in the community. The habits, the feelings, all the prejudices of society—prejudices which neither refinement, nor argument, nor education, nor religion itself can subdue—mark the people of colour, whether bond or free, as the subjects of a degradation inevitable and incurable. The African in this country belongs by birth to the lowest station in society; and from that station he can never rise, be his talents, his enterprise, his virtues what they may.[19]

The slaveholders had a special interest in maintaining the degradation of the free Negro. If the fugitive slave was the "Safety Valve of Slavery,"[20] the subduing of the free black population of the North was what kept the safety valve from turning into a massive tear which would allow all the power to escape from the chamber. The slaveholders were aware that the harsh conditions faced by free Negroes in the North helped keep their laborers down on the farm; hence they did their best to publicize the cold reception that awaited any slave so foolish as to run away from the security of the plantation. They did more than observe events in the North: because they had a strong interest in maintaining the free Negro there in a condition as much like slavery as possible, they sought an alliance with Northern white labor based on the defense of color caste.[21]

"It is a curious fact," wrote John Finch, an English Owenite who traveled the United States in 1843, "that the democratic party, and particularly the poorer class of Irish immigrants in America, are greater enemies to the negro population, and greater advocates for the continuance of negro slavery, than any portion of the population in the free States."[22] Finch attributed this attitude to labor competition, noting that

> ten or twelve years ago, the most menial employments, such as scavengers, porters, dock-labourers, waiters at hotels, ostlers, bootcleaners, barbers, etc., were all, or nearly all, black men, and

nearly all the maid servants, cooks, scullions, washerwomen, etc., were black women, and they used to obtain very good wages for these employments; but so great has been the influx of unskilled labourers, emigrants from Ireland, England, and other countries, within the last few years, into New York, Boston, Philadelphia, and other large towns in the eastern States, who press into these menial employments (because they can find no other), offering to labour for any wages they can obtain; that it has reduced the wages of the blacks, and deprived great numbers of them of employment, hence there is a deadly hatred engendered between them, and quarrels and fights among them are daily occurring.

Some modern scholars have joined Finch in pointing to labor competition as the cause of intergroup animosities within the working class, and in particular animosity between Irish- and Afro-Americans, who together made up the bulk of America's unskilled proletariat.[23] However, there is nothing distinctively racial in what Finch recounted of the relations among black and immigrant workers. He might have been describing conflicts between Irish and Germans, or among Irish from different counties, with no assumption of racial favoritism.

While labor competition explains some things, unless its operation is specified, identifying it as the source of intergroup tensions raises more questions than it answers. In the ideal situation, workers contracting for the sale of their labor power compete as individuals, not as groups. And this is even true to some extent in the real world: no employer ever hired "the Irish" or "the Afro-Americans"; individual persons compete to fill specific openings. Under the capitalist system, all workers compete for jobs. The competition gives rise to animosity among them; but normally it also gives rise to its opposite, unity. It is not free competition that leads to enduring animosity, but its absence. Race becomes a social fact at the moment "racial" identification begins to impose barriers to free competition among atomized and otherwise interchangeable individuals. To the extent it does so, the greatest individual competition takes place not between groups but within each group. In the period under consideration the most intense and desperate labor competition was not between Irish and free Negroes, but within each of the two groups, and no one has ever suggested that it presented an insurmountable obstacle to the cohesion of either. If the experience of Cork and Longford men killing each other on the canal projects taught them that it was to their mutual advantage to come together, and if the rivalry among Irish and Germans eventually gave way to cooperative relations, why did the competition among Irish- and Afro-American laborers fail to lead to a mutual appreciation of the need for unity? The answer is that the competition among these two groups did not take place under normal circumstances, but was distorted by the color line, what O'Connell called something in the "atmosphere" of America.

Finch himself recognized that what was going on was more than simple labor competition. "The working people reason thus," he continued.

> Competition among free white working men here is even now reducing our wages daily; but if the blacks were to be emancipated, probably hundreds of thousands of them would migrate into these northern States, and the competition for employment would consequently be so much increased, that wages would speedily be as low, or lower here, than they are in England; better, therefore, for us, that they remain slaves as they are. Hence we see why the American abolitionists of slavery are more unpopular among these parties in America, than Socialists are among the priests and upperclasses in England—hence we see why the repeal associations in Cincinnati wrote to O'Connell in defence of slavery, and why many repeal associations in the United States, particularly in the south, broke up and refused to give any more assistance to the repealers in Ireland, after receiving his denunciations of that accursed system.

Finch here located the source of the tensions between Irish immigrants and Afro-Americans in the slavery question. That is getting close, but it is necessary to be even more specific. Slavery has existed for thousands of years without prejudice of color, language, or tribe. Even the singling out of one group to be enslaved does not require that nonslave members of the designated group be branded as inferior. What distinguished nineteenth-century America was not the existence of slavery, but the way it was enforced: In parts of the West Indies, by contrast, people who in the United States would have been identified as "black" were enlisted in the policing of the slaves. In those places color prejudice did not take the same form as in the United States, nor did free people of color commonly show solidarity toward the slaves.[24] Slavery in the United States was part of a bipolar system of color caste, in which even the lowliest of "whites" enjoyed a status superior in crucial respects to that of the most exalted of "blacks."[25] As members of the privileged group, white workers organized to defend their caste status, even while striving to improve their condition as workers. They prohibited free Afro-Americans from competing with them for jobs, in effect curtailing their right to choose among masters (a right which contemporary labor activists declared the only essential distinction between the free worker and the slave).

During the eighteenth century, Africans and Afro-Americans in Pennsylvania had produced a substantial group of slave artisans, including bakers, blacksmiths, bricklayers, carpenters, coopers, distillers, refiners, sailmakers, shoemakers, tailors, and tanners.[26] "When white Philadelphians were furiously debating the Stamp Act in 1765, their city contained about 100 free blacks and 1,400 slaves." The Revolutionary crisis contributed to the ending of slavery; by 1783 the number of slaves had fallen to 400, while the free black population had grown to more than 1,000.[27] For many former slaves, emancipation was followed by a period of servitude and apprenticeship, during which they continued to labor at the occupations they had pursued under slavery.[28]

One scholar has characterized the period from 1790 to 1830 as one of "considerable advancement" for black people ended by "growing hostilities from whites in general and increased competition from immigrants in particular."[29] Others believe that the decline began earlier, pointing to the increasing appearance of pauperism among them and manifestations of street violence against them.[30] Whatever the truth of the matter, it is universally agreed that there was "a remarkable deterioration in the socioeconomic conditions of blacks from 1830 to the Civil War."[31]

One of the marks of the deterioration was the gradual elimination of the black artisan. A survey by the Pennsylvania Abolition Society in 1838 noted that thirty percent of the 506 male black mechanics and tradesmen in Philadelphia in 1838 did not practice their trades because of "prejudices."[32] An 1856 survey recorded that, while the number of those claiming trades had gone up, "less than two-thirds of those who have trades follow them...on account of the unrelenting prejudice against their color."[33] White artisans and mechanics were able to gain control of the labor market by withholding apprenticeships and training from black youth. In 1834, students from Lane Seminary, near Cincinnati, investigated the conditions of free Negroes in that city:

> A respectable master mechanic stated to us...that in 1830 the President of the Mechanical Association was publicly tried by the Society for the crime of assisting a colored young man to learn a trade. Such was the feeling among the mechanics that no colored boy could learn a trade, or colored journeyman find employment. A young man of exceptional character and an excellent workman purchased his freedom and learned the cabinet making business in Kentucky. On coming to this city, he was refused work by every man to whom he applied. At last he found a shop carried on by an Englishman, who agreed to employ him—but on entering the shop, the workmen threw down their tools and declared that he should leave or they would....The unfortunate youth was accordingly dismissed.
>
> In this extremity, having spent his last cent, he found a slaveholder who gave him employment in an iron store as a common laborer. Here he remained two years, when the gentleman finding he was a mechanic, exerted his influence and procured work for him as a rough carpenter. This man, by dint of perseverance and industry, has now become a master workman, employing at times six or eight journeymen. But, he tells us, he has not yet received a single job of work from a native born citizen of a free state.[34]

"If a man has children," asserted *A Colored Philadelphian* in 1830, "it is almost impossible for him to get a trade for them, as the journeymen and apprentices generally refuse to work with them, even if the master is willing, which is seldom the case."[35] An 1832 Memorial from the People of Color to the State Legislature complained of "the difficulty of getting places for our sons as apprentices, to learn mechanical trades, owing to the prejudices with which we have to contend."[36] James Forten, a wealthy Afro-American sailmaker and employer of black and white labor, complained in a series of public letters of the lack of opportunities for Negroes in the trades, as shown in the difficulty he had in obtaining apprenticeships for his sons.[37] Frederick Douglass observed that prejudice against the free colored people had shown itself nowhere in such large proportions as among artisans and mechanics.[38]

The artisans and mechanics of whom Douglass complained pioneered in the building of unions, and it was natural that the unions reflected their outlook. In 1822, a carpenter and thirty-four other proletarians were hanged in Charleston, South Carolina, for planning an uprising against slavery. At the same time, journeymen millwrights and machine workers, reawakening after the depression of 1819 to 1822, were meeting at a tavern in Philadelphia, plotting to establish the ten-hour day as standard for their trades.[39] Just as racial slavery was the distinctive feature of American growth, the distinctive feature of American labor history is that these two conspiracies of labor, instead of coming to form part of a single movement, profoundly diverged.

The first formal organization of wage earners in different trades occurred in Philadelphia in 1827, when skilled workmen, following a strike of building-trades workers for the ten-hour day, combined their craft organizations into the Mechanics' Union of Trade Associations. This gave rise the following year to the Philadelphia Working Men's Party. In 1829, mechanics in New York, following the Philadelphia example, called their first general meeting and plunged into electoral politics. The early unions and Working Men's Parties sought, among other things, to prohibit chartered monopolies, regulate apprenticeship, restrict female, child, and convict labor, abolish imprisonment for debt, and establish a system of public education. Within a short time Working Men's Parties appeared up and down the east coast, and as far west as Missouri. Most folded in 1831 and 1832, but local organizations composed of associations of workers of different trades soon reappeared. At about this time, workers made their first efforts to form national unions. The depression of 1837 to 1843 wiped out these early unions, concluding that chapter in the history of labor reform.

If the conditions of the Irish laborers on the canals led them to adopt methods similar to those of the slave, their situation as wage earners in the cities led them into contact with the organizations of workers that have conventionally been termed the labor movement. It is difficult to specify the Irish role in these early unions, partly because records are few and newspapers did not take an interest in the movement comparable to that which they showed two decades later. It is known that the Irish formed the largest portion of the immigrants during those early years and that, while most were unskilled, there were a fair number of skilled workers among them. Although there is a sprinkling of Irish surnames among the union leaders of the pre-Famine period, the Irish took part in the movement more as rank-and-file members than as leaders, forming an integral part of the unions and sharing their policies and aims.[40] The early labor unions, therefore, should be regarded not so much as Irish institutions, in the way they later became, but as institutions for assimilating the Irish into white America. The Philadelphia general strike of 1835 provides an example of how the unions aided in the assimilation process.

It has already been noted that the Mechanics' Union of Trade Associations in Philadelphia grew out of a strike for the ten-hour day. Boston carpenters struck in 1825 and again in 1832 for the same demand. In 1835 they struck again. They were defeated, but their effort inspired the Philadelphia general strike of the same year, the first general strike in an American city. One sentence in the Boston strike circular, which had been written by Seth Luther, evoked a particularly enthusiastic response in Philadelphia: "We claim by the blood of our fathers, shed on our battlefields in the war of the Revolution, the rights of American citizens, and no earthly power shall resist our righteous claim with impunity."[41]

The strike began with a group of laborers who in fact could not claim, by the blood of their fathers, the rights of American citizens—the Irish workers on the Schuylkill River. In May 1835, coal heavers demanding the ten-hour day shut down the wharves. One contemporary account reported that "three hundred of them, headed by a man with a sword, paraded along the canal, threatening death to those who unload or transfer the cargoes to the 75 vessels waiting in the river."[42] The press denounced the leaders of the strike as "freshly imported *foreigners*—who despise and defy the law."[43]

On June 3, shoemakers struck for higher wages and, shouting "We are all day laborers," marched in a procession to the docks, declaring their intention to boycott coal until the coal heavers had won the ten-hour day.[44] The carpenters joined in, followed by the bricklayers, plasterers, masons, and hod carriers. On June 10, the *Saturday Evening Post* reported twenty trades on strike for higher wages and shorter hours.[45]

On June 6, the strikers held a rally at the State House, at which not only mechanics but lawyers, physicians, merchants, and politicians spoke in favor of the ten-hour day. Strike leader John Ferral wrote, "each day added thousands to our ranks. We marched to the public works, and the workmen joined with us...."[46] The Whig-controlled City Council responded quickly, instituting the ten-hour day for city employees. In the heavily Irish suburb of Southwark, the board of commissioners not only reduced the hours of labor but granted an increase in the daily wage.[47] Among private employers, the master carpenters were the first to grant the ten-hour day; on June 6, the master bricklayers agreed to it; and before the month was out, the master shoemakers had conceded the wage demands of their employees.[48]

The unrest spread to nearby towns. Mechanics at Germantown won their demands without a strike, and journeymen shoemakers at Norristown gained a wage increase.[49] The movement was not confined to craftsmen. At Norristown, three or four hundred railroad workers struck successfully for the ten-hour day. The laborers and carters employed by the Borough of Reading walked off their jobs, demanding higher pay. Boatmen in the coal mining area upriver on the Schuylkill, many of them Irish immigrants, refused to allow coal to be shipped out until their wage demands were met. When several hundred of them marched into Pottsville, the sheriff and his men attacked their procession.[50] Before the movement was over as many as 20,000 workers had taken part in walkouts.[51]

Ferral called it a "bloodless revolution," at which "the blood-sucking aristocracy...stood aghast."[52] Commons concurs that it was a revolution, declaring that the Philadelphia general strike "marked the turning point in this country from the 'sun to sun' agricultural system to the 'six to six' industrial system." Its influence extended up and down the east coast, so that by the close of the year, ten hours was the standard day's work for mechanics everywhere except for Boston.[53]

One of the reasons for the success of the movement was its rejection of anti-immigrant and anti-Catholic sentiment. As early as 1828, the *Mechanic's Free Press,* organ of the Working Men's Party, urged its readers to "LET THE SUBJECT OF RELIGION ALONE—or the death knell of our Associations will soon be sounded."[54] In 1834, John Ferral, himself Irish born, convened a meeting of Irish Americans, where he appealed to Protestant and Catholic workers in the Manayunk textile mills to recall their experiences in Ireland, where the "aristocracy" exploited religious differences in order to "keep the honest and industrious population divided, rendering them…an easy prey to their enemies."[55]

The Report on the Ten-Hour Movement at the National Trades' Union Convention of 1835 recognized the Irish immigrant as the spearhead of the general strike. "Previous to that time," the report stated, "nearly all who worked by the week, were obliged to toil from sun to sun, for a bare existence. The coal heavers on the banks of the Schuylkill first began the struggle against the tremendous power of wealth and avarice. The strike was justice against oppression; and the issue, for a time, was considered doubtful." The report went on to describe the difficulties which the immigrant had to overcome. "All our enemies joined against these powerless people, and denounced them as disorderly and riotous. Merchants met in the Exchange, and offered large sums to all who would take the places of the strikers."[56] Summing up its experiences, the Philadelphia Trades' Union declared, "The Union makes no distinction between natives and foreigners. All alike are welcome to its benefits. If he is a workingman in favor of the emancipation of all who labor from the thraldom of monied capital, he is welcome to our ranks."[57]

Although craftsmen had shouted "We are all day laborers" in 1835, it was not until the following year that they admitted unskilled laborers to the Trades' Union. In the spring of 1836, the coal heavers on the Schuylkill struck again, this time for higher wages. After a strike parade, Philadelphia city officials arrested several leaders; the mayor, in fixing bail at $2,500 each, was said to have declared his determination to "lay the axe at the root of the Trades' Union." The Trades' Union responded by admitting the coal heavers as members and underwriting the cost of the trial. Following the court's dismissal of charges against the workingmen, the Trades' Union launched a campaign to unseat Mayor Swift.[58]

In the Philadelphia strike wave of 1835 and 1836, the labor movement by and large adopted the cause of the Catholic Irish laborers as its own. Not only did Philadelphia artisans admit the coal heavers to the ranks of the union, thus becoming the first skilled workers in the nation to join in the same union with the unskilled, they explicitly recognized their vanguard role in the strike. Moreover, in carrying out their campaign (unsuccessful as it happened) to unseat the mayor, they showed their commitment to solidarity with the Irish laborers. The actions of the Philadelphia artisans by no means signaled the death of nativism among the workingmen. But they were a significant early step, foreshadowing the ultimate rejection of anti-Irish, anti-Catholic sentiment in the ranks of labor.

The welcome Philadelphia artisans gave to the newcomers did not extend to a group that had been a traditional part of the local scene, free persons of color. At one of the strike processions there appeared a delegation of wood sawyers, described by one newspaper as "some ten or a dozen who claimed affinities with whites and the rest the cullings of a lot of blacks...." "The woodcutters had a regular turn out, ebonies, mulattoes and whites," reported another paper. "They raised a dust, made a good deal of noise, marched up street and down again, and 'strait were seen no more'!"[59] The tone of the reports indicates that the participation of the black laborers was viewed by all as an anomaly. A few months before the strike it will be recalled that a number of black men at work in a coal yard on the Schuylkill had been attacked and severely beaten by the coalheavers who would soon become the heroes of organized labor.[60]

Universally hostile to the free Negro, many white workers nevertheless considered slavery unjust, and some went so far as to sign abolitionist petitions and join abolitionist societies as individuals.[61] However, they never viewed slavery as part of the labor question.[62] The programs of the Working Men's Parties did not mention slavery, although they addressed such questions as convict labor, imprisonment for debt, and even public lotteries. When spokesmen for white labor did talk about slavery, it was usually to compare rhetorically the condition of the slave favorably to that of the free wage worker. The following from the *Mechanic's Free Press* is a typical example: "What is the condition of the 'free' laborer? He works more for his employer than the slave does for his master...The slave is regularly supplied with the necessaries of life—has no anxious care for the future....The free laborer, with greater toil, cannot secure to himself and children the necessaries of life....The black slave is secured from want and a necessity to crime, in lieu of which the free laborer sometimes has a choice of employers....Although the Southern master can use only the lash, yet the other has a more powerful means of enforcing servitude..."[63] Seth Luther, the itinerant agitator who wrote the circular that sparked the Philadelphia general strike, was fond of drawing the parallel between the free laborer and the slave, to the disadvantage of the former.[64] To those who insisted that the lot of the free white laborer was worse than that of the slave, Frederick Douglass liked to point out that his old position on the plantation had been vacant since his departure, and encouraged them to apply.

A writer for the National Trades' Union, in a review of James Kirke Paulding's book *Slavery in the United States,* criticized the abolitionists for ignoring the plight of white labor, and denounced Daniel O'Connell, who "could not bear to have his ebony brethren whipped even enough to arouse them to a sufficient degree of exertion to digest their hominy, pigs and poultry." The writer went on to praise slavery, which benefited both the slave, who was better off than he had been as a free man in Africa, and the country, because it provided people to perform the tasks that were too low for whites.[65] Among labor attacks on abolition, the review was unusual only in that it went beyond denunciations of the abolitionists to a positive defense of slavery.

In 1836, the Working Man's Association of England, parent body of the Chartist movement, addressed an appeal to American workers, urging them to launch a national campaign to abolish chattel slavery. Philadelphian Lewis G. Gunn joined in the appeal, declaring, "As long as the pulse beats in my frame the poor Negro in chains shall have my sympathy and much of my attention....Let me entreat you also never to forget the slave....Our voice should *thunder* from Maine to Georgia, and from the Atlantic to the Mississippi—the voice of a nation of *Republicans* and *Christians* demanding with all the authority of moral power, *demand-ing* the immediate liberation of the bondsmen."[66] Although his appeal was published in the *National Laborer,* it did not lead to the desired effect. A few days later the paper replied that, while it opposed "slavery in every form, either over the body, mind, color, or degree," it was "the duty of organized labor to begin to secure to the workingmen the right of dispos-ing his own labor at his own price, and to make that price just and equivalent to his toil."[67]

Labor activists denounced the abolitionists not for opposing slavery but for placing the cause of the slave ahead of the cause of the free worker. Luther complained, "We have the philanthropists moaning over the fate of the Southern slave when there are *thousands* of children in this State as truly slaves as the blacks in the South."[68] Ely Moore, president of the New York General Trades' Union and the first representative of the working men elected to Congress, declared that support for abolitionism would strengthen "the pro-Bank, anti-Jackson aristocracy."[69] George Evans, editor of the *Workingman's Advocate,* told his readers that aboli-tionists were men "actuated by a species of theological fanaticism, [who] hoped to free the slaves more for the purpose of adding them to their reli-gious sect, than for love of liberty and justice."[70] A number of labor papers of the day published a verse describing the death from starvation of a factory girl. The last stanza went:

> That night a Chariot passed her,
> While on the ground she lay;
> The daughters of her master,
> An evening visit pay.
> Their tender hearts are sighing,
> As Negroes woes are told;
> While the white slave was dying,
> Who gained their fathers' gold.[71]

If abolitionism, in Melville's words, "expresse[d] the fellow-feeling of slave for slave," participation in the organized labor movement was likely to harden the hearts of working-class whites to any abolitionist sentiments they held, by providing them with arguments for why they should turn their backs on their fellow workers in chains.[72]

In the South the slave figured prominently in both skilled and unskilled labor, and although working-class whites sought to restrict the use of slaves, the political power of the slaveholders generally prevented them from doing so.[73] In some cases Irish immigrants were preferred to slaves, for reasons having nothing to do with race. Frederick Law Olmsted cited an official of an Alabama stevedoring company who explained why Irish workers were employed on the docks: "The niggers are worth too much to be risked here; if the Paddies are knocked overboard, or get their backs broke, nobody loses anything."[74] When the commissioners of the (New Orleans) New Basin Canal corporation began building in 1831, they knew that the mortality rate among the laborers would be high; consequently they hired Irish. A song commemorates those who died:

> Ten thousand Micks, they swung their picks,
> To dig the New Canal.
> But the choleray was stronger 'n they.
> An twice it killed them awl.

The horrible conditions did not deter a group of Corkmen from attacking other Irish in a battle over jobs in 1834, killing four. In the early 1850s, Irish were hired to build a wagon road across a swamp in southwest Louisiana, by a landowner who stated that he would not risk his slaves in the marsh.[75] Surely no one would argue that in situations like these the employment of free Irish in place of black slaves, who represented a great initial outlay of capital and who could not be easily discharged when the job was completed, was the result of racial bias.

Even in the free North, the initial turnover from black to Irish labor does not imply racial discrimination; many of the newly arrived Irish, hungry and desperate, were willing to work for less than free persons of color, and it was no more than good capitalist sense to hire them. In domestic service the shift began fairly early: the New York Society for the Encouragement of Faithful Domestics reported that between 1826 and 1830, it had received applications for employment from 3,601 Americans, 8,346 Irish, 2,574 Negroes, 642 English, and 377 foreigners from other countries.[76] By 1849, only 156 of 4,249 black women, and none of the men, were listed as living with white families.[77] A Negro newspaper, the *Colored*

*American,* wrote that "these impoverished and desperate beings—transported from the transatlantic shores, are crowding themselves into every place of business and of labor, and driving the poor colored American citizen out. Along the wharves, where the colored man once done [*sic*] the whole business of shipping and unshipping—in stores where his services were once rendered, and in families where the chief places were filled by him, in all these situations there are substituted foreigners or white Americans."[78] By 1855, Irish immigrants made up eighty-seven percent of New York City's 23,300 unskilled laborers, while Negroes accounted for three percent.[79] In Philadelphia, "P.O.," in an 1849 letter to a local newspaper, wrote

> That there may be, and undoubtedly is, a direct competition
> between them (the blacks and Irish) as to labor we all know. The
> wharves and new buildings attest this fact, in the person of our
> stevedores and hod-carriers as does all places of labor; and when
> a few years ago we saw none but blacks, we now see nothing but
> Irish.[80]

The 1850 U.S. Census listed a total of twenty-eight black hod carriers and twenty-seven stevedores in the city, a drop in both cases of more than half in only three years.[81] One of the consequences of the closing off of occupations to black men was the rise to prominence of the Negro washerwoman, who became in many instances the principal wage earner of the family, washing and ironing while her husband brought in and carried the clothes to the homes. Nearly half of all black female adults in Philadelphia in 1849 worked as washerwomen.[82]

One black writer, looking back in 1860, explained the changes he had witnessed:

> Fifteen or twenty years ago, a Catholic priest in Philadelphia said
> to the Irish people in that city, "You are all poor, and chiefly labor-
> ers; the blacks are poor laborers, many of the native whites are
> laborers; now, if you wish to succeed, you must do everything that
> they do, no matter how degrading, and do it for less than they can
> afford to do it for." The Irish adopted this plan; they lived on less
> than the Americans could live upon, and worked for less, and the

result is, that nearly all the menial employments are monopolized by the Irish, who now get as good prices as anybody. There were other avenues open to American white men, and though they have suffered much, the chief support of the Irish has come from the places from which we have been crowded.[83]

All the information on displacement of Afro-Americans (except for the artisan trades) can be read without the slightest reference to race. The race question comes up *after* the Irish have replaced the Afro-Americans in the jobs. Now it was the black workers who were hungry and desperate, willing to work for the lowest wage. Why, then, were they not hired to undercut the wages of the Irish, as sound business principles would dictate? Why did the thrifty Yankee employers, always on the lookout for a bargain, fail to take advantage of the cheapest labor power available regardless of color? It is here that the organization of labor along race lines makes itself felt.

In 1851, the *African Repository* reported

In New York and other eastern cities, the influx of white laborers has expelled the Negro almost en masse from the exercise of the ordinary branches of labor. You no longer see him work upon buildings, and rarely is he allowed to drive a cart of public conveyance. White men will not work with him.[84]

"White men will not work with him"—the magic formula of American trade unionism! Before it could do the Irish any good, however, it was necessary to establish that they were white. In 1853 Frederick Douglass noted, "Every hour sees us elbowed out of some employment to make room for some newly-arrived emigrant from the Emerald Isle, whose hunger and color entitle him to special favor. These white men are becoming houseservants, cooks, stewards, waiters, and flunkies. For aught I see they adjust themselves to their stations with all proper humility. If they cannot rise to the dignity of white men, they show that they can fall to the degradation of black men." "In assuming our avocation," warned Douglass, the Irishman "has also assumed our degradation."[85]

Douglass's words pointed to the difficulty the Irish faced: it was not always clear on which side of the color line they fell. How to determine their status? In American history, "white" has not meant all scrambled together without regard to religion, language, or country of origin. At every period, however, the "white race" has included only groups that did "white man's work." But what was "white man's work?" In the case of the Irish, "white man's work" could not be defined as work they did, when it was precisely their status as "whites" that was in question.[86] Since "white" was not a physical description but one term of a social relation which could not exist without its opposite, "white man's work" was, simply, work from which Afro-Americans were excluded. Conversely, "black man's work" was work monopolized by Afro-Americans.[87] The distinction was entirely arbitrary: many of the occupations from which free black laborers were excluded were those which slaves had performed earlier in the free states and were still performing in those parts of the country where slavery existed.[88]

To be acknowledged as white, it was not enough for the Irish to have a competitive advantage over Afro-Americans in the labor market; in order for them to avoid the taint of blackness it was necessary that no Negro be allowed to work in occupations where Irish were to be found. Still better was to erase the memory that Afro-Americans had ever done those jobs.[89] Charles H. Wesley described their reasoning: "While the foreigners were willing to take the menial places which Negroes had been filling, they were unwilling, as a rule, in the North as well as in the South, to work at the same occupations with Negroes...and through the operation of this racial attitude the Negroes were excluded very gradually from many occupations."[90]

In antebellum Philadelphia neither the artisanal nor service trades nor outdoor labor would prove decisive in establishing the place of the Irish. That was fixed only through access to the new industries which were then growing up in the city.

These new industries were principally represented by the large textile mills along the banks of the Schuylkill. "In the 1820s, Philadelphia's textile industry, which had long resisted mechanization, made the move into the water-powered mill and the era of industrial factory production. This process, unfolding rapidly, took place along a recently completed section of the Schuylkill Navigation Canal in the township of Roxborough.

By 1828, the newly named mill town of Manayunk was being likened to Lowell and Manchester." By 1840, Manayunk's eight mills operated forty-four percent of the spindles in Philadelphia county, employing over a quarter of the whole country's textile operatives, more than 1,000 women, children, and men.[91]

Unlike the labor force in the New England textile mills, the bulk of Manayunk's workers were immigrants from Germany, Ireland, and England (many of the latter Irish), particularly from areas where the transition from handloom to powerloom weaving had led to distress. "The experienced and skilled positions in the Manayunk mills were generally filled by British (and sometimes German) workers, whereas the native and Irish groups were more commonly present in lower-skilled jobs."[92] Some came directly to Manayunk after disembarking from the middle passage, while others underwent additional seasoning in other Philadelphia mills, in neighboring counties, or in the New England textile districts. The family system prevailed, with women and children comprising a majority of loom tenders, while the men were concentrated in the more skilled occupations.[93]

The wages and hours of work in the textile mills were typical of those in newly industrializing societies, and hardly need recounting here.[94] Of special interest to this study are the labor recruitment practices. The mills relied entirely upon immigrant labor. Possible explanations for this pattern fall into several categories: 1) employer prejudice; 2) rational decisions by employers, made in response to pure market considerations; 3) choices by various groups of potential employees; and 4) extra-market pressures from workers or other sectors of the public.[95]

No record has been found to indicate that Manayunk textile manufacturers were motivated in their hiring practices by color prejudice. This absence is especially significant given, for example, the remarks by numerous contemporary observers that pressure from white laborers played an important role in driving free persons of color out of artisanal and service trades and certain branches of common labor, or the abundant documentation of explicit race discrimination in the Southern textile mills a half-century later.[96] While it is difficult to prove a negative proposition, the failure to discover a single statement by anyone in a responsible position that he allowed his personal feelings toward one or another group to govern his hiring policies, from a time when neither government commissions nor public opinion would have inhibited anyone from making such statements, suggests that color prejudice as such on the part of the employers simply did not play any important part in determining the mill work force.

The absence of color prejudice as an operative factor does not mean that no preferences existed in hiring. It must not be forgotten that not only were Afro-Americans absent from the mill labor force, but native whites as well. It is possible that immigrants brought with them skills at the handloom or at old-fashioned weaving, skills possessed by no other group, but since the majority of the operatives were children or women lacking those skills, their importance in the new mechanized operations was questionable. Moreover, since children or women with no previous experience in mechanized production formed the basis of the industry, the lack of specific skills could not have posed any serious barrier to employment.

The need for specific skills in textile making would not have been the only possible reason why the mill owners preferred immigrant labor. Their preference may have resulted from the recognition that the immigrants, coming from areas where capitalist production was firmly established, had already acquired habits of work discipline that would enable them to adjust to the mills; they had already learned to submit to the long hours, strict supervision, and uninterrupted pace characteristic of the new mode of production. This explanation, though, while it is plausible for the early period of industrialization, breaks down for the period of the Famine and after, when the majority of the immigrants were fleeing from rural areas, with no more experience in the capitalist factory than native Americans, black or white.

Choices made by potential workers would reflect the history of capitalist development from the other side. The composition of the work force may have resulted from the unwillingness of any but immigrants to work in the new mills. Could native blacks as well as whites have shared a similar reluctance to do so, notwithstanding the very different scope of the alternatives open to them? The possibility should not be discounted, although the extent to which it operated is probably unmeasurable, and must therefore be left to speculation.

Unlike the situation in artisanal or service trades, or in various spheres of common labor, where persons of color had made up a large portion of the traditional labor force before they were ousted by prejudice, it is not likely that the racial attitudes of the laborers played any significant part in shaping the employment policies of the textile mills— at least not initally. In the first place, before their arrival in America, the immigrant laborers were not able to form any definite ideas of the proper place for black and white labor; and in the second place, as impoverished newcomers they were in no position to impose their views on employers.

The textile mills of Manayunk were representative of industry generally: in 1847 less than one-half of one percent of the black male work force of Philadelphia was employed in factories.[97] While no single factor by itself accounts for the racial contours of the mill labor force of antebellum Philadelphia, it is possible to combine a couple to provide a logical story of cause and effect. I would suggest that, in the formative period, the factory owners hired immigrants from the industrial districts of Britain and Ireland because they were most suitable to their needs, both in their experience with the sort of regime that prevailed in the factories and their willingness to work for low wages.[98] Later on, after the immigrants had established their place in America, they were able to exert enough pressure on the employers to maintain the factories as "white" preserves.[99] In this second stage, organizations of laborers, including unions, played a considerable part.

Whatever the origins of the employment practices of the new industries, they had different consequences for Afro-Americans, Irish, and native whites. Black workers, already being driven out of artisanal trades by prejudice, and squeezed out of service trades and common labor by competition, could find no refuge in the manufacturing area, and hence were pushed down below the waged proletariat, into the ranks of the destitute self-employed: ragpickers, bootblacks, chimneysweeps, sawyers, fish and oyster mongers, washerwomen, and hucksters of various kinds. In contrast, native-born whites and Irish immigrants, coming, to be sure, from different social backgrounds and by no means perfectly homogenized, were being transformed into the waged labor force of industry. The distinction between those who did and those who did not have access to the most dynamic area of the economy became a principal element defining "race" in the North.[100]

The depression that followed the panic of 1837 brought to an end the early period of labor organization. It took the discovery of gold in California in 1849 to lift the country out of protracted hard times and allow unions and other forms of workers' organization to revive. The new unions came into existence during a period of major recomposition of the working class: from 1840 to 1849 there were 1,400,000 immigrants; from 1850 to 1859 the total was 2,700,000. Of these, the Irish formed the largest group, 41.4 percent of the total immigration. If the unions of the 1830s, headed largely by native-born and British Protestants, functioned at that time as schools for teaching the Irish the meaning of whiteness, the unions later were to become to a considerable extent Irish institutions.[101]

New York was the capital of labor unionism. By the 1850s, the Irish were well on their way to establishing their prominence in the labor movement there: all the officers of the New York Tailors' and Laborers' Unions were Irish in 1854, and Irish dominated the unions of boilermakers, boot and shoe workers, bricklayers and plasterers, cordwainers, masons and bricklayers, quarrymen, and stone cutters, in addition to holding important posts or making up a large share of the membership in the unions of bakers, cartmen, cigarmakers, coachmen, coopers, longshoremen, painters, piano makers, plumbers, printers, porters, smiths, and waiters. In fact, of 229 antebellum labor leaders in New York City whose ethnicity could be unambiguously determined, 106 were Irish.[102]

One scholar comments, "In examining these unions it will be seen that they are exactly the same as those of the American workers, for a history of the Irish immigrant in the labor movement reduces itself to a history of the American labor movement."[103] To reverse the order of the phrases in her formulation would hardly be an exaggeration.

What stands out in the above list of Irish-dominated and -influenced unions is that, with the exception of the laborers, longshoremen, porters, and coachmen associations, all represented workers in the mechanic trades. This is not surprising to those familiar with the unionism of that era, which was largely a phenomenon of the mechanic trades, but it shows that, while the Irish made up the majority of laborers, they were also a strong presence in many trades with large populations of native-born whites and English and German immigrants. "We venture to say," wrote the editor of the (New York) *Irish American* in 1852, "that One-Half (at least) of the mechanics of New York—machinists, turners, shipwrights, carpenters, cabinet-makers, smiths of all kinds, practical engineers &c., &c., &c., are Irish."[104]

That the Irish were disproportionately concentrated as laborers and servants is well known. In New York in 1855, servants formed a quarter of the Irish working population, exceeding the number of laborers by one-fourth.[105] In Boston in 1850, forty-eight percent of the Irish working population worked as laborers, compared to eleven percent for the German and less than five percent for the U.S. born. Another fifteen percent were servants, compared to four percent for U.S. born. At the same time, there were a total of 362 occupations listed among them, higher than the number for any group except those born in New England, who were more than twice as numerous.[106] In Philadelphia in 1840, four out of ten Irish workers were hod carriers, laborers, draymen, and stevedores.[107] Ten years later, thirty percent were day laborers, and another eleven percent worked as sweated handloom weavers; at the same time, nearly a third were employed in skilled trades.[108]

Kerby Miller has written that "Often without capital or skills, unaccustomed to work practices in their adopted country, the Famine Irish usually entered the American work force at the very bottom, competing only with free Negroes or—in the South—with slave labor for the dirty, backbreaking, poorly paid jobs that white native Americans and emigrants from elsewhere disdained to perform. Even if they aspired to higher status, most Irish males probably worked at least part of their lives in North America as canal, railroad, building construction, or dock laborers. Those who rose later to more remunerative or respectable employment remembered bitterly that as 'Labouring men' they were 'thought nothing of more than *dogs*...despised and kicked about' in the supposed land of equality."[109]

Miller is right overall. Yet in spite of the misery to which the Irish immigrants were subjected—misery so severe that it was estimated that their average length of life after arrival was six years[110]—no system of caste confined them to the pick and shovel in the way color discrimination kept black workers as "hewers of wood and drawers of water."

An 1857 novel depicts a scene in an engraver's shop in Philadelphia on the first day a newly employed colored lad appears on the job.

Charlie...found some dozen or more journeymen assembled in the workroom; and noticed upon his entrance there was an exchange of significant glances, and once or twice he overheard the whisper of "nigger."

...Mr. Blatchford, noticing Charlie, said, "Ah! you have come, and in good time, too. Wheeler," he continued, turning to one of the workmen, "I want you to take this boy under your especial charge: give him a seat at your window, and overlook his work."

At this there was a general uprising of the workmen, who commenced throwing off their caps and aprons....

"We won't work with niggers!" cried one; "No nigger apprentices!" cried another; and "No niggers—no niggers!" was echoed from all parts of the room.

..."What is the occasion of all this tumult—what does it mean?" [asked Mr. Blatchford].

"Why, sir, it means just this: the men and boys discovered that you intended to take a nigger apprentice, and have made up their minds if you do they will quit in a body."

"It cannot be possible," exclaimed the employer..."Come, let me persuade you—the boy is well-behaved and educated!"

"Damn his behaviour and education!" responded a burly fellow; "let him be a barber or shoe-black—that is all niggers are good for. If he comes, we go—that's so, ain't it, boys?"

There was a general response of approval....

In the novel, the employer accedes to the demands of his employees, and discharges the Negro.[111] Another novel, written a decade later and set in New York on the eve of the Civil War, depicts a similar scene, in which seven hundred workmen threaten to walk off the job in protest against the presence of a black clerk. "You can't get an Irishman, and, what's more, a free-born American citizen, to put himself on a level with a nigger," says one of the characters. The result is the same: the black man is dismissed. "The contest would have been not merely with seven hundred men," explains the employer, "but with every machinist in the city." The writer appended a note stating, "almost every scene in this book is copied from life."[112]

When Frederick Douglass, a caulker, sought to board a ship in New Bedford to work, he was told that "every white man would leave the ship in her unfinished condition if I struck a blow at my trade upon her."[113] In Baltimore in 1858 and 1859, mobs of whites rioted against Negroes working as caulkers, and succeeded in having whites hired in their places; the *American* reported that "until the riot Baltimoreans were not aware that any white caulkers even existed in [the city]."[114]

In August 1862, a largely Irish mob in Brooklyn attacked the black employees, chiefly women and children, who were working in a tobacco factory. The mob, having driven the black employees to the upper stories of the building, then set fire to the first floor. The factory was allowed to reopen only when the employer promised to dismiss the Negroes and hire Irish.[115]

It would be possible to extend almost indefinitely the list of examples of organized white labor hostility to the black worker, without even citing any cases where it might be said that the black workers were acting as strikebreakers (although by that time, at the insistence of white labor, almost the only employment open to Negroes was to take the places of whites during strikes). To white labor, black people were, by definition, a race of strikebreakers. One British traveler, who spent three years working in America, reported on working-class attitudes toward the Negro:

> the strongly expressed opinion of the majority was, that they are a soulless race, and I am satisfied that some of these people would shoot a black man with as little regard to moral consequences as they would a wild hog.

He went on to note that "it is in the Irish residents that [the men of colour] have, and will continue to have, their most formidable enemies."[116]

In 1853, black waiters in New York, who had just won a wage increase that lifted their wages above the standard for whites, attended, at the invitation of a white waiters' union, two mass meetings called by the white union to prepare for a strike for higher wages. Philip S. Foner, who probably has done as much research as anybody living on the relations between the black worker and organized labor in the nineteenth century, has called it the only known example of a white union before the Civil War asking a union of black workers to take part in a joint meeting. Even in that case, though, the Negroes were not invited to join the white union.[117]

To what extent did the unions speak for working-class whites? Most workers did not belong to unions, and black workers were excluded from places that did not have unions as well as from places that did. It seems reasonable, therefore, to view unions in the period under consideration more as a gauge of working-class white attitudes than a significant shaper of them.[118]

On the docks, the Irish effort to gain the rights of white men collided with the black struggle to maintain the right to work; the result was perpetual warfare. Black workers had traditionally been an important part of the waterfront work force in New York, Philadelphia, and other Northern cities, as well as Baltimore, Charleston, New Orleans, and other Southern ports. By the 1850s the New York waterfront had become an Irish preserve; few black men could find work on the docks except during strikes under police protection, and even Germans were unwelcome. In 1850, Irish laborers had struck demanding the dismissal of a black laborer who was working alongside them. During the strike of 1852, and again in 1855, 1862, and 1863, Irish longshoremen battled black workers who had been brought in to take their places. The Longshoremen's United Benevolent Society, formed in 1852, was exclusively Irish, even marching annually in the Saint Patrick's Day parade. It is significant, however, that at no time did the Society declare its commitment to an Irish monopoly of jobs, stating instead that it sought to ensure only that "work upon the docks…shall be attended to solely and absolutely by members of the 'Longshoremen's Association,' and such white laborers as they see fit to permit upon the premises." In fact, the banner of the Society was decorated with flags of France, Germany, the

Netherlands, Sweden, Ireland, Denmark, Hungary, and Italy, under the American flag and the word "unity." At the top of the banner was the inscription: "We know no distinction but that of merit."[119] These Irish showed they had learned well the lesson that they would make their way in the U.S. not as Irishmen but as whites.

In Philadelphia, as in New York, "Irish gangs not only drove Blacks out of jobs, they also served as surrogate unions."[120] There, the race riot of 1849 and the longshore strike of 1851 were simply different tactical phases of the same struggle. As one historian, apparently unaware of the irony, has remarked, "Ethnic identity was a shaping force for labor solidarity."[121]

The wars along the docks led directly to the so-called draft riots of 1863 in New York. The riots were the coda to the theme with which this chapter began—and the most dramatic illustration of how the laborer McManus acquired the will and power to help the newcomer O'Rourke find employment in the new country.

" A cry at once arose that a white man was shot, and the
corner of Sixth :

of the mob was directed to the California House, at the
ary street."—page 30

# V

# THE
# TUMULTUOUS REPUBLIC

Why you see, a party of us one Sunday arternoon, had nothin' to
do, so we got up a nigger riot. We have them things in Phil'delphy,
once or twice a year, you know? I helped to burn a nigger church,
two orphans' asylums and a school-house. And happenin' to have
a pump-handle in my hand, I aksedentally hit an old nigger on the
head. Konsekance wos he died. That's why they call me Pump-
Handle.

That is a passage from *The Quaker City*, an 1844 novel by one of the
most remarkable writers the country has ever known, George
Lippard. Now forgotten, Lippard was the best selling author in America
before Harriet Beecher Stowe. Before he died in 1854, two months shy
of his thirty-second birthday, he wrote twenty-three separate books,
ranging from thick volumes to pamphlets, scores of uncollected stories
and "legends," hundreds of news and editorial columns, and wrote or
collaborated on several plays; he also founded his own publishing
house, edited his own weekly paper, and lectured widely. Among other
accomplishments, he was responsible for naming Philadelphia the
"Quaker City," and for popularizing the Liberty Bell as the symbol of the
republic. All these efforts were subordinate to his life's work, founding
and directing a secret society, the Brotherhood of the Union, to
"espouse the cause of the Masses," a society which may have laid the
foundation for the Knights of Labor and that survives to this day as an
association providing burial insurance.

To Lippard, "a literature which does not work practically, for the
advancement of a social reform, or which is too dignified or too good to

picture the wrongs of the great mass of humanity, is just good for nothing at all." In case there was any doubt as to the social reform he had in
mind, or the means he advocated to achieve it, he declared, "When
Labor has tried all other means in vain—when the Laborer is deprived
of Land, of Home, and of the Harvest of his toil—when the Few will not
listen to the voice of Justice, nor the Gospel of Nazareth—then we would
advise Labor to go to War, in any and in all forms...."

The overwrought plots and flat characters make Lippard's novels
unreadable today. But they are unsurpassed as sources of information
about the life and attitudes of the "Lower Million" (to borrow from one
of his titles).[1]

A "n—— riot" in "Phil'delphy" once or twice a year, said Pump-Handle.
Scholars have been able to document only nine major mob attacks
against black people in Philadelphia in the years 1834 through 1849, of
which seven occurred between 1834 and 1838. Undoubtedly there were
other incidents too small to make the newspapers. One of the best studied has been the "Flying Horse Riot" of 1834.[2]

On a lot near Seventh and South Streets in Philadelphia, an entrepreneur had for some time been operating a merry-go-round called
"Flying Horses." It was popular among both black people and whites, and
served both "indiscriminately." Quarrels (not necessarily racial) over
seating preference and so forth were frequent. On Tuesday evening,
August 12, a mob of several hundred young white men, thought to be
principally from outside the area, appeared at the scene, began fighting
with the black people there, and in a very short time tore the merry-go-
round to pieces. The mob then marched down South Street, to the adjacent township of Moyamensing, attacked a home occupied by a black
family, and continued its violence on the small side streets where the
black people mainly lived. On Wednesday evening a crowd wrecked the
African Presbyterian Church on Seventh Street and a place several blocks
away called the "Diving Bell," operated by "a white man, and used as a
grog shop and lodging house for all colors, at the rate of three cents a
head." After reducing these targets to ruins, the rioters began smashing
windows, breaking down doors, and destroying furniture in private
homes of negroes, driving the inmates naked into the streets and beating any they caught. One correspondent reported that the mob threw a

corpse out of a coffin, and cast a dead infant on the floor, "barbarously" mistreating its mother. "Some arrangement, it appears, existed between the mob and the white inhabitants, as the dwelling houses of the latter, contiguous to the residences of blacks, were illuminated, and left undisturbed, while the huts of the negroes were signaled out with unerring certainty."[3]

By the time the riot subsided Friday evening, two black people were killed and many beaten. Two churches and upwards of twenty homes were laid waste, their contents looted or destroyed. Many black families took refuge in other parts of the city or across the Delaware in New Jersey. A Town Meeting appointed a committee to investigate the riot. It cited no immediate incidents that might have sparked the outbreak, although several had been reported in the newspapers in the week before, including a battle between members of one of the local fire companies (always centers of rowdyism) and a group of black people known to frequent the Flying Horses; an attack on the son of James Forten, Philadelphia's most eminent Afro-American, by a mob of fifty or sixty whites; and a disturbance at the Flying Horses the night before the riot. Another possible contributing factor the committee did not cite was the mob attacks on the homes of black people and prominent abolitionists in New York City a month earlier, which Phildelphia papers reported extensively and blamed on abolitionist "incendiaries."[4]

As a principal cause of the riot the committee identified the belief that some employers were hiring black workers over whites, and that as a result, many white laborers were out of work while people of color were employed and able to maintain their families. To underscore their complaint, five days after the riot ended, whites attacked a group of black men who were at work in a coal yard on the Schuylkill.[5] The matter of white right in employment the committee proposed to leave "for correction, to the consideration and action of individuals."

The committee concluded its report by calling upon all citizens to join in suppressing riot, recommending compensation for the victims, and advising the black people to conduct themselves "inoffensively, and with civility at all times...taking care...not to be obtrusive, [to avoid] giving birth to angry feelings." John Binns was the reporter for the committee.[6]

The rioters appear to have been predominantly, though not entirely, young men of "the most brutish and lowest cast of society," that is, indentured apprentices and laborers, including some with criminal records. Among them were a number of Irish, as evidenced by the names of those arrested (of eighteen arrested on the first night six had definite Irish surnames, and of the remaining twelve only six had names that were clearly not Irish) and by the testimony of black victims interviewed by a visiting English abolitionist.[7]

The rioters were organized. On the second and third evenings, they assembled in a vacant lot, at a spot "right well known" to those intent on criminal assault, arson, and pillage, and there planned the evening's recreation. In one instance, a group was dispatched early Thursday evening with ropes, axes, and the other requisite paraphernalia, and proceeded systematically to tear down the Wharton Street Church (a mile and a half from the main riot scene), retiring when its task was complete. The rioters used signal words, "Gunner," "Punch," and "Big Gun," perhaps to warn of the authorities' approach.

While the "object of the most active among the rioters, was a destruction of the property, and injury to the persons, of the colored people, with intent...to induce, or compel them to remove from [the] district," places of interracial fraternization were attacked with particular wrath: the Flying Horses itself, the Diving Bell, and the homes of two employers suspected of hiring Negroes. Racial antagonism gained virulence when inflamed by envy: the rioters made a point of targeting successful persons and institutions, including the well-dressed younger Forten, and the Afro-American Masonic lodge; on the second night of rioting, the mob passed over a number of easy-to-destroy frame houses in order to attack more substantial black-owned brick houses in the same street.[8]

The South Street area in which the riot occurred, including the southernmost wards of Philadelphia and the townships of Moyamensing and Southwark, was both poor and diverse. Heavily populated by "immense numbers of emigrants weekly arriving on our shores—bringing with them ignorance, poverty and vicious habits," the area was a refuge for many of the victims of Philadelphia's housing squeeze. "High rents drive them from the city...they are naturally or necessarily led to choose their residence here." "The heart sickens, and the feelings revolt at the scenes of degradation and misery which constantly meet our view."⁹

The poor lived in small alley houses built by speculators on the cheap land located between the large streets. These "trinity" houses were three stories high with one room on each floor; the occupants shared wells and outhouses. Few of the alley people owned their homes; most paid rent that could be made even cheaper by subletting. It was not unusual to find ten to twenty people living in one trinity home. Here is Lippard's description:

> Runnel's Court was one of those blots upon the civilization of the Nineteenth Century, which exist in the city and districts of Philadelphia, under the name of Courts. It extended between two narrow streets, and was composed of six three story brick houses built upon an area of ground scarcely sufficient for the foundation of one comfortable dwelling. Each of these houses comprised three rooms and a cellar. The cellar and each of the rooms was the abode of a family. And thus, packed within that narrow space, twenty-four families managed to exist, or rather to die by a slow torture, within the six houses of Runnell's Court. Whites and blacks, old and young, rumsellers and their customers, were packed together there, amid noxious smells, rags and filth, as thick and foul as insects in a decaying carcase.¹⁰

Although there were criminals, prostitutes, and paupers among them, the population consisted largely, in the words of a contemporary journalist, of "the immense army of *proletaires* which exist in every city, who live hardby in poor cabins and shanties, and whose labor supplies the profits upon which the merchant-princes and their aristocratic families subsist in luxury."¹¹ A study of Gaskill Street in 1839, considered representative of the area, showed thirty different occupations being pursued among the ninety-two households on the block, including laborer, cook, cordwainer, carpenter, and even one commercial merchant and broker—testimony to the relative absence of economic segregation in the nineteenth-century walking city.¹²

If the area was diverse economically, it was even more so ethnically. To those accustomed to the hyper-segregated twentieth-century city, it is difficult to imagine that there was no such thing as a ghetto. Over three-fifths of Philadelphia County's 1830 black population of fifteen thousand lived in the Cedar, Locust, New Market, and Pine Wards of Phildaelphia and the adjacent townships of Moyamensing and Southwark, and yet no ward was even one-third black. Even if we disregard ward lines and limit our attention to the South Street corridor, where African-Americans congregated most heavily, we find that they accounted for no more than half the population. If the area is broken down still further into blocks, then patterns of segregation appear; but even Bedford Street, where Negroes made up a large majority of the residents, housed a number of white families.[13] Two first-hand accounts from the time suggest that the area was popularly seen as poor rather than black. In both of these works black characters appear only briefly.[14]

The Irish were even more spread out than the Negroes. They began in the 1830s to increase substantially in the city's population, and by 1850 were concentrated in seven clusters throughout the city. These clusters were not ghettos; only five percent of the Irish immigrants lived in areas in which the majority were immigrants. Even in Moyamensing, where the concentration of immigrants was highest, the Irish represented only forty-five percent of the population.[15] Although the figures lack precision, it seems clear that, from the beginning, Irish lived among native-born Americans, German immigrants, and Afro-Americans.

In the trinity houses, black people, Irish, and native poor could literally live on top of one another. Many observers commented on the association of Irish, Afro-Americans, and poverty. An 1847 census taker in Moyamensing–Southwark, describing the black population, wrote "My heart is sick, my soul is horror-stricken at what my eyes behold....The greater part of these people live in with the Irish."[16] When Philadelphia was hit by the cholera in 1832, the highest mortality rate was in Moyamensing. Two of the streets later torn by the riot, Small and St. Mary, had to be closed temporarily and the residents evacuated to makeshift housing on the common. One eyewitness referred to the exodus of "men women and children, black and white, barefooted, lame and blind, half-naked and dirty...," illustrating both extreme misery and the absence of effective separation of the races there.[17]

Let us imagine two families, one Irish and one black, living next door to each other in one of the maze of alleys off Seventh Street. In good weather the women wash clothes together at the well they share in the courtyard, and exchange news, complaints, and household advice. In emergencies, they care for each other's children. Both families are desperately poor; the Irish husband works on the docks, when he can get work; the other goes up and down the streets with a sandstone wheel, crying "Knives and scissors to grind." Or perhaps one or the other husband, discouraged by poverty, has fled the home or taken to drink, and is more of a burden than a help to his poor wife. Each family depends on the little extra money brought in by a daughter just entering womanhood who cleans houses occasionally for the saloon-keeper around the corner, and whose mother worries about what will become of her. Each has a son entering manhood who has recently quit attending church services and is spending time hanging out with his friends on the corner, or at the Flying Horses carousel that recently opened. Their smaller children chase cats together and race paper boats in the garbage-strewn gutters that fill up with water after a rain. Each of the mothers has watched a child die of croup in the drafty, ill-heated flat.

A riot breaks out and a mob sweeps through the miserable street like some natural force. The word reaches the Irish woman: if she puts a burning candle in her window, her house will be spared. She does, and it is. The next morning she comes out to discover her next door neighbor weeping at the pile of rubble in front of her door that was once her bed, table, and dishes.

What can the Irishwoman say to her neighbor? That she is sorry? When the black woman looks at her reproachfully because her home was spared, will she feel guilty? And if so, how long will it take for her guilt to be replaced by resentment and rationalization?

We begin with the knowledge that some Irish had reasons to hate and fear people of black skin. We also assume that not all Irish felt that way, at any rate not strongly enough to join a white supremacist mob; this we know from our general knowledge of humanity, of Irish history, and, most of all, from the fact that the mob numbered only hundreds in a community of many thousands. Yet that organized force of hundreds was able to batter those who opposed it, or even those who held back, into silence and submission, so that in time it came to speak for the entire community. Rioters do not merely reflect public opinion; they shape it.[18]

The urban riot was a common occurrence in the Jacksonian period, and by no means all of the riots turned on race questions. One historian found that at least seventy percent of American cities with over 20,000 people experienced some major disorder in the 1830–65 period. Another counted thirty-five major riots in Baltimore, Philadelphia, New York, and Boston from 1830 to 1860. The year 1834 alone saw sixteen riots, and the following year thirty-seven. No less a witness than Abraham Lincoln warned in 1837 that "accounts of outrages committed by mobs form the every-day news of the times."[19]

Disorder on such a scale becomes order. The social function of the riot in Jacksonian America can be best understood in the light of Machiavelli's notion of the "tumultuous republic" (developed in *The Discourses*). According to Machiavelli, aristocratic republics (like Sparta and Venice) do not grow. In the chapter entitled "The Disunion of the Senate and the People Renders the Republic of Rome Powerful and Free," he declared that "the Roman republic has always been a theatre of turbulence and disorder," and that this was the key to its success. "Every free state," he wrote, "ought to afford the people the opportunity of giving vent, so to say, to their ambition."

"The market system," observed Polanyi, "was more allergic to rioting than any other economic system we know."[20] In the novel with which this chapter opens, one of the characters asks Pump-Handle if he was ever tried for killing the Negro. "Yes I was. Convicted, too," responds Pump-Handle. "Sentenced, in the bargain," he continues.

> But the Judge and the jury and the lawyers, on both sides, signed a paper to the Governor. He pardoned me. But I couldn't keep my hands in the ways o' virtue, so here I am agin, hidin' from the poleese!

Here another character joins in the conversation. "Rusty Jake"

> had been a small politician in his time. Two years past he had been an influential party man, on a limited scale. In procuring forged naturalization papers for verdant foreigners, or in swearing native paupers and thieves into the inestimable knowledge of voting, he was alike efficient and skillful....

"Genelmen, feller citizens, freemen!" he shouted, ascending the table, and gazing upon the assembled crowd of ruffians.

"Wot was it that our forefather's fit, bled and died for? Wot did they go in the cold for, without a mint-julip to make 'em jolly, or a sherry cobbler to warm their insides? Wos it to have *this* item o' human rights wiped off the slate o' liberty, with the sponge o' tyranny? Was it to have the Pardenin' Power struck out o' th' Constitooshun? The idee is redikulus! Why the fact is, tho' it ain't ginerally known—that the whole Revolution was on account o' the Pardenin' power! Gineral Washington—as history will tell you— was put in jail, for killin' an injun' in a nigger riot down South! That old curmedgeon, George the Third, refused to pardon Gineral Washington. The Revolution, gentlemen, wos the konsekence o' that refusal! I refers you to history, gentlemen, for further per-tik'lers."

Francis Grund, a Jacksonian publicist, wrote that direct action by a mob "is not properly speaking an opposition to the established laws of the country...but rather...a supplement to them—as a species of *common law.*" If he was expressing a Machiavellian idea, so were Pump-Handle and Rusty Jake; the reader is referred to history for further pertik'lers.[21]

Every institution in American life takes on a new hue when examined through a color-sensitive lens. So with the riot: in antebellum America a citizen (or potential citizen) was distinguished by three main privileges: he could sell himself piecemeal; he could vote; and he could riot.[22]

If the Constitution did not formally guarantee to whites the right to engage in mob attacks on black people, that right was safeguarded in the Jacksonian age by the absence of anything like a modern state. The city relied on volunteers to defend public order. When the call came to "Assist the mayor!" citizens were expected to, and did, step forward to apprehend a law-breaker or stifle disorder. In case of need, special posses were sworn in, whose members neither carried guns nor wore badges. Behind the *ad hoc* volunteers stood the militia, a slightly more regular but also nonprofessional force. While the reliance on amateurs to main-tain order may have kept down the number of serious injuries inflicted on crowds, it often left minorities unprotected.[23]

An ordinance of 1833 provided for twenty-four constables to patrol the city during the day, and 120 watchmen at night. The bulk of the constables' income came not from a salary for keeping order but from fees earned serving papers, delivering warrants, and collecting debts. They were all politically connected, and therefore extremely sensitive to public opinion. Moreover, as city employees, they were normally prohibited from crossing into the working-class suburbs, where a great deal of the rioting took place. Furnished with only a wooden mace, they were at least formally outarmed by the one-third of the city's males "between youth and middle age" who customarily carried knives. Between the end of the constables' watch and the setting of the nightwatch, the city was without any police force at all. Philadelphia, after the ordinance of 1833, had one patrolman for every 3,352 inhabitants. London in the same year had one patrolman for every 434 persons. At that time Paris was kept secure "by virtue of a hundred thousand bayonets" (as a Philadelphia paper of the day boasted). Two years later, Philadelphia actually reduced the number of day police because they were deemed too expensive.[24]

In that kind of extreme democracy, official response could not be separated from public opinion. On the first two nights of the August 1834 rioting, the authorities had been conspicuously absent. In the Moyamensing district, one of the centers of the riot, not a single public official of any rank was called out. "One or two watchmen were to be seen at a distance, but they had evidently no intention of disturbing the operations of the rioters." The best the mayor of Philadelphia could do was station police on the city line.[25] Some of the problem was due to the inevitable inefficiency of a force composed of a citizen's posse, militia, and the constabulary of several townships attempting to coordinate maneuvers in an area of clouded jurisdiction; for Thursday evening, the sheriff authorized the mayor to cross into the adjoining townships; he assembled a large force, including three hundred special constables and an infantry company under arms. In fact it appears that the authorities responded more effectively in 1834 than they did on several subsequent occasions.

A year later there was a similar outbreak. On that occasion city police did not cross over into Southwark and Moyamensing but "remained on the city line with their hands in their pockets."[26]

Racial attitudes were mixed up, in the minds of many, with attitudes towards abolition. In August of 1835 the Pennsylvania Anti-Slavery Society was forced to call off a planned public meeting after city officials informed them they could not guarantee their safety against a hostile crowd. A week later prominent citizens assembled to denounce the abolitionist cause, and especially the "dissemination of incendiary publications throughout the slave-holding states." The following day, a trunk-load of antislavery literature bound for various Southern states and the District of Columbia "accidentally" broke open on the docks. The officers at the previous night's meeting, heading a delegation of "a hundred of our most respectable citizens," took possession of the literature and dumped it in the Delaware. "We need only add," they concluded, "that Philadelphia is perfectly tranquil, and is likely to continue so."[27]

In 1837 a state constitutional convention disenfranchised black people. The following year a mob burned the just-completed Pennsylvania Hall, built by subscription to serve as a center for public meetings, including those devoted to abolition.[28] Mobs had been gathering at the hall for several days before the fire, and there was open talk of violence. According to reports, what most inflamed the mob was the sight of Negroes and whites walking arm-in-arm to and from the sessions of the convention of the Female Anti-Slavery Society, the first important event held at the new hall. The commander of the Philadelphia militia, Colonel August James Pleasonton, recorded in his diary his reactions to these scenes:

> There are serious apprehensions that the injudicious, to say the least, but as many think highly exciting and inflammatory proceedings of the Abolitionists, which have recently taken place here, and the disgusting intercourse between the whites and the blacks, as repugnant to all the prejudices of our education, which they not only have recommended, but are in the habit of practising in this very Abolition Hall, will result in some terrible outbreak of popular indignation, not only against the Abolitionists, but also, against the colored people.

In an addition to the entry, dated the same day, he noted that his prediction had come to pass: "a large mob of near 2,000 persons assaulted the Abolition Hall."[29]

No one who reads Pleasonton's diary will doubt the depth of his opposition to mob violence, regardless of his personal distaste for abolitionism; in that sense he was a perfect Whig. In an entry dated May 18 he reported on a meeting he had with a delegate from the mayor: "I told him, I would gladly offer any assistance to the legal authorities if regularly called upon—but that I would not act with a municipal mob, an unorganized mass of police officers against another mob."

Of the position of other officials it is not possible to be so certain. Mayor Swift's daughter had just married a Southern slaveholder. When the managers of Pennsylvania Hall, fearing an attack, called upon him to solicit protection, he informed them that he did not have enough police to secure the hall, and that only the governor had the authority to call out the troops. The managers then visited the sheriff, who told them that with the men under the mayor's command he could easily prevent violence, but with his three deputies he could do nothing. He said nothing about swearing in special deputies or calling out a posse. The mayor did address the crowd in front of the hall, informing them that the meeting was canceled and asking them to disperse. He also assured them that he had no police with him, a bit of information that brought forth three cheers from the crowd. As soon as he departed, all the street lights were broken and the destruction began. Fire companies were called to the scene, but limited their intervention to saving the surrounding buildings.

The next day a mob attacked the still-unoccupied, Quaker-sponsored Shelter for Colored Orphans. Another gathered to throw stones at the First Colored Presbyterian Church. A large mob gathered at the office of the *Public Ledger* (which had strongly denounced the violence of the past few days), but was deterred from attacking by public knowledge of the presence of armed men within.[30]

At about midnight, word came of fighting in front of the Presbyterian Church. The mayor, the sheriff and their forces headed that way, together with a large crowd, and arrested a number of people, most of whom were black.

After the riot was over, the whitewash began. The city councils instructed the Police Committee to investigate the attack on Pennsylvania

Hall. The Committee duly reported that the attack was the fault of the abolitionists, who had offended public opinion by advocating amalgamation. The report also blamed the riot on outsiders, since none of the rioters could be identified. One correspondent to a local paper, defending the mob, appealed to revolutionary authority. He captured the essential quality of Jacksonian democracy when he wrote, "But there was a law that authorized the destruction of the very tabernacle of abolitionism. The law was made on the spot—the very act itself was law."

In a by-now-familiar pattern, Irish figured prominently in the rioting.[31] A month later there was another riot after an Irish watchmen and an Irish butcher were killed by black men in two separate incidents in the southern suburbs. The militia was called out, but only twenty men mustered. The owner of the horses normally used by the company refused to let his animals, claiming that some Irish had threatened to burn his stables if he did so. Meanwhile, some of the militia, who were mostly German bakers, asked to be allowed to return to the bakery before the dough spoiled. At that point Colonel Pleasonton went home, consigning "all citizen soldiers most heartily at the devil."[32]

"We have had a serious time lately with the colored people and the whites, the catholicks being the worst of the two," wrote one Philadelphia Irish in a letter back home, dated August 22, 1842.[33] The writer was referring to the riot three weeks earlier, which, more than any other Philadelphia riot of the period, was a distinctively Irish affair. It was provoked by a black temperance parade on the anniversary of the emancipation of the slaves in the British West Indies. The combination of temperance and praise for Britain undoubtedly inflamed the Irish, but there were other factors present as well. "Nearly every man," wrote another correspondent, "who was guilty of cruelty and violence to the colored people, was an Irishman." He explained,

> Philadelphia has suffered, and is now suffering, more than any
> other city in America, from bad debts to the South. It is now in a
> state of almost complete paralysis; and as a large portion of the
> laboring population of Moyamensing and the banks of the
> Schuylkill are Irish, the consequence is, there is among them a

great deal of distress, arising from an inability to find work. To add to the difficulty, large numbers have recently emigrated from Ireland to this country, and are now living in various parts of the county and city, unable to find sufficient employment....Suffice it to say, that the Irish in this city seem to have imbibed the idea, that the blacks, not being citizens, have no right to stay in the city, and that if they can drive them out of the city, they will have their places, and have work enough to do...."There's a house," said an Irish woman to the mob in Gaskill street, "that I want to have mobbed—there's some negroes living there, who are living just like white folks." I could fill a sheet almost with cases of this kind, showing that what was once contempt is now envy, and the most ferocious hatred, arising from the fact that a large portion of the blacks can find work, and they cannot.

Another correspondent echoed the first: "Since I began this letter a friend has informed me that an Irishman came into his [illegible] office, and wished to know if he had need for any men. He was told no. 'I have been been in this country 16 years,' said he, 'and if it was not for the infernal naygurs, I could find work enough.' He defended the conduct of the mob, and declared that these 'naygurs,' as he called them, who were so cruelly beaten, were served just right. 'They have no business,' said he, 'to live among white folks.'"[34]

On the second day of the riot, Irish laborers in coal yards on the Schuylkill River attacked black men working nearby. In a naive ethnic appeal the sheriff dispatched a posse of sixty unarmed men wearing green ribbons on their coats; as can be imagined, that action only infuriated the rioters.[35] Three weeks before the riot, 1,500 Irish coal miners from Pottsville had downed tools in the first recorded strike in the anthracite region. Many of these working-class heroes had made their way to Philadelphia, and when the riot broke out they displayed the highest degree of white race consciousness by taking an active part in it.[36]

The riot began in Moyamensing, a southern suburb that boasted 450 liquor dealers, most of them Irish. Due to recent efforts of the Moyamensing Temperance Society, 1,047 black and 120 white persons had signed the temperance pledge, including even one liquor dealer.

Daily receipts in the rum shops fell drastically, creating a particular vested interest in bringing about an end to the temperance crusade. "Father Mathew had ruined many, said one who had left a rum-shop in Ireland, and in this land of liberty they expected to do as they liked."[37] Arsonists had tried twice without success to burn the Temperance Hall. In the aftermath of the riot, the civil authorities accomplished what arsonists and rioters had failed to do. A petition was presented to the Court of General Sessions, charging that the Temperance Hall was a nuisance, because if it were burned the flames could spread to neighboring houses. A judge gave the matter to a grand jury, which found that in the "present excited state of feeling," the building—itself a new, secure brick building—was indeed a nuisance; accordingly, the town of Moyamensing ordered it torn down, and it was done. The judge who presided over these proceedings and charged the grand jury was Joseph M. Doran, who six months later would assume the presidency of one of the two Irish Repeal associations in the city.[38]

Judicial responses to the riots also revealed public attitudes: of sixty persons arrested during the 1834 riots, only ten were ever brought to trial and none was ever fined or imprisoned. This remarkable leniency was due, no doubt, to the presence of magistrates like John Binns, and to the benevolent effects of the "Pardenin' Power."[39] After the Pennsylvania Hall incident of 1838, twelve accused white rioters were bound over from the Mayor's Court to stand trial, along with a number of black men.[40] In the 1842 temperance march riot, most of the first twenty people arrested were black; the few whites arrested were "unarrested" by the crowd.[41] One historian has calculated that eighty-three riot-related charges betwen September 1841 and August 1843 produced sixty-eight indictments and six convictions.[42] In 1849, Judge Parsons, sentencing eleven men who had been convicted for their actions in a series of riots, declared, "It is a melancholy fact, yet nevertheless true, that from 1844, down to this time, scarce an individual, who has been convicted of an aggravated riot, in this county, has served out his imprisonment; no matter whether short or long. The ink is hardly dry in which the sentence is recorded, before a petition is prepared and circulated, asking for the pardon of the offender." The judge came under attack for the impropriety of his remarks, but another newspaper defended him, denouncing Governor Johnston's "flagrant abuse of the pardoning power."[43]

Perhaps the most most decisive indication of public attitudes to white race attacks was in the response to black people's efforts to defend themselves. Nothing seemed to provoke white hostility like black resistance. One of the worst outrages of the 1834 riot, the organized destruction of the Wharton Street Church, took place in response to a widespread belief that a shot had been fired from it. Of course the rule that nothing provokes the aggressor like resistance by his intended victim did not apply only in cases of black people defending themselves against white attacks; it was characteristic generally of mob attitudes in the Jacksonian period.[44] For most groups, however, the appeal of a policy of self-defense outweighed the drawbacks, with the result that the nineteenth-century city came to be a battlefield where relations among various warring ethnic groups were regulated daily through hand-to-hand combat. Only black people were excluded from equal participation in the war of each against all, and in restricting them to nonresistance the leaders of the tumultuous, white republic found the secret of government.[45]

Any sympathy black people might might have enjoyed from respectable elements was quickly dissipated when they took steps to defend themselves. On the first morning after the 1834 riot began, a black man was arrested and jailed for haranguing a crowd in front of the State House. When, on Thursday evening of the riot week, the mayor discovered a number of black people (estimates vary from sixty to one hundred) in Benezet Hall, a large brick house in the riot area, prepared to resist a surrounding mob, he informed them that he would offer them no protection and would not be accountable for their safety. They left through the back door, under police escort. After the riot ended, one of the Whig papers published a letter from a black man "of considerable property," inquiring how to protect himself. The paper admitted it had no answer.[46] During the riot of 1838, the sheriff authorized private individuals to arm themselves for protection, and an attack on the *Public Ledger* office was probably forestalled by the general knowledge that those inside were armed. However, during the riot, thirty black men armed with knives, razors, and pistols were arrested at the Presbyterian

Church that was under attack, suggesting that the right of self-defense was not intended to apply to them.[47]

"God sent the blight, but the British sent the famine," runs a popular Irish expression. From 1841 to 1851, the population of Ireland declined from eight million to six and one-half million. If the increase in population that would have occurred normally is taken into account, it is likely that during those years a million persons died of hunger and diseases brought on by hunger, or were not born, and another million and a half emigrated.[48] While people in the Irish countryside were eating the bark off the trees, the British government's adherence to market principles ensured that Ireland would continue to export food.[49] The torture did not end at the dock; in the worst year, 1847, one-sixth of the emigrants to British North America died on board ship in the middle passage, or in quarantine, or in the provincial hospitals where they were confined on debarkation.[50]

Once landed in Boston, New York, or Philadelphia, however, the Irish enjoyed one marked advantage over refugees from Southern slavery: no one was chasing them with dogs. Not only fugitive slaves but free Negroes as well were subject to capture and sale into slavery. As Julie Winch has observed, "there were two 'underground railroads.'…Both employed black and white agents, both had a network of 'safe houses' and both made liberal use of forged documents—in one case free papers and in the other fraudulent bills of sale."[51]

In New York City, gangs of men, known as "Blackbirders," roamed the heavily Irish- and Afro-American Five Points district, kidnapping free Negroes and hustling them at night onto southern-bound boats. In self-defense black people banded together in groups, which may have been the origin of the more famous of the two Underground Railroads.[52]

Because of its proximity to the slave states of Delaware and Maryland, Philadelphia was a center for persons escaping from slavery, as well as for the activities of kidnappers. Forty children were abducted there in one year, sixty another.[53] In the years 1826–27 there were frequent alarms of the kidnapping of black children. In one case five boys were transported on one ship to Virginia, then shipped to Alabama. They were finally stopped in Mississippi, and returned to the city, whereupon it was discovered that their kidnappers formed part of a large and well-organized ring. The case led the City Councils to offer a reward for the arrest and conviction of abductors, and prompted the State Assembly to impose strict penalties for kidnapping.[54]

However, the big profits to be made in the trade, combined with widespread white hostility to the growing black presence in the city, made the law of little value as a deterrent. It fell largely on the city's black population to protect its members from kidnapping. They formed vigilance committees, which brought together well-known abolitionists like Robert Purvis with sailors, dockers, teamsters, and other men who "could do heavy work in the hour of difficulty." Black women played a key role in keeping committee members informed of suspicious whites they encountered in hotels, boarding houses, and in the streets.[55] According to Purvis, the Philadelphia vigilance committee aided 9,000 fugitives between 1830 and 1860—a number far greater than the number of fugitive slaves calculated by the federal census.[56]

In some cases the activities of these vigilance committees broke out into the light of day, as attempts were made to rescue people from the hands of legal authorities. The *Mechanic's Free Press* of April 24, 1830, reported a rescue attempt by about "sixty coloured people" of a man in the custody of police officers who were taking him to prison as a runaway. In 1833 a case came to trial growing out a successful rescue eleven years earlier "by a mob of 40 or 50 persons."[57] On June 18, 1835, the *Pennsylvanian* reported three hundred "coloured people of both sexes" surrounded and broke into the house of "an aged coloured woman" who had testified for a slaveowner attempting to reclaim his disputed property. Incidents like these were apparently frequent enough to lead the committee investigating the Flying Horses riot of 1834 to identify as a principal cause the conduct of some black people, who had on numerous occasions crowded into courtrooms and attempted forcibly to rescue prisoners who were being held as "fugitives from justice" instead of leaving such cases to the judicial system and the "untiring exertions of benevolent citizens, who promptly interest themselves in their behalf."[58]

The denial to black people of the most elementary right of citizenship (to say nothing of humanity), the right of self-defense, was long enshrined in law. A Pennsylvania statute of 1777 had limited the militia to white men. The U.S. militia law of 1792 had placed the congressional stamp on the policy, and every militia law passed in Pennsylvania after 1790 had expressly limited enrollment to white men. "Not a black man in the union lifts even a cooks-spit to help defend our liberties," wrote Thomas Branagan, "(indeed this is an excellent piece of policy not to permit them to bear arms)...."[59] During the debate on whether free Negroes were citizens, one of the arguments advanced was that they were not required to perform militia duty.[60]

Of course black people had frequently borne arms in the Union's cause (including the War of Independence), but the policy came to be that Afro-Americans could be used only in nonmilitary capacities. Thus in the War of 1812, a black-led Committee of Defense mobilized more than a thousand black Philadelphians to work on fortifications outside the city.[61]

The exclusion of Negroes from militia duty contrasted with the openness with which Irish and other foreigners were welcomed to the colors. As early as the eighteenth century, William Duane organized an Irish militia regiment in Pennsylvania. Later on the Irish formed other militia units, including the Hibernia Guards, Irish Volunteers, Montgomery Guards, Repeal Volunteers, Emmett Guards, Tyler Guards, and Patterson Guards. By 1846 nine Philadelphia companies out of thirty were composed entirely of immigrants, and the outbreak of the Mexican War provided the occasion for still others to come together.[62]

These various militia companies were not all to be taken seriously as military formations. In fact, they came in for a great deal of popular scorn. In 1824 one unit elected a known mental defective to the post of colonel, outfitted him with a preposterous uniform and set him at the front of the parade. The following year one of the papers declared that "the military is a farce. Demagogues have been using commissions in the militia as stepping stones to offices of profit and honor." In 1828 a working men's paper denounced "that burlesque upon military etiquette, militia training,...the truly ludicrous scenes which characterize a militia muster day,...the useless waste of time; the increased consumption of whiskey."[63] Whether the militia ever provided anything in the way of real military training, through it various groups asserted their right to bear arms, and the exclusion of black people from it was at least symbolically important. One curious feature of the militia system was the attachment of Negroes to various militia companies. Frank Johnson, the famous bugler, band conductor, and composer, regularly accompanied one of the militia companies. On one occasion the company was scheduled to parade in Boston when they learned that the white bands of Boston would not attend their reception because of Johnson's presence; the militia colonel thereupon refused to go to Boston.[64]

Far more important than the militia as a street-fighting force was the so-called volunteer fire company. It began in colonial times as a middle-class institution, but was transformed during the second quarter of the century by the emerging city proletariat. The companies became notorious as centers of riot and disorder, always "at deadly feud among themselves, and fighting freely with pistols, knives, iron spanners, and slung shot, whenever they met, whether at fires or in the streets." With firefighting as a pretext, they fought continuously over control of territory within the working-class districts of the city or suburbs. Arson was high on their list of weapons: one of their favorite tactics was to set a fire near the territory of a rival company, and then lie in wait to attack it when it showed up; they also extorted money from nearby homeowners who had good reason to anticipate fire if they failed to contribute. An investigating committee reported in 1853, "There is scarcely a single case of riot brought before the courts that has not its origin in the fire companies, their members, or adherents."[65] They bring to mind Mark Twain's remark that in those days people insured their homes not against fire but against the fire company.

Although the early fire companies were not segregrated along national lines, each later became identified with a particular ethnic group and played an important role in establishing the place of that group within the city. It is therefore significant that only the free Negroes were without their own fire company; in 1818 some black people had attempted to organize one, but the initiative aroused such universal antagonism, especially among existing companies, that the project was dropped. It is also significant that the controversy took place at a time when the fire companies still represented to a considerable degree the respectable element of society.[66]

Each fire company was allied with (and in some cases indistinguishable from) one or another street gang, which had infiltrated it and taken it over. The gangs, with names like Bouncers, Rats, Stingers, Skinners, Flayers, Bleeders, Blood Tubs, Pluckers, Garroters, Hyenas, Deathfetchers, and (in one exceptional case) Dock Street Philosophers, held "nightly conclaves on the corners of by-streets or in unoccupied building-lots, sneaking about behind the rubbish-heaps, and perhaps now and then venturing out to assault an unprotected female or knock down a lonely passenger"; among their duties was assisting the local fire company in its battles with its rivals.[67] One of the largest and most violent, and the most notorious of all the gangs was the "Killers." They were the subject of an anonymous 1847 fictional account entitled *The Almighty Dollar: or, the Brilliant Exploits of a Killer*, in which they were likened to the Jacobins of revolutionary France, leading an uprising of "the ground down and oppressed."[68] According to another fictional account by Lippard, members of the Killers

> were divided into three classes—beardless apprentice boys who after a hard day's work were turned loose upon the street at night, by their masters or bosses. Young men of nineteen and twenty, who, fond of excitement, had assumed the name and joined the gang for the mere fun of the thing, and who would either fight for a man or knock him down, just to keep their hand in; and fellows with countenances that reminded of the brute and devil well intermingled. These last were the smallest in number, but the most ferocious of the three. These, the third class, not more than ten in number, were the very worst specimens of the savage of the large city. Brawny fellows, with faces embruted by hardship, rum and crime; they were "just the boys" to sack a Theatre or burn a Church.[69]

Like other cities, Philadelphia eventually made a transition from a tumultuous republic to a (more or less) orderly republic. The story of how that happened is linked to the conflict between Irish and nativists in those years.

# A FULL

### AND

## COMPLETE ACCOUNT

#### OF THE LATE

# AWFUL RIOTS

## IN PHILADELPHIA.

### EMBELLISHED WITH TEN ENGRAVINGS.

PHILADELPHIA:
JOHN B. PERRY, No. 198 MARKET STREET.

# VI

# FROM
# PROTESTANT ASCENDANCY
# TO
# WHITE REPUBLIC

In the antebellum years, Protestant Englishmen constituted the upper class of Philadelphia. Many were descended from Quaker families which had become prominent in the eighteenth century—Ingersoll, Morris, Mifflin, Biddle, Cadwalader, Wharton, and Binney, and there was an infusion of new names from commerce, publishing, and industry—Girard and Drexel, Curtis and Bok, and the locomotive manufacturer Matthias Baldwin. This class ruled the city through the Whig Party, and maintained the voluntary, charitable, public, and semi-public institutions like the Penitentiary, the University, the Central High School, the Franklin Institute, the Museum of Art, the Hospital, the Meeting House, and the Episcopal Church.[1]

As large numbers of working-class and disorderly (from a bourgeois standpoint the two terms were synonymous) Irish settled in Philadelphia, there arose a certain opposition to them among the existing population. The hostility had several origins and manifestations, which are ordinarily grouped under the heading of nativism. First was snobbery, the disdain of the members of an upper class for their social inferiors; this was shared by many who, while not themselves members of the upper class, aped its manners. Second was partisan: the Irish were Democrats while the upper class, except for a few black sheep like Charles Jared Ingersoll and Richard Vaux, was Whig. Third was doctrinal: most of the Irish were Catholic, and therefore suspect as Mary-worshippers and idolaters. Fourth was historical: the Catholic Church was for many Protestants the Whore of Babylon, an institution they viewed (not without cause) as incompatible with republican principles. Fifth was economic: native-born workers, primarily artisans but including others as well, feared that the Irish were degrading the conditions of labor. Sixth was political: as the slavery controversy moved to center stage, Irish support for the slave power came increasingly to vex those who sought to end its sway over the Union. And of course under the heading of what may be called moral there was the temperance issue. In actuality the various causes of anti-Irish feeling cannot be separated so conveniently as a simple list implies, but it will be useful to bear the distinctions among them in mind as the story develops.[2]

Nativists had been trying for years to gain a foothold in Philadelphia. In 1837 they held their first meeting in the Philadelphia area, in Germantown, and in 1843 organized the first American Republican club, in the Spring Garden district. Its program called for a twenty-one-year waiting period for naturalization and for barring foreign-born citizens from holding any government office. In 1842 a Catholic teacher in Southwark had been fired for refusing to start the school day by reading from the King James version. A deal had been worked out whereby Catholic children could be excused from the exercise, but the controversy sparked the growth of several more nativist branches. In 1844, Catholic alderman Hugh Clark, a member of the Kensington school board, ordered an immediate suspension to Bible-reading in public schools. The Catholic plot to "kick the Bible out of the classroom" provided the stimulus the nativists needed, and they were emboldened to call a rally for Friday afternoon, May 3, 1844, on Master Street in Kensington, one block away from the Nanny Goat market.

"Let us wander into the northern districts of the city," invites Lippard. "Two miles northward from the State House....

We will leave the Germantown Road, and turn down Master Street. Some few paces toward the east, and where do we stand?

In front of a market-house...Yonder to the south-east, the heavy outlines of a red brick school-house...

A few paces from the school-house to the east, lies Second Street. Northward on this street...arise the walls of St. Michael's Church, and southward...you may behold the Catholic nunnery.

These localities are worthy of your serious recollection, for let me tell you, in a few days this quarter of Kensington, will become the scene of strange and terrible events....

Here we behold a house of time-worn brick, there a toppling frame; on every side the crash of looms, urged on by weary hands even at this hour, disturbs the silence of the night. And faint rays of light steal out from narrow windows along the street, revealing the exterior of these haunts of misery and want.[3]

The Kensington district, at night illuminated only by faint gleams of light, its stillness broken only by the crash of the looms, was a center of hand-weaving. "Of all the workers in competition with machinery," wrote a contemporary observer of English life, "the most ill-used are the hand-loom cotton weavers....Great numbers of them are Irish or of Irish descent."[4] As in Yorkshire, so in Kensington, where nearly all the hand-loom operators were Irish, both Protestant and Catholic, refugees from the poverty of rural Ireland as well as the effects of the power-loom. The hand-weavers of Kensington had already furnished the labor movement with John Ferral, leader of the 1835 strike.

Along with the concentration of Irish in hand-weaving, Kensington had the highest proportion of native-born residents of any district in the city.[5] The "strange and terrible events" Lippard refers to are the Riots of 1844.[6]

The residents of Kensington had a long tradition of direct action. As early as 1828, the sheriff had mobilized a posse to suppress weavers there, several of whom beat to death a watchman who called them "bloody Irish transports."[7] In the fall of 1842 weavers in Kensington and Moyamensing had struck against a cut in the piece rate. They paraded through the textile districts, forcing their way into the homes of nonstriking weavers and throwing their unfinished work into the street. In November, strikers dispersed a meeting of master weavers by threatening to tear down the house where it was taking place, and in January of 1843 a crowd of some 400 weavers armed with bricks and boards drove off a sheriff's posse attempting to arrest a strike leader. On that occasion it took four militia companies patrolling the streets, plus eight more at the armories, to suppress the strike and send the weavers back to work.

Another strike in the spring of 1843 won a small raise. During the same period the local population carried on a protracted war, now peaceful now violent, against the building of a railway through the district, culminating in the "Nanny Goat riot." Their determination finally forced the state legislature to cancel construction.

The location the nativists chose for their rally was in the heart of Irish Catholic turf. It is likely they chose the spot with a desire to provoke. If so, they got their wish; local Catholics broke up the rally by heckling and throwing rocks and garbage. Nativists responded by calling another rally for three days later at the same location, inviting supporters from all over the city to attend. A crowd of local Irish rowdies were waiting for them, fighting broke out, and this time weapons were fired on the rally from buildings adjoining the lot. The first person killed was a man named George Shiffler, a Protestant, whom nativists promptly designated a martyr. Returning that night with reinforcements, including snipers, they destroyed Irish homes and attacked a school run by the Sisters of Charity. The next day the *Native American* shrieked that "another St. Bartholomew's day has begun on the streets of Philadelphia."[8]

On Tuesday afternoon, a crowd marched from a nativist rally at Independence Hall to Kensington and attacked the headquarters of an Irish fire company from which gunshots had been fired the day before. Armed defenders opened fire, leaving four nativists dead and eleven wounded. Nativist forces set fire to the surrounding buildings, causing many Irish to flee to the nearby woods. When arsonists managed to set fire to St. Michael's Church, volunteer firemen, mostly native-born Protestants, contented themselves with hosing down adjacent buildings to keep the flames from spreading. That night, a mob burned St. Augustine's Church in the center of the city.

The Governor placed Philadelphia under martial law. Two thousand soldiers patrolled the streets; all meetings were banned. The burning of St. Augustine's Church marked the last major violence in that phase of the riots.

On July 4, 1844, nativists called a rally at Independence Hall; 5,000 paraded through the streets, while 100,000 cheered from sidewalks, windows, and rooftops. The next day a mob gathered at a Catholic church in Southwark, provoked by information that Catholics were storing rifles there. The Sheriff and militia arrived on the scene, persuaded the Catholics to surrender their arms, and managed to disperse the crowd. On Sunday, July 7, a mob returned and battered down the doors of the church, milling about inside, searching for additional weapons.

That night soldiers arrived on the scene, and became the targets of rocks, bricks, and occasional gunshots. For the first time in a Philadelphia civic disorder, troops, under the command of General George Cadwalader, fired into a crowd. Two were killed. The mob scattered, but returned with a cannon from a ship docked nearby. Its first blast killed two soldiers, but cavalry reinforcements succeeded in capturing the weapon. That proved to be the turning point, and order was soon restored, although there was one minor incident the next night in Moyamensing.

A total of twenty were killed in Kensington and Southwark together, and perhaps a hundred seriously wounded. But the two riots were different: in Kensington what took place was a confrontation of Catholic Irish against Protestant nativist civilians, with the forces of the state playing a marginal role; Southwark was the scene of a battle between a nativist mob and the more-or-less regularly established forces of law-and-order. It was an important precedent.

Historians have noted that the two decades before the Civil War were the crucial years in the transformation of Philadelphia from an eighteenth-century commercial town into an industrial city, and that the 1844 riots were a turning point. In reaction to these upheavals there arose the two characteristic features of urban life: bureaucratized administration, especially a professional police force, and racially defined ethnic politics.[9]

At a rally following the Kensington events, Horace Binney, a long time spokesmen for the city's old elite, called for the use of "all necessary force" to uphold the law. For years the *Public Ledger*, voice of the city's respectable classes, had been calling for stricter law enforcement. Now, after the events in Southwark, when it declared that "the State is at war," it found itself no longer alone. Even the Democratic *Spirit of the Times* proclaimed:

We are in the midst of a civil war! Riot and anarchy are around us! Death and destruction stare us in the face; and for once we behold the strange anomaly in this country, of an open and regularly organized rebellion on the part of a certain faction....[10]

Part of the reason for the alarm on the part of the city's elite was the willingness and ability of the Catholics to defend themselves. While there were criticisms from some (including Bishop Hughes, who threatened to turn New York into "another Moscow" if a single Catholic Church were harmed) of the lack of resolve on the part of Philadelphia's Catholic hierarchy, in fact the armed resistance contrasted with the one-sided mob violence of previous outbreaks, in particular the riot of 1838. (No Catholics died in the riots of 1844, and most Catholic injuries resulted from the misfiring of their own weapons.)[11]

In 1843 the *United States Gazette* had condemned fire company disorders because they "hinder the city of gains from the residence of capitalists who seek comfort and ease."[12] This sentiment could only have increased after 1844. An anonymous wag satirized these concerns:

> Oh in Philadelphia folks say how
> Dat Darkies kick up all de rows,
> But de riot up in Skensin'ton,
> Beats all de darkies twelve to one.
>
> > An' I guess it wasn't de niggas dis time
> > I guess it wasn't de niggas dis time,
> > I guess it wasn't de niggas dis time,
> > > Mr. Mayor,
> > I guess it wasn't de niggas dis time.
>
> Oh, de "Natives" dey went up to meet,
> At de corner ob Second and Massa' Street,
> De Irish cotch dar Starry Flag,
> An' tare him clean up to a rag.
>
> > An' I guess it wasn't, etc.
>
> De Natives got some shooting sticks,
> An' fired at dar frames and bricks,

De Pats shot back an' de hot lead flew,
Lord! what's creation comin' to?

    Oh, guess it wasn't, etc.

Cat-wallader he walk in now,
An' wid his brave men stop de row,
Den wicked rowdies went in town,
An burn de St. Augustine's down,

    Oh, whar was de police dat time,
    Oh, whar was, etc.

Oh, den de big fish 'gin to fear,
Dey thought the burnin' was too near,
Dey call'd a meetin' to make peace,
An' make all white folks turn police.

    If dey'd been a little sooner dat time
    If dey'd been a little sooner dat time,
    If dey'd been a little sooner dat time,
      Mr. Mayor,
    Dey might a stopt all dis crime.[13]

The riots convinced many of the city's leaders that the days of rely-ing on personal intervention to guarantee the peace were past, and that a professional force of some sort was needed to serve an unruly crowd a "whiff of grapeshot." With the cannon smoke still thick in the air, the City Council passed an ordinance providing for an armed force of one battallion of artillery, one regiment of infantry, and one or more troops of cavalry. By September 26, the full complement was enlisted, consist-ing of 1,326 men. The following spring, the State Legislature passed an act providing for at least one police officer for every 150 taxable inhab-itants of Philadelphia and the surrounding districts, at the same time making coordinated operations easier.[14]

In fact, little actual change occurred. Over a year after the riots, Mayor Peter McCall complained to the city council that during the day only four high constables and eleven policemen patrolled the entire city; at night there were twenty-seven officers on duty. He did not even mention the watch.[15] Life went on as usual. A survey of the *Philadelphia Bulletin* over a three-month span turned up the following stories: April 29, 1847, a murder of a black man by three Bouncers; May 1 an editorial stating, "Philadelphia, for a long time distinguished for its love of order, celebrated for its quietude, and characterized by the peaceful temper of its people, is now notorious for an opposite character"; May 3 the news, "no rioting yesterday"; June 1 a small riot at 11th and Locust; June 5 arrests and reprimands by the mayor of firemen making noise racing through the streets; July 5 a riot between two fire companies; several people arrested, then freed by the crowd; the same day a fight between "Killers" and local citizens at Gloucester Point, New Jersey, undoubtedly part of the gang's Fourth of July celebration cruise; July 7 two whites attacked by "colored ruffians" in Moyamensing; July 8 the complaint that "the citizens of Southwark are constantly kept in dread of the frequent street fights of the rowdies. Gangs attack each other in open day"; July 9 "more rowdying"; July 12 "another of those disgraceful fire riots," with the comment, "The 'mob city' is the familiar term for our beautiful town....There are perhaps, in the city and suburbs of Philadelphia, five thousand riotous and disorderly persons, principally boys and young men between the ages of fifteen and twenty-six"; July 28 four Killers arrested for an attack on a constable.

In June of 1849 a battle took place between the (nativist) Franklin and the (Irish) Moyamensing Hose Companies, in which at least seven people were shot, one fatally. The police arrested only two people at the scene; both were later acquitted by a jury.[16] Things reached such a pass that in one riot in Moyamensing in August 1849 the authorities were forced to enlist the services of one of the gangs to restore order—a rather extreme example of reliance on autonomous popular activity.[17]

The disorder reached a peak on October 9, 1849, election evening, when a mob led by the Killers attacked a four-story building at Sixth and St. Mary Streets in Moyamensing.[18] The building housed a popular tavern, called the California House, which was owned by a black man who had recently married a white woman. As the mob approached the building with a wagon carrying a blazing tar barrel, black people who had mobilized in defense began hurling stones at them. The mob attacked the tavern, which was defended by firearms, and succeeded in forcing their way in, smashing the furniture and tearing out the gas fixtures to release the gas, and then set it on fire. Wielding guns and knives, they drove away the city police and the fire companies who arrived at the burning building, destroying one engine. The militia arrived about two in the morning and, finding everything quiet, withdrew.

As soon as they had done so, the whites renewed their attack, and fighting between Negroes and whites continued until the soldiers returned in the morning and placed cannon in front of the ruins of the California House, systematically sealing off the area. The following day two companies of militia were sent into Moyamensing to search for weapons.

George Lippard provides an account of the riot in *The Bank Director's Son*. It agrees in important respects with newspaper accounts, adding only an element of conspiracy on the part of the wealthy and respectable citizen Cromwell Hicks, leader of the Killers. Another novel of the day, *The Garies and Their Friends* (first published in London, 1857) by the Afro-American writer Frank J. Webb, also portrays the riot and includes as well an element of conspiracy in which a speculator provokes it in order to gain possession of a certain piece of property he covets. An Irishman named McCloskey acts as his agent. Webb depicts the mayor as unwilling to protect the black population.

Whether these accounts of conspiracies were founded in fact, the California House riot was one of the bloodiest the city had experienced; three whites (including two firemen) and a Negro were killed; nine whites and sixteen Negroes were hospitalized, and many more were injured. It revealed the continuing inability of the existing police to prevent civic disorder notwithstanding the 1845 measures.

On May 3, 1850, the State Legislature responded by creating a single police district including the city and the suburbs of Northern Liberties, Spring Garden, Kensington, Richmond, and the townships of Southwark, Moyamensing, and Penn, and assigning it a new police force, commanded by a marshall, of one policeman per 400 inhabitants, independent of the old watch and the police of the city and districts.[19] The Legislature did not, however, abolish the existing police, who continued to function as arms of local aldermen and political bosses.

One of the obstacles to an effective police presence had always been multiple jurisdictions in the county. Even after the riots, consolidation of the districts continued to meet with resistance from elite conservatives, including municipal bondholders who feared a drop in the value of their holdings, city Whigs who feared merger with Democratic suburbs, and office holders of all parties who feared for their sinecures. However, having tasted a military version of consolidated government, many began to see that it would be better to institute it under civil authority. Moreover, as the city's population was growing and the demand for housing was increasing, the outlying districts took on new importance to real estate interests. Perennial Mayor Swift, who spearheaded redistricting, spoke to that point when he said, "Let us have a consolidation of the districts and a union of the police, and real estate in Moyamensing will pay a fair interest."[20] In addition, professional office holders were won over to consolidation by changes in voting patterns, which undermined the traditional division between the Whig city and the Democratic districts, so that each of the traditional parties could now hope to benefit by consolidation.[21] Part of the change, of course, was due to the new element in politics, the Native American Party of the 1840s and the Know Nothings of the 1850s, to which we shall return.

Although the new marshall's police was intended by some to stave off consolidation, it proved to be a step toward it. In 1853 supporters of consolidation triumphed in the election, and on February 2, 1854, the Consolidation Act became law. It merged all the districts and townships of Philadelphia County into a single jurisdiction, created a single police force under the mayor's command, and, most important of all, ended the direct dependence of police on local elected officials.[22]

Consolidation of the districts under a single authority was above all a police measure, but, as Steinberg points out, by itself it was largely an illusion.[23] It could not achieve its desired effect until a way was found to institutionalize the tensions between nativist- and Irish-Americans. To explain why this was so it will be necessary to go back a bit.

Trade unionists in Philadelphia, for the most part, had set aside nativism during the strike wave of 1835–36, but it surged up again during the depression of 1837 to 1843. While by no means all workmen were swept up in the sectarian tide, the riots of 1844 and the nativist triumph at the polls showed that many among the native born had abandoned even the white labor solidarity achieved earlier. Orestes Brownson, a native-born convert to Catholicism, explained:

> The Yankee hod-carrier, or Yankee wood-sawyer, looks down with ineffable contempt upon his brother Irish hod-carrier or Irish wood-sawyer. In his estimation, "Paddy" hardly belongs to the human family. Add to this that the influx of foreign laborers, chiefly Irish, increases the supply of labor, and therefore apparently lessens relatively the demand, and consequently the wages of labor, and you have the elements of a wide, deep, and inveterate hostility on the part of your Yankee laborer against your Irish laborer, which manifests itself naturally in your Native American Party.[24]

As David Montgomery writes, "by making strikes futile, destroying the Trades' Union beyond even hope of resurection and stimulating th[e] new emphasis on self-improvement…the depression opened the way for the rise of nativism among the artisans." For their part the Catholic Irish responded by electing ethnic politicians who "mounted the hustings to champion their right to a drink and the consciences of their children."[25]

The use of military force against the civilian population in 1844 provoked bitterness. Residents of Southwark refused even a drink of water to soldiers patrolling the streets in July heat, instead emptying slop buckets on them from the second story. In the Fall elections the nativist American Republican Party reaped the benefit at the polls. Although it narrowly lost the city mayoralty contest to the Whigs, its heavy pluralities in working-class districts and industrial suburbs (Protestant) permitted it to finish in first place county-wide, ahead of Whigs and Democrats, and gave it two of four congressional seats, the county's seat in the State Senate, and other important county offices. The following year the nativist tide began to ebb, but the American Republicans were able to maintain their grip in Kensington and elsewhere, which allowed them to appoint the police, the school board, and other officials. In addition, nativist groups sprung up everywhere, including "Shiffler" fire companies, Young Native clubs, and a volunteer militia company, the Native American Rifles (whose enemy of choice, it may be presumed, was neither Great Britain nor the Six Nations).

If nativism reflected fissures in white society, its demise reflected efforts to close them, a process essential to the formation of the white republic. Previous to the riots many members of Philadelphia's elite had sympathized with nativism. Sidney G. Fisher wrote in his diary:

> This movement of the "native" party is decidedly conservative, because by excluding foreigners so much of democracy is excluded, so much of the rabble, so much ignorance and brutality from political power. The natural ally of this party are the Whigs. Their object harmonized with the instincts and secret wishes and opinions of the Whigs. The consequence is they have combined forces so far in this election, and I hope to see the one merged in the other....

Yet during the riots Fisher stood guard to defend a Catholic church from rioters.[26] The Philadelphia Bar turned out seventy people to patrol the neighborhood around St. Mary's Church. What accounts for this apparent contradiction? The explanation is that, while the city'e elite loved the Protestant virtues of thrift, sobriety, the sabbath, and the wage system, they loved order more, and the riots in Kensington revealed the extent to which ethnic tensions among whites strained the limits of the tumultuous republic.

When the marshall's police was established in 1850, nativist John Keyser, formerly a police lieutenant in Spring Garden, was chosen as the first marshall. He picked for his force men connected to nativist gangs and fire companies. The Irish responded by treating them as their traditional enemies with badges. The Buffers mocked:

> Go and get John Keyser and all of his Police;
> Come up to the Market, and there you will see fun,
> To see the Buffers thump old Keyser,
> And make his puppies run.

The Bleeders told of being attacked one night "by a band of ruffians...they called themselves Police."[27] In 1853 when the marshall's police were asked to wear uniforms, they refused, claiming that they did not wish to be in the same category as trolley conductors. The *Public*

*Ledger* declared that they "were afraid to wear the uniforms because of the ill favor in which they are held by the firemen."[28] The first consolidation mayor, Robert T. Conrad, elected on a Whig-Nativist ticket, continued the tradition of appointing nativists to the police force.

The individual who, more perhaps than any other, embodies the Irish triumph in Philadelphia was William McMullen. He was born in Moyamensing in 1824. His father, a native of Ireland, was able to save enough money as a drayman on the docks to open a grocery store, where his son helped him after school. After a few months in high school, a short service in the navy, and brief apprenticeships in printing and carpentering, young William came to work for his father full-time. He soon became a member of the Killers and, as such, a member of the Moyamensing Hose, the fire company allied with them. It was at that time he acquired his first nickname, "Bull."[29]

McMullen was an active participant in the Kensington phase of the 1844 riots. He was among those who shot the Protestant Shiffler. For two days after the riot, he stood guard at Catholic churches in Moyamensing.[30]

McMullen's physical strength, talents, and connections were invaluable to the Polk Democrats. On election day in 1844 he served as the bookman for his district, formally charged with checking residency requirements of prospective voters and distributing printed ballots. His actual job was to keep opposition voters from the polls.

Elections and the ballot box are wonderful inventions, but before they can come into play it is necessary to determine who gets to use them. McMullen left this account of an antebellum Moyamensing election:

> The Whigs and Democrats would line the curb on either side of the street, to be counted as most numerous, the majority to be entitled to all the officers, to receive the votes, count them and make the returns. Those lines on the curb would be made up, not only of legal voters, but grown up lads, and after being counted once, would go to the far end to be counted again, so it would be seen that there could be no reliance on the count. Then a rush would be made for possession of the polls and the best fighters would get possession.[31]

After several scraps with the police, McMullen was jailed in 1846 for stabbing one policemen and injuring another. To avoid trial he joined the army, along with other Killers, who had enlisted en masse when the Mexican War broke out. After the Killers forced out an officer suspected of nativist sympathies, McMullen assumed leadership of his company. Waiting to be shipped off, he and his men were accused of beating some New Orleans police, but the troop ships arrived before arrests could be made.

The U.S. army in Mexico had the highest desertion rate of any army in U.S. history—eight percent. Foreign-born soldiers made up almost half of General Zachary Taylor's force; of these, half were Irish. McMullen and the Killers were just what the Army needed for that proud war. During the battle of Mexico City, they were cited for "the extremest of bravery."

The Killers' Mexican adventures stand in sharp contrast to the activities of another group of American Irish, the Saint Patrick Battalion. Motivated by solidarity between Catholics, opposition to slavery, promises of land, and romance, these men fought on Mexico's side during the War. Their leader was a man named John Riley, who had been born in Galway, deserted from the British Army in Canada, and joined the U.S. Army before the Mexican War; while posted on the Rio Grande he defected to the Mexican side. After Mexico surrendered, the Battalion joined General Paredes's anti-Treaty rebellion, which itself became part of a war within Mexico to recover Indian land rights. Regarded as traitors and deserters by the U.S. conquerors, abandoned by the government of Mexico which had capitulated to the U.S., many were whipped, branded, hanged, and crucified. Some managed to evade punishment and settle in Mexico, where their descendents still reside. The men who fought with the Saint Patrick's Battalion are today revered as heroes in Mexico.[32]

On his return to Philadelphia McMullen resumed his activities with the Killers and the Moyamensing Hose, and also his career in electoral politics. In 1850 he was elected president of the Democratic Party Keystone Club. In 1852 the marshall's police raided the club's headquarters, located in a saloon. McMullen met them at the door with knife in hand. The raid had been prompted by the Club's support for the Democratic candidate for district attorney Horn R. Kneass in the upcoming elections. Kneass won, but the election was overturned due to the large number of votes cast by illegally naturalized Irish. In 1854 McMullen opened a saloon in the heart of Moyamensing, which became a head-quarters for the Killers and the Moyamensing Hose Company.

Nativism had subsided with the outbreak of the Mexican War, but it rose up again in the mid-1850s with the sudden appearance of the Know Nothing movement. The explosion of the Know Nothings was due to an increase in immigration (which reached a peak in 1854) and to popular exasperation at the inability of the Whigs and Democrats to deal with the slavery crisis, an inability which became particularly evident with the repeal of the Missouri Compromise in 1854. As various historians have demonstrated, part of the appeal of nativism was resentment of the role of the Irish as the Swiss guards of the slave power. In Boston, Irish mili-tia companies had to be called out to return former slave Anthony Burns to his owner, after native companies refused to do so. It was at that time that a correspondent wrote to Massachusetts Senator Charles Sumner that from the moment an Irishman landed in America, he "identifies himself with slavery upon the shallow pretext of upholding the law."[33]

In Philadelphia in 1854, Robert T. Conrad was elected the first mayor of the consolidated city. Nativists celebrated, while Democrats mourned. "I take it for granted," wrote one, "that hereafter, no foreigner or *Catholic* can be elected to any office in this city. At bottom this is a deep seated religious question—prejudice if you please, which nothing can with-stand. Our party is made to bear the sin of *catholicism*."[34] A Know Nothing city councilman hailed the millenium:

> We can truly say that the reign of law and order is established and maintained among us. Our religious rights, our social rights, are secured and protected. The Sabbath day is remembered, and our people are allowed to keep it holy. Violence and outrage, once so familiar to our streets, are almost unknown.[35]

Yet two years later, the Democrat Vaux triumphed, partly as a result of a falling out between Whigs and Know Nothings. Vaux, a scion of an old Quaker family but a long time Democrat, had established a record as a friend of the Irish. At the time of the 1844 riots, when he was serving as

County Recorder, he had ordered nativist editors Lewis Levin (later a congressman) and Samuel Kramer arrested for "inciting to treason" in the pages of their newspapers. He had also arrested former sheriff John Watmough for using "inflammatory language" against the militia. In boosting Vaux to victory, the Irish proved themselves masters of ballot-box stuffing, intimidation, and other arts of big-city politics, demonstrating the truth of the assertion made ten years earlier by Brownson:

> the opposition to naturalized citizens is, in fact, not that they do not understand the genius of our government, but that they do understand it; not that they do not adhere to it, but that they do adhere to it....It is not their ignorance of the real nature of our institutions, but their intelligence of them, that constitutes their disqualification in the eyes of the natives.[36]

McMullen's support was instrumental in Vaux's victory; as a consequence six members of the Moyamensing Hose were immediately named police officers. McMullen himself was rewarded with an appointment to the Board of Inspectors of Moyamensing Prison. He used this position to secure the release of numerous of his friends and followers who had been convicted of various offenses. The following year he was elected alderman, a position he chose over police lieutenant because, as his biographer says, it allowed him "the opportunity to help his Moyamensing neighbors."[37] It was then he acquired his second nickname, "The Squire." In 1857 Vaux appointed as police commissioner Samuel Ruggles, a trunkmaker with no previous police experience, formerly affiliated with the Columbia Hose Company, whose principal qualification for office was that he had never been a nativist. Under his leadership, "Dick Vaux's police" established a formidable reputation for dispensing curb justice—free, for the first time, of nativist bias. Although Vaux was defeated for reelection in 1858, Ruggles held on to his position as police commissioner, serving under the Peoples-Unionist (as the Republican coalition was known in Philadelphia) administrations of Alexander Henry and Morton McMichael, which lasted until 1869.[38]

The Irish cop is more than a quaint symbol. His appearance on the city police marked a turning point in Philadelphia in the struggle of the Irish to gain the rights of white men. It meant that thereafter the Irish would be officially empowered (armed) to defend themselves from the nativist mobs, and at the same time to carry out their own agenda against black people. The Protestant Ascendancy had given way to the White Republic. As the writer of the doggerel about the 1844 riots had predicted, the key to stability was to "make all white folks turn police."[39]

The Civil War and Reconstruction were many things, but one thing they were, taken together, was an effort to redefine the basis of the republic. The war began, as Frederick Douglass remarked, with both sides fighting for slavery—the South to take it out of the Union, the North to keep it in. At first the government in Washington followed a policy of attempting to conciliate the slaveholders, and especially the Border States, by refusing to touch slavery where it existed. But the demands of war compelled a change, and in 1863 Lincoln shifted from a constitutional to a revolutionary policy. Three measures signaled the turn: the Emancipation Proclamation (which in fact freed no one, since it applied only to those areas of the country then in revolt, that is, the areas where Union authority did not reach, but was important as a declaration of intent and an encouragement to the slaves); the enlistment of black soldiers; and the replacement of McClellan by Grant (who, at the battle of Vicksburg, introduced the technique of waging war not solely against the enemy's armies but against the enemy's capacity to wage war).[40] And so the war that began with not one person in a hundred foreseeing the end of slavery ended with the Grand Army of the Republic marching through the land singing, "As He died to make men holy, let us fight to make men free."

The abolition of slavery called into question the existence of the white race as a social formation, for if the main underpinning of the distinction between the "white" worker and the black worker were erased, what could remain to motivate poor "whites" to hug to their breasts a class of landowners who had led them into one of the most terrible wars in history? And if class interest replaced "race" interest in their hearts, who could say where it might end?[41]

After the Civil War, Southern recalcitrance pushed the Republican Party to embrace Negro suffrage in the South (although many Republicans continued to oppose it in the North). That bold step opened the door to a far-ranging social revolution, the establishment of a degree of proletarian political power in the governments of Southern states under reconstruction. For a brief moment the abolitionists—men like Wendell Phillips, and women like Sojourner Truth and Lydia Maria Child—stood at the head of a nation struggling to find its soul. In this struggle the Irish threw their weight on the scales, and not, it may be said, on the side of the angels.[42]

Philadelphia's old commercial upper class was economically and socially tied to the South, and the city's political sympathies followed. No major paper endorsed antislavery. The Republican Party got nowhere under its own banner, and as late as the 1860 election, the Lincoln ticket was forced to call itself the People's party and mute its antislavery views. When South Carolina declared secession, the city council called for a conciliatory rally at Independence Square, at which speakers urged the South's case. During the course of the war, the federal government saw need to arrest a number of the city's old elite, whose public stance as "Peace Democrats" provided the thinnest of veils to "the most treasonable sentiments."[43]

The firing on Fort Sumter provoked an outpouring of patriotic emotion, but it soon subsided as Philadelphians settled into a prolonged apathy. There still remained the problem of defining the war aims and, by extension, the character of the republic that would emerge from the war. In July 1862 the state Democratic convention, with Philadelphia leadership conspicuous, resolved that "Abolitionism is the parent of secessionism," and "That this is a government of white men, and was established exclusively for the white race...." That year Frederick Douglass remarked that "There is not perhaps anywhere to be found a city in which prejudice against color is more rampant than in Philadelphia."[44] Sidney G. Fisher recorded "an incident significant of the times." A man of his acquaintance

discharged an Irish servant and in his place employed a Negro. Shortly after, his garden was trespassed on, plants and shrubbery destroyed and a paper stuck on one of the trees, threatening further injury if he did not send away the Negro. The Irish hate the

Negroes, not merely because they compete with them in labor, but because they are near to them in social rank. Therefore, the Irish favor slavery in the South, and for the same reason the laboring class of whites support it—it gratifies their pride by the existence of a class below them. The Democrats have industriously represented that the Republicans intend to emancipate the Negroes and make them the equals of the whites; also, that when the slaves are free, there will be a great emigration of them to the North to the injury of the white workingmen. The Irish are all Democrats and implicitly believe and obey their leaders.[45]

It is interesting that Fisher in this entry makes a distinction between the "Irish" and "the laboring class of whites." Another observer reported prevailing attitudes toward the war aims and the future republic:

> I found, most gladly, no secession;
> But hatred strong of abolition,
> A willingness to fight with vigor
> For loyal rights, but not the nigger.

Even after Lincoln's order to enlist black soldiers it was thought unwise to permit them to parade armed and uniformed in Philadelphia, until Lee threatened the city in the summer of 1863 and whites proved slow to enlist in its defense.[46]

If Philadelphia's working-class voters proved themselves no more loyal to the goal of emancipating the slaves than did their upper-class mentors, they did show themselves less willing to embrace treason. Despite the population's lethargic response to the danger, the Peace Democrats had gone too far in aligning themselves with the invader. In the October gubernatorial elections following Lee's invasion, an upstate Republican actually carried the city against a local upper-class Peace Democrat. In 1864, a group of Democratic politicians, headed by Lewis Cassidy, an Irishman, sought to distance the Party from the disastrous policy of the Peace Democrats. Using the Keystone Club as their vehicle they captured the Party leadership from the upper-class Central Democratic Club. The move came too late to regain the Party's former ascendancy; that October the Unionists (Republicans) won majorities in the city council and four of five congressional seats (the one exception was the district that included McMullen's home base, Moyamensing). Thereafter, McMullen would have to adjust to a Republican majority in the city.[47]

In 1860 McMullen attended the Democratic Party national convention in Charleston, which took place while the mayoralty election in Philadelphia was held. One historian credits McMullen's absence from the streets of Philadelphia for the election that fall of the People's Party candidate, Alexander Henry.[48] When war broke out McMullen immediately enlisted for a three-month duty tour. In a similar burst of patriotic fervor, eighty-four members of the Moyamensing Hose Company enlisted along with him, electing him captain of the company. Their stint was uneventful, coming as it did during the early phase of the war when Union military strategy was passive.

Returning to Philadelphia on August 12, 1861, McMullen resumed his activity in local politics. In the fall of 1862 the Democrats narrowly captured the State Legislature, which would elect a United States senator. The Republican candidate was Simon Cameron, who had a history of association with the Know Nothing movement. To avoid the possibility of some Democratic legislators bolting to the Republicans, Party leaders sent McMullen to Harrisburg. When the joint session of the Legislature convened, McMullen and his men were stationed around the hall, firearms in hand, cocked and ready to fire. Their presence kept the legislators in line, and the Democrat, Charles R. Buckalew, was elected. McMullen's success in preventing any wavering brought him a greater voice in Democratic Party circles. In the election of 1864 he supported McClellan; the Keystone Club pledged to defend the "Constitutional rights of white men against Republicans and negro equality." In January 1865 the Club held a banquet to celebrate the capture of New Orleans. Every important Democrat was there to hear speeches lauding Andrew Jackson and General McClellan; Lincoln's name was not mentioned.

In 1863 the federal government opened Camp William Penn for black soldiers. The mistreatment of families of the soldiers on city streetcars on the way to and from Camp Penn sparked a demand for their desegregation. Some of the lines acceded to the demand and began admitting

Negroes. It became an issue in the mayoral election of 1865. The Republican candidate Morton McMichael refused to take a stand. His Democratic opponent Daniel Fox opposed it, arguing that it would be followed by "demands for political equality including the right to vote and hold office." On one occasion McMullen hired two black men, who had been cleaning cesspools and whose clothing emitted the appropriate odor, to ride a streetcar on one of the desegregated lines, in order to provoke opposition. Nevertheless, in 1867 the state legislature, responding to a campaign led by local black leaders William Still and Octavius Catto, passed a law outlawing segregation on streetcars. McMullen's stance, however, did not hurt him with his Moyamensing constituents.[49]

McMullen's links with the fire company continued to provide him with his political base, and the city with adventures. In 1865 Moyamensing suffered one of its most serious fires, in which one fireman died, as a result of a fire which the Moyamensing Hose Company was rumored to have set deliberately in order to ambush the Protestant Shiffler Company. In 1866 Philadelphia found itself in the grip of a cholera epidemic. The mayor and the city council decided to convert Moyamensing Hall, which had previously served as a hospital for Civil War wounded, into a cholera hospital. The night it was scheduled to open, the two watchmen assigned to the building left early, and an hour later a fire broke out. McMullen and the Moyamensing Hose Company were first on the scene; they brought hoses too short to reach the building, and when other fire companies arrived, they cut their hoses. For the remainder of the night, the firemen sat and watched the building burn, calmly eating sandwiches and cake and drinking coffee provded by women of the neighborhood. The next day, alderman McMullen exonerated the watchmen of all wrongdoing. In 1867 a brawl with another company led to impeachment proceedings against McMullen, but charges were dropped. In 1869 he threw a splendid ball for the Moyamensing company, at which the entertainment was a blackface performance. The highlight of the evening was the award of a diamond-studded breast pin and gold tobacco box to the Squire himself. Firemen and politicians from all over the city attended. That same year there was another brawl, and the Moyamensing Hose Company was suspended for a month. In 1870 the Moyas got into it once more, this time with another

Irish company, the Hibernia Hose. There were calls for an investigation, but everyone knew that "the Squire was always in the lead of these bloody engagements, wildly cheering on his men and dealing out broken heads and black eyes with a brass nozzle or a spanner." After the battle, the men returned to the Hose House to sing their fighting song:

> The Moyas made a rally,
> The Shifflers said, "Hurray,"
> The Killers rushed upon them,
> And the Shifflers ran away.[50]

In 1871 the city finally established a full-time paid fire department, abolishing the volunteer fire companies. Although the Moyas tried to keep together after that, even McMullen was forced to accept the inevitable. According to Geffen, however, technology and not legislation finally destroyed the volunteer system, for the steam-driven engines which began to arrive in 1859 required professional, full-time operators.[51]

The saloon business also came under attack, as the Republican administration in Washington attempted to impose taxes on liquor. On one occasion in 1869, two men, one a friend of McMullen's and a member of the Moyamensing Hose House, shot a revenue agent. McMullen helped them escape the city, but they were captured and brought back to stand trial. In the trial McMullen testified in their defense, but they were found guilty and sentenced to twelve years in prison. He then arranged pardon for them after two years.[52]

In 1868 the Republican-controlled city council passed a Registry Act, which gave it the authority to appoint voter registrars. McMullen promised defiance: "We will crowd the place with men....You will have club law there on election day." In the end, he accepted a compromise that allowed one of three canvassers in each ward to be a Democrat; this meant, as one historian writes, that "the Democratic canvasser would just have to work that much harder."[53]

Aside from general resentment of any attempts to meddle with his ability to determine who could vote, McMullen had special reasons for alarm. Republicans were calling for replacement of aldermen by a system of judges elected at large. Moreover, the Fifteenth Amendment, which took effect in 1870, gave black men the franchise in Pennsylvania; at that time there were approximately 5,500 eligible black voters in Philadelphia, including many in his Fourth Ward.[54] They could of course be expected to vote Republican, and McMullen saw the Registry Law as a Black Republican plot.[55] He was not the only Democratic politician to worry over the effect of black votes: another noted that "if it were not for the Negroes we would have everything our way," and even Congressman Samuel J. Randall showed concern, although a friendly correspondent assured him that the Republicans were having a "hallucination" if they thought the "Nigger vote" would give their party a chance in his district.[56]

In spite of predictions of fraud and violence, the election went off fairly peacefully, in part due to the discipline of black voters, who took the opposition by surprise by showing up at the polls early with ballots filled out beforehand. The only disturbance took place at Sixth and Lombard Streets in Moyamensing, where whites tried to keep Negroes from voting. The *Bulletin* charged that police on the scene aided the whites.[57] The Mayor called for federal troops, who put down the disorder. McMullen himself attempted to remove a black man from the polling place, but failed. Later he congratulated the man, "the first black man not to show fear in my presence." After the election, which resulted in a Republican victory, the Republican *Press* confirmed that but for black votes, "the Republicans would have been beaten in many places, and especially Philadelphia."[58] Of the Negroes who voted, the majority were in McMullen's Ward.[59]

Silcox comments that it must have seemed to McMullen that the world had turned against him. The Moyamensing Hose Company was outlawed, his position as alderman was threatened, the Republicans had come within reach of control of the city, liquor-law enforcement was hurting his saloon business, and black people were beginning to vote in his ward. McMullen prepared for a new conflict in the 1871 mayoralty election.

That election pitted incumbent Democrat Daniel Fox, under fire for signing the bill outlawing volunteer fire companies, against Republican William S. Stokely, who had spearheaded the campaign to abolish them. Violence again accompanied the election, and this time Mayor Fox turned his back. Two days before the election a rock-throwing mob broke up a meeting of black and white Republicans at Seventh and Lombard. The next day a black man was shot; he died three weeks later. Election day saw continuous fighting between Negroes and whites, often initiated by Democratic police who feared for their jobs. Hundreds were injured, and three Negroes were killed; among them was Oliver Catto, a prominent figure in the Afro-American community and leader of the campaign to desegregate the streetcars, shot in the back by a white man who was then ushered from the scene and out of the city by a policeman. The day after the election, a white poll worker was killed, probably by black men retaliating for the murders of the day before.

The Republican candidate won the election but no one was ever convicted of any of the murders. Of the accused, one was a neighbor of McMullen's, two others were members of the Moyamensing Hose Company, a fourth was a friend. Two of the accused, including Sergeant John Duffy of the Eighth and South station, were each implicated in two killings. McMullen managed to secure freedom for all of them. The death of one black man was ruled "accidental" when it was discovered that the man suffered from a chronic kidney disorder which would have killed him at some point even if the bullet had not.[60]

McMullen's line of work was not without its risks: he sustained various wounds earned in fire company brawls, innumerable scraps with the police, brief service in the navy and stints in the army in two wars; he survived two attempts on his life in which guns were stuck in his chest and the trigger pulled (both times the weapons failed to fire, giving rise to a popular belief that he possessed mystical powers); and in 1872 he was shot right below the heart by a man who had rendered him loyal service, gone to jail for it, and subsequently resented McMullen's failure to spring him in what he considered a reasonable time. On that occasion he was generally expected to die; newspapers ran his obituary and political dignitaries, including the mayor and Congressman Randall, paid their respects, but he recovered and was back on the street within three weeks.

McMullen was evidently no altar boy. Lest, however, it be thought that his opponents wore halos, let it be noted that the Philadelphia Republican Party of that day was in the hands of as infamously corrupt a gang as ever feasted at the public trough. That was why he was able to come to terms with them.[61]

There is no need here to detail the kaleidoscopic turns of Philadelphia politics in the 1860s, '70s, and '80s. Suffice it to say that city politicians ate their share at the Great Barbecue, that there were "reform" movements in both parties, and that McMullen skillfully maneuvered among the various forces. On several occasions he was expelled from the Democratic Party for supporting Republican candidates on the municipal level, but he always managed to preserve intact his political base in the Fourth Ward. In 1881 Rufus E. Shapley wrote a satirical novel about Philadelphia politics entitled *Solid for Mulhooley*. It was a popular success, with illustrations by Thomas Nast, and even gave rise to an eponymous term for corruption—*Mulhoolyism*. Many thought it was intended as a portrayal of McMullen.[62]

Throughout the entire period, with all its alliances and betrayals, one of the certainties of political life in the city was the bond between McMullen and Samuel J. Randall. Although they occasionally diverged on tactics, each was careful to do nothing to jeopardize the interests of the other. They first met in 1862 when McMullen supported Randall's successful campaign for Congress, and maintained a close working relationship for thirty years thereafter. While historian Harry C. Silcox describes Randall as McMullen's "boss," it would be more accurate to say that they operated in different spheres; what McMullen did in the ground, Randall did at the peak; one was foundation, the other was steeple. In 1873, when McMullen ran for the Common Council, and traded support with Republicans in order to be elected, Randall supported him, even though the city's Democratic Party expelled McMullen for it. Later, when Randall needed to ensure that only his men were elected to a state Democratic convention in Harrisburg, McMullen employed his uglies to break up anti-Randall meetings. It was at one of those meetings that, for the second time, a pistol stuck in his chest failed to fire; Randall wrote him, "I rejoice that your life was spared although in peril." On the rioting, he remarked, "The fight was made where it was right and best to make it, to wit, within the rules of the party." As one newspaper commented editorially, "There's sweet little Sammy who sits up aloft, to look out for the life of Dear Bill." For his part, McMullen ridiculed the idea that anyone could unseat Randall so long as he, McMullen, controlled the district.[63] In order to appreciate the full significance of their relationship, it is necessary to turn back to the national scene.

As we know, Radical Reconstruction did not last. When Northern capitalists realized that they had less to fear from the former slave-holders than from the former slaves, they withdrew their support from Reconstruction. Their decision to do so met with general approval from the mass of white labor, including the subjects of this study. As W. E. B. Du Bois wrote, "When white laborers were convinced that the degrada-tion of Negro labor was more fundamental than the uplift of white labor, the end was in sight."[64] The Reconstruction governments were over-thrown, and night descended once again.

If the abolition of slavery had called into question the meaning of whiteness, the overthrow of Reconstruction marked the restoration of the color line on a new basis. No longer did it coincide with the distinc-tion between freedom and slavery; it now came to correspond to the distinction between free, wage labor and unfree, semi-feudal labor, and between those who had access to political power and those who did not.

In these momentous events, Congressman Randall played a key role. He gained national prominence through his filibuster against the Civil Rights and Force bills in January and February 1875, bills intended to preserve the voting rights of Southern Negroes against white-suprema-cist terror. But his real service came during the famous Compromise of 1877.

The Democratic candidate in the 1876 presidential election, Samuel J. Tilden of New York, had won a majority of votes in the electoral college over his Republican opponent, Rutherford B. Hayes of Ohio—if he was awarded the electoral votes of South Carolina and Louisiana. However, because the results of the popular vote in both of those states were in dispute, the election was thrown into the House of Representatives. After a prolonged stalemate, the House decided to award their votes, and thereby the election, to Hayes, with the proviso that he withdraw the last of the federal troops from the South and recognize the white-suprema-cist Redeemer governments in the two states. As Woodward summarizes the classical account, "In effect the Democrats were abandoning the cause of Tilden in exchange for control over two states, and the Republicans were abandoning the cause of the Negro in exchange for the peaceful possession of the Presidency."[65]

Randall had been elected Speaker of the House by the Democratic majority in December 1876. In that capacity he made several key rulings that facilitated the bargain. Early in the parliamentary wrangling, he had encouraged a Northern Democratic filibuster by his rulings from the chair (Northern Democrats were less willing than their Southern counterparts to accept another four years of Republican control of patronage, etc.), and warned the Southerners who favored the bargain that they were buying a pig in a poke. At that time he "predicted that Hayes would revive bayonet rule and that his policy would be of 'such a character as to overwhelm any Southern man in ruin who aided in carrying out their agreement in good faith.'"[66] Later, when he was satisfied that Hayes had given sufficient guarantees that he would fulfill his part of the bargain, Randall reversed himself and ruled the filibuster out of order, isolating the last of the die-hard Tilden supporters. The bargain was struck, Hayes was declared President with the promise that the white South would be as free of federal interference as Connecticut, and the Redeemer regimes were recognized as the legitimate governments of Louisiana and South Carolina.

It should be noted that the electoral votes of the two states were in dispute because of widespread "irregularities" in the voting. In each of them there existed two rival claimants to legitimacy, one elected with the participation of black voters, the other chosen under a reign of Ku Klux Klan terror that barred Negroes from the polls.[67] Thus it may be said that the Compromise of 1877 represented the application of the Philadelphia Plan for elections on a national scale.[68] The South went "solid for Mulhooly."

As Silcox reports, because of his role in restoring white supremacy in the South, "Randall became a popular figure with Southerners and with Irish Democrats like McMullen through this victory for local control and denial of centralized authority."[69] The precious Home Rule of Daniel O'Connell was transmuted by the malign alchemy of America into the base "home rule" of the Redeemers. Of course no one would claim that the triumph of the Southern Redeemers was solely the consequence of McMullen's activities in South Philadelphia. But it is no exaggeration to say that in 1877, when the Irish flexed their political muscle in the national arena, as they had done in 1844, it marked not the dedication of the Union to a new birth of freedom but the restoration of the White Republic.

As for McMullen, he continued to do well. In 1873, when he felt that the aldermanic post was played out, he ran successfully for one of the Fourth Ward's seats on Common Council, the lower of the two city councils. Four years later he was elected to fill a vacancy on the Select Council, a much smaller body than the Common Council, wielding considerably more power. During those years he maintained close relations with his fishing buddies William Leeds and James McManes, who were nominal Republicans but whose real strength lay in their control of the city's notorious Gas Ring. As a member of the Gas Works Committee in the city council, McMullen was able to help them, and they in turn did what they could for him.

There is no evidence that McMullen enriched himself financially from his various arrangements; on his death he bequeathed only a modest legacy to his heirs.[70] The main thing he got from his connections were jobs and services for his constituents. Aside from the gas works, he was able to place "his people" in the custom house, federal construction projects, the U.S. Mint, the federal arsenal, the Eastern State Penitentiary, and the Navy Yard (which he and Randall preserved for the district when there was a threat of relocation). He also had influence with private employers, including the giant Baldwin Locomotive Works. As Silcox puts it, he became "Philadelphia's best-known Irish employment agency."[71]

He helped his constituents get Civil War veterans' and widows' pensions, not always being to careful to demand verification of the validity of their claims. He was able to obtain the release of prisoners from various prisons, and of soldiers and sailors from military service. And of course he made sure that the streets were kept well lit and the sidewalks in good repair.

In 1885 McMullen sought the post of tax assessor for his ward. After a newspaper campaign to clean up his image, with references to his service in two wars, he got the job, with Randall's help.

It was the last important service Randall could perform for him, as

Randall himself lost influence under the Cleveland Administration for his high-tariff policies. When Randall died in 1889, McMullen managed to place in his seat his old friend, Richard Vaux, then unseated him when he proved insufficiently responsive to the district.

And so forth. When he died in 1901, the city councils passed a memorial resolution. One of his obituary writers quoted a comment someone had made earlier: "His life was worthy of a book, but not one in all its chapters, fitted for Sunday-school instruction."[72]

# AFTERWORD

The reader will note that I have written a book about racial oppression without using the term "racism." I consider the term useless. As Barbara J. Fields points out, it is applied to the view that one "race" is inferior to another, as well as to its direct opposite, the view that its members must be held down because they are *superior,* and has been devalued to mean little more than a personal preference for one complexion over another.[1] The sooner the term is retired, the better it will be for clear thinking all around.

This book is an attempt at the collective biography of a couple of million people—clearly an impossible task. In writing it, therefore, I have aimed not so much at facsimilitude as plausibility: aware that no historical study can account exactly for the life of a single person, I have tried to tell the story as it might have happened, and I ask that it be judged for its coherence and explanatory power. If there is any value in what I have done, I believe it lies not so much in the answers I have come up with as in the questions I have posed.

In the course of my research I learned that no one gave a damn for the poor Irish. Even the downtrodden black people had Quakers and abolitionists to bring their plight to public attention (as well as the ability to tell their own stories effectively), but there is no Irish-American counterpart of the various Philadelphia studies of the condition of free colored people,[2] let alone an autobiography to stand alongside the mighty work of Frederick Douglass. Why this should be so is a matter for speculation; perhaps it reflects a perception that the striving of the Negro for full freedom carried within itself the vision of a new world for everyone, while the assimilation of the Irish into white America meant merely more of the same. Moreover, I found not one single diary, or letter, or anything of that sort in which an ordinary Irish man or woman recorded in any detail the texture of daily life and relations with the black people who were often his or her closest neighbors. Consequently, like a paleontologist who builds a dinosaur from a tooth, I have been forced to reconstruct from fragments, and to infer.

This book draws upon the work of scholars in at least three areas: ethnic studies, Afro-American studies, and labor history (although in part I seek to knock down, or at least dig under, the walls between them, as well as those that separate political, social, and intellectual history). My aim in surveying them is not to provide a comprehensive guide to the literature, but to indicate a stance. In that connection I insist that, as C. L. R. James remarks somewhere, historical controversy is always contemporary.

As regards the first, the monumental work is, of course, Oscar Handlin's *Boston's Immigrants*.[3] Handlin's book has been cited so frequently in other works and reviewed so highly that anything I say about its merits would be superfluous. I wish, however, to record a disagreement with Professor Handlin: one of his main themes is that the Irish in America were decisively shaped by a stubborn peasant conservatism brought over from Ireland; I hope I have shown that they were as radical in spirit as anyone in their circumstances might be, but that their radical impulses were betrayed by their decision to sign aboard the hunt for the white whale (which in the end did not fetch them much in our Nantucket market). Nevertheless, it was a passage in *Boston's Immigrants* that first drew me to my own question: it recounts the complaints of Boston Irish "that colored people did not know their place."[4] How, I wondered, did an Irish immigrant, perhaps fresh off the boat, learn "the place" of the Negro?

The second great work in the field of Irish immigrant studies (here the term "emigrant" is more fitting, since the focus is at least as much on the departure of the Irish as on their reception) is Kerby Miller's *Emigrants and Exiles*, cited previously in these pages. That book leaves the reader feeling that the author knows everything there is to know about the Irish and what he does not know is not worth knowing. Miller has also written a study (so far unpublished) of the origins of Irish-American antipathy toward the Negro, a study I consulted frequently. Both of these works combine a deep sympathy for his subjects with the critical stance of the serious historian.

In addition to Handlin's and Miller's works, I also benefited from one-volume histories of the Irish in America by Carl Wittke and George Potter, and from Robert Ernst's study of immigrant life in New York.[5] For Philadelphia, I drew upon studies of the Irish by Dennis Clark.[6] Dale Knobel sheds light on the formation of Irish identity.[7] All these studies provide valuable information about the Irish in America. Although most note the widespread animosity between Irish- and Afro-Americans, they do so in passing, apparently taking it for granted as natural. Only Miller, in his unpublished study, probes at any length into how it developed.

Various studies of Afro-American life (cited in the text) have shed light on the question. While I reject the term "Afrocentric," loaded as it is with notions of inherited racial superiority, these works show that Afro-American studies at its best, when it looks at everything from the stand-point of those on the very bottom, provides a new understanding of American life as a whole and not simply a glimpse of an interesting and little-known group of people. The same thing is true of writings by and about the abolitionists, who were the intellectual expression of the striv-ing of the Negro to do away not only with slavery but with racial oppres-sion, and who paid a great deal of attention to the Irish, recognizing in them one of their greatest problems.

For general political and social history, labor history, abolitionism, nativism, Philadelphia, and Ireland I used various works cited in the text.

If this book has a target, it is the New Labor History, associated in America with the name of Herbert Gutman. The New Labor History shifted attention away from unions and other institutions toward the daily life of working people. It broke new ground in examining the role of the family, the community, and culture in forming the working class. In treating working people as the subjects of their own activity, it broke with the labor historians who preceded it. However, in its attitude toward the race problem it continued the tradition established earlier within Old Left circles, of substituting an abstract notion of the working class for the lived experience of working people.[8] Unable to deny entirely the record of white labor in accepting and promoting racial distinctions, the new labor historians treated it as peripheral to the main line of working-class formation and struggle. Rarely did they ask what the labor movement looked like from the perspective of the slave worker kept in bondage by the alliance of slaveholders, financiers, and white laborers known as the Democratic Party, or the free black worker denied land and employment, or the Chinese worker barred from the country, by the power of organized labor. In failing to do so they were reneging on their promise to write history "from the bottom up."

One explanation that can be offered for the Gutman school's blind spot on race is that it was motivated by the search for a tradition that could serve as the starting point for the sort of labor movement they hoped would emerge—the famous "usable past." But the selective lens used in the search involved denial, and denial led to apologetics. Among the earliest and certainly the most influential of the white labor apologetics to come out of the New Labor History was Gutman's own 1968 essay, "The Negro and the United Mine Workers of America," in which he portrayed the turn-of-the-century UMWA, despite shortcomings, as an outpost of working-class solidarity. "Any authoritative history of the UMW," he wrote

> will surely tell of the endless and formidable difficulties and frustrations that accompanied early efforts to build this inter-racial union. It will include grimly detailed pages about racial and ethnic quarrels and even death and violence. But it will also make much of the successful early confrontation between the UMW, its predominantly white leaders and members, and Negro workers. And it will explain why...enormous sacrifices by white and Negro miners made this union a reality.

"The essential fact," wrote Gutman, is that about 20,000 Negroes belonged to the UMW in 1900."[9]

Twenty thousand black members may have been a fact, but whether it was the essential fact is open to question. Workers join unions for many reasons, among them the desire to improve their living standards. To conclude from the presence of black miners in the UMW that either they or their white coworkers ever saw it as a champion of racial equality is to show considerably less sophistication than the workers themselves.

The year before he published his essay on the UMW, Gutman wrote a preface to a new edition of the 1930 classic by Spero and Harris, *The*

*Black Worker.*[10] In that preface, Gutman wrote, "We turn time and again to Spero and Harris" (xi). I suggest that had he turned to them a bit more often while writing his own essay, he would have found a corrective to his celebratory tone. According to them:

> the most frequent complaint one got from the Negro unionist in the coal fields was his inability to use his union card at some mines where the employment of a Negro had caused the white union miners to strike, or where it was believed by the operators that the employment would cause a strike. Indeed the frequent manifestations of racial antipathy against the Negro on the part of the white miners were in large measure accountable for the great defections among Negro members of the United Mine Workers during the 1927 strike. But even before 1927 many Negroes deserted the union because of the race prejudice of their white fellow unionists.

Spero and Harris cite an investigation reporting the refusal of whites in strong union areas to permit the employment of black miners in a number of the more desirable above-ground categories, "even though the Negroes are members of the union also." Some mines became known as "white men's mines."[11]

Gutman's assertion of the UMW's "conspicuous success" was bound to provoke a response, and in 1988 Herbert Hill published "Myth-Making as Labor History: Herbert Gutman and the United Mine Workers of America." In that essay, Hill, examining the sources Gutman had used, arrived at very different conclusions, and accused Gutman of fostering "a revived populist neo-Marxism that advanced the ideology of working class consciousness and solidarity against the social realities of race."[12] His essay touched off a new round of debate; Nell Irvin Painter wrote, "Much of the new labor history has downplayed or completely overlooked racism, and for years I have been nipping at the heels of some of the best-known, if not the greatest offenders, David Montgomery and Sean Wilentz, insisting that their writing as well as their teaching needs to recognize the ugly fact of racism, and not simply as a problem for nonwhites or a minor theme in American life."[13] Pivotal to the debate was an examination of the dual character of the white worker. As Steven Shulman wrote, the white working class is composed of whites as well as of workers. Both aspects of its identity are social relationships in the sense of being socially constructed processes which define group identities and interests. Just as the class-for-itself bears a systematic relationship to the class-in-itself, the racial ideologies of the white working class (as well as of all other classes) are systematically related to its construction and reconstruction of a racial hierarchy. The origin of its racial ideologies is not external to itself. The white working class adopts racial ideologies because it exists racially.[14]

The most egregious example of the blind spot of the new labor historians on race is Sean Wilentz's book, *Chants Democratic*. It is all the more objectionable because the book is so well-researched and well-written and has won so many prizes. As Herbert Hill notes, it contains only two references to Afro-Americans, one in a footnote. Wilentz, like any historian, can write about what he pleases, but by writing about white workers without reference to the black presence, he ignores one of the essential forces that shaped his subjects. In fact, there are no references to white workers in the book either, revealing that he regards their "whiteness" as a natural attribute, something they are rather than something they do.

Earlier I suggested that one reason for the blind spot of the New Labor Historians on the subject of race is the search for a usable past. There is another explanation: the historians who are writing about white workers without reference to their race have abandoned any hopes they once held for the constitution of the working class as a class for itself, a class in opposition to capital. If the workers are doomed to toil forever in the service of capital, and can only hope for heaven when they die, why scrutinize too closely the deals they make to ease their lot in this world below? Thus, the sympathy with the working people that virtually all the New Labor Historians express as a matter of course is no more than a sentimental attachment to the losers. For my part, my insistence on addressing problems of race as central to the formation (or nonformation) of an American working class stems from my view that there have been (and continue to be) moments when an anticapitalist course is a real possibility, and that the adherence of some workers to an alliance with capital on the basis of a shared "whiteness" has been and is the greatest obstacle to the realization of those possibilities. In this, as in other matters, I take my lead from Jim, who, on being asked by Huck if he knew any signs for good luck, answered, "Mighty few—an *dey* ain't no use to a body. What you want to know when good luck's a-comin' for? Want to keep it off?"

The summation of the New Labor History is the textbook *Who Built America*.[15] It brings together the accomplishments and shortcomings of the Gutman school. While it recounts the struggles of black people and their allies for justice, they form no part of the movement against capital. It acknowledges the hostility of white labor to abolition and the free Negro, but does so only in the discussion of slavery; the hostility was not important in defining the movement of free labor. One quote, from the introduction to the section on the Civil War and Reconstruction, will capture its general outlook: "Decades of conflict about the status of slavery had ended; now a new drama pitting capital against labor was about to begin."[16]

There we have it: David Walker's *Appeal*, Nat Turner's rebellion, the development of the Afro-American church and the black press, the underground railroad and the vigilance committees, abolitionism, John Brown, the Civil War, the withdrawal of labor from the plantation, the black soldiers, Negroes as voters and citizens, forty acres and a mule, the overthrow of Reconstruction—all these were prelude, part of the debate over slavery and the Negro; the "real" struggle between capital and labor is about to begin. It is now sixty years since Du Bois wrote:

> The most magnificent drama in the last thousand years of human history is the transportation of ten million human beings out of the dark beauty of their mother continent into the new-found Eldorado of the West. They descended into Hell; and in the third century they arose from the dead, in the finest effort to achieve democracy for the working millions which this world had ever seen. It was a tragedy that beggared the Greek; it was an upheaval of humanity like the Reformation and the French Revolution. Yet we are blind and led by the blind. We discern in it no part of our

labor movement; no part of our industrial triumph; no part of our religious experience.[17]

Apparently the labor historians have made little progress since Du Bois wrote those lines. The survey of the history of class struggle in America is yet to be written.

There are, however, several recent books that represent a new departure. The first of these is *The Rise and Fall of the White Republic* by Alexander Saxton.[18] The author sees little difficulty in understanding how the theory of white superiority arose out of the need to vindicate a class of people that grew rich from the slave trade, slavery, and the expropriation of land from nonwhite populations; the more formidable problem is to explain why nonslaveholding whites acquiesced either in planter dominance or its justifications. *The Rise and Fall*, then, is a study of the role of white supremacy in legitimating the changing class coalitions that ruled the U.S. in the nineteenth century.

Contrary to the fictions of the white labor apologists, "the hard side of racism generally appeared in nineteenth-century America as a corollary to egalitarianism" (186). Whiggery was shaped, above all, by class position; within the Whig social hierarchy, "racial difference could be viewed...[as] simply one among many" (70). Northern Whig employers felt the greatest threat from the insurgent immigrant population, while their attitude toward nonwhites was often one of tolerant condescension. For the Jacksonians, needing to cement a coalition based on white egalitarianism, racial distinctions were central. "Their natural proclivity was to the hard side of racism" (120). Accordingly, "class differentials dissolve into a sentimental oneness of the white *herrenvolk*" (123).

David Roediger also explores the problem of white ideology, with specific attention to the working class. He asks "why the white working class settles for being white" (6) and finds the answer in Du Bois's notion of the "public and psychological wage." The "pleasures of whiteness could function as a wage" (13) which led "many workers [to] define themselves as white" (6). To trace the evolution and effects of that wage is the task of *The Wages of Whiteness*. Although Roediger locates himself within the "broad tradition" of the New Labor History, and uses Marxist tools, he acknowledges that "the new labor history has hesitated to explore 'whiteness' and white supremacy as creations, in part, of the white working class itself" (9) and that "the main body of writing by white Marxists in the United States has both 'naturalized' whiteness and over-simplified race, reproduc[ing] the weaknesses of both American liberalism and neo-conservatism" (6).

"Working class formation and the systematic development of a sense of whiteness went hand in hand for the U.S. white working class," writes Roediger (8). If the color line paid a "public and psychological wage," the cost was a "debased republicanism," condemnation to "lifelong wage labor" (55). He concludes with an appropriate symbol: by the end of Reconstruction, "white workers were still tragically set on keeping even John Henry out of the House of Labor" (181).[19]

Both of these books are welcome challenges to the old and new myth-makers. Another study which sheds light on race formation is Richard Williams, *Hierarchical Structures and Social Value*. According to Williams, some people from Africa became unfree laborers in America because, at a time when the plantations of the Western Hemisphere were crying for labor, West African societies produced a surplus population that could not be exploited at home. "If Europeans had been assigned to [the unfree labor slot] the mark of vertical classification…would have been something other than skin pigmentation" (85–6). In short, people from Africa were not enslaved because they were black; rather, they were defined as black because they were enslaved.

Turning his attention to Ireland, Williams traces the developments that ultimately led to the formation of a massive surplus population following the Napoleonic Wars. "The expulsion of a portion of the peasantry from Ireland has become the 'Irish migration'…" (132).

"Ethnicity," he argues, "cannot exist without race" (2). In Britain, the Irish constituted a subject race. Because blackness was the badge of the slave in America, people from Ireland who went there entered the free labor system, which made them part of the dominant race. As unskilled workers, they occupied the lowest place within it. Ethnicity marked the spot. Through a process parallel to the creation of race, "a segment of Irish society became identified as the Irish in the United States" (100).

Another work searching out the origins of whiteness is Theodore W. Allen's, *The Invention of the White Race*. Allen declares that, when the first

Africans arrived in Virginia in 1619, there were no "white" people there, nor would there be any for another sixty years. How the English, Scots, and other European servants, tenants, merchants, and planters in the American colonies were assigned a single status, so that the most degraded "white" was exalted over any "nonwhite," is the subject of his study. Using Ireland as a mirror of America, Allen traces the development of Protestant supremacy. The meanest "Protestant" was granted a status above the most exalted "Catholic." After having spent centuries perfecting this system, Britain was compelled in the nineteenth century to abandon it—everywhere except in Ulster—and allow the task of administering Ireland to pass from the Ascendancy to a developing Catholic bourgeoisie. But Anglo-America, writes Allen, is "Ulster Writ Large," stressing the parallels between the two places: the oppressors' refusal to acknowledge the family structure of the oppressed, the persecution of their religions, the prohibition of literacy, the massive and forcible removal of populations.

Racial oppression does not depend on a difference in "phenotype," insists Allen. The two most formidable objections to his thesis are: why no chattel slavery in Ireland; and why did Irish Catholics not escape their oppression by converting to Protestantism? His answers: slavery was not established in Ireland because under the conditions that prevailed in agriculture there it was cheaper to maintain a force of seasonal laborers than year-round slaves; and the Protestant Ascendancy made it virtually impossible for Catholics to convert. In fact, the number of American slaves who gained manumission was greater than the number of Irish Catholics whose conversions to the (Protestant) Church of Ireland were officially recognized. In these details Allen reveals the essential identity of the Irish and American cases, and thus refutes those who attach suprahistorical importance to "natural" affinities and aversions. As Barbara J. Fields has said, "race" explains nothing; it is something that must be explained.

In his last two chapters Allen examines the change that Catholic Irish underwent on emigration to the United States, from being victims and opponents of racial oppression to upholders of slavery and white supremacy. His account is a welcome departure from sentimental histories that gloss over an ugly reality.

The appearance of these studies, and others not mentioned here, gives rise to the hope that there is at last emerging, more than a half-century after Du Bois pointed the way, a school of American working-class history free of both white labor apologetics and the scholastic dismissal of the working class as "a concept long past its sell-by date."[20]

# NOTES

## INTRODUCTION

1. For a consideration of these and other absurdities, see Barbara J. Fields, "Ideology and Race in American History," in J. Morgan Kousser and James M. McPherson, *Region, Race and Reconstruction* (New York, 1982), 143–177.

2. Theodore W. Allen, *The Invention of the White Race, Volume One: Racial Oppression and Social Control* (New York, 1994), 28, 32.

## I ❧ SOMETHING IN THE AIR

1. A useful biography of O'Connell, focusing on the period under consideration, is Angus Macintyre, *The Liberator: Daniel O'Connell and the Irish Party, 1830–1847* (New York, 1965). The fullest account of the American abolitionist side of the events around the Irish Address is Gilbert Osofsky, "Abolitionists, Irish Immigrants, and Romantic Nationalism," *American Historical Review* 80: 4 (October 1975): 889–912. From the other side of the Atlantic it is Douglas C. Riach, "Daniel O'Connell and American Antislavery," *Irish Historical Studies* XX: 77 (March 1976): 3–25. Also useful is Owen Dudley Edwards, "The American Image of Ireland: A Study of its Early Phases," *Perspectives in American History* 4 (1970): 255–72.

2. The reality was more complicated: there was some actual involvement by Irish merchants in the slave trade, and some ships to Belfast numbered slaves among their crews. See Douglas C. Riach, "Ireland and the Campaign Against American Slavery, 1830–1860" (Ph.D. dissertation, Edinburgh University, 1975).

3. Kenneth Charlton, "The State of Ireland in the 1820s: James Cropper's Plan," *Irish Historical Studies* XVII: 67 (March 1971): 320–39; O'Connell referred favorably to Cropper's plan at a Catholic Association Meeting in 1825. Cropper himself had interests in the East Indies.

4. The story was told by Wendell Phillips, in his speech on the O'Connell centenary meeting in Boston, August 6, 1875. Phillips cited the English abolitionist and member of parliament at the same time as O'Connell, Thomas Fowell Buxton, as the person who told it to him. Wendell Phillips, *Speeches, Lectures, and Letters: Second Series* (Boston, 1891), 407.

5. *The Irish Patriot: Daniel O'Connell's Legacy to Irish Americans* (Philadelphia, 1863), 6.

6. *The Irish Patriot,* 8.

7. *The Irish Patriot,* 11.

8. *The Correspondence of Daniel O'Connell* (Dublin, 1972) VI, letter 2,499: 129. The letter has five signatures, of which three are legible as the names of prominent Philadelphia Irish: Alexander Diamond, William Dickson, and John Binns. The speech that had touched their nerves was delivered at a public meeting of antislavery delegates from all parts of the United Kingdom, held in London in November of 1837. In his talk O'Connell had denounced the seizure of Texas from Mexico and the plan to merge it with the U.S. and reimpose slavery on territory where it had been abolished.

9. *O'Connell Correspondence* VI, letter 2,566: 193. Wright's letter was occasioned by O'Connell's denunciation of the U.S. Ambassador to Britain, Andrew Stevenson of Virginia, as a slave-breeder. O'Connell's remarks started a flap: Stevenson challenged him to a duel; letters between the two were widely covered in the British and American press; and O'Connell was attacked by newspapers in the South. The American Anti-Slavery Society published copies of O'Connell's speech and his correspondence with the Ambassador. See Douglas C. Riach, "Daniel O'Connell," 5, and "Ireland and the Campaign," 149–50.

10. *O'Connell Correspondence* VI, letter 2,673 (Jan. 11, 1840): 295. Haughton's letter followed a visit by the eminent Irish writer, R. R. Madden, who had just returned from a trip to America. For Madden, see Riach, "Ireland and the Campaign," 161–2.

11. *O'Connell Correspondence* VII, letter 2,951, n2: 145–6.

12. *Liberator,* August 28, 1840, cited by Osofsky.

13. There is no separate enumeration of clergymen among the signers. Richard Allen reported that forty-three of the first fifteen thousand signers were Catholic clergymen, including one bishop. The *Liberator* of March 18, 1842, carried a letter from Ireland dated October 27 of the previous year stating that on one sheet of paper containing eighty-seven names the writer had collected the signatures of twenty-eight Catholic clergymen, bringing his total of priests to seventy-three, including one bishop. (See Riach, "Ireland and the Campaign," 162.) Father Theobald Mathew, the leader of the Irish total abstinence crusade, was a signer, and his name was normally singled out with O'Connell's in copies of the Address. For Mathew's course, see Colm Kerrigan, "Irish Temperance and U.S. Anti-Slavery: Father Mathew and the Abolitionists," *History Workshop* 31 (Spring 1991): 105–119.

14. Riach, "Ireland and the Campaign," 162–64; *The Letters of William Lloyd Garrison,* ed. Walter Merrill (Cambridge, Mass., 1973) III: 47.

15. *Liberator,* December 18, 1841, cited by Osofsky.

16. The Address was reprinted in the *Pennsylvania Freeman,* the *Liberator,* the *Philadelphia Public Ledger,* and any number of places. The excerpt here, representing about half of the Address, is taken from the *Liberator* of March 25, 1842, with its layout.

17. John A. Collins to Webb, January 1, 1842, Garrison Papers, Boston Public Library, cited by Osofsky.

18. Letter from George Thompson, cited by Oscar Sherwin, *Prophet of Liberty: The Life and Times of Wendell Phillips* (New York, 1958), 130.

19. Anne Warren Weston to Elizabeth Pease, January 30, 1842, William Lloyd Garrison Papers, cited by Osofsky.

20. *Liberator,* February 4, 1842. Other reports listed Abby Kelley as one of the speakers, but there is no mention of her in the *Liberator* account, nor in Garrison's letters in the days following.

21. *The Letters of William Lloyd Garrison,* Vol. III *No Union with Slaveholders 1841–1849,* ed. Walter M. Merrill (Cambridge, Mass., 1973), 48.

22. Reprinted in the *Liberator,* February 18, 1842.

23. Hughes's statement was in a letter which was published in (and cited from) various places, including the newspaper he controlled, the *Freeman's Journal* (NY). It is taken here from the *Liberator* of March 25, 1842, which reprinted it from the New York *Courier and Enquirer.*

24. John A. Collins to R. D. Webb, cited by Riach, "Ireland and the Campaign," 166.

25. Boston *Pilot,* September 23, 1839, cited by Madeleine Hook Rice, *American Catholic Opinion in the Slavery Controversy* (New York, 1944), 79.

26. This article was reprinted in the Boston *Morning Post* and then in the *Liberator* of February 25, from which it is quoted here.

27. Boston *Pilot,* February 12, reprinted in the *Liberator,* March 18, 1842.

28. Reprinted in the *Liberator,* March 4, 1842.

29. *National Anti-Slavery Standard,* March 24, 1842, cited by Osofsky.

30. James G. Birney had replied to Bishop Hughes by saying that either Hughes was not a repealer, in which case he had no right to interfere in Irish American affairs, or he was, in which case he was interfering in British affairs. (*National Anti-Slavery Standard,* March 24, 1842, cited in Riach, "Daniel O'Connell and American anti-slavery.") The business of foreign influence was largely a question of whose ox was being gored. Phillips took every opportunity to cite the antislavery declarations of various popes.

31. Garrison *Letters* III: 51.

32. Garrison *Letters* III: 53.

33. *National Anti-Slavery Standard,* February 6, 1842, cited in Riach, "Ireland and the Campaign," 167; virtually every number of the *Liberator* for months starting March 18, 1842 carried letters, speeches, and resolutions from Ireland upholding the Address and reiterating Irish support for the abolition cause.

34. The following account of the formation of the Repeal movement in the U.S. is, except where noted, taken from George Potter, *To the Golden Door* (Westport, Conn., 1960), 388–94. Potter's book, published after his death from

copy furnished by his widow, is without footnotes. In those cases where it has been possible to check his research, it has proved reliable.

35. The first president of the New York society, Robert Emmett, resigned after an attack on the Rising of '98 by O'Connell, who, of course, was absolutely committed to the nonviolent path. The personal discord, which had nationwide repercussions, mainly centered around one Thomas Mooney, who was a type of adventurer and charlatan that abounds in exile organizations.

36. These were the same methods O'Connell used to build the movement in Ireland.

37. Most of the political supporters were associated with the Democratic Party. John Quincy Adams, the Whig, sympathized with the Irish against British oppression, but did not take a position on the specific issue of Repeal. Herman Melville, whose brother Gansevoort was a popular Democratic stump speaker and supporter of Repeal, took a stand similar to Adams.

38. *Irish Patriot,* 8, 12.

39. Garrison *Letters* III: 57. This letter was reprinted in the *Liberator,* April 8, 1842.

40. *Liberator,* March 22, 1842.

41. For an illuminating discussion of this and other issues, see Aileen F. Kraditor, *Means and Ends in American Abolitionism* (New York, 1967).

42. Phillips to Allen, March 30, 1842, Garrison Papers, Boston Public Library, cited by Riach, "Ireland and the Campaign," 166.

43. *New Orleans Jeffersonian* account of an Irish Repeal meeting on February 21, reprinted in the *Liberator,* April 1, 1842.

44. *New-Orleans Bee,* reprinted in the *Liberator,* April 1, 1842.

45. Philadelphia *Public Ledger,* February 23, 1842.

46. Philadelphia *Public Ledger,* February 24, 1842.

47. *O'Connell Correspondence* VII, letter 2,951, March 28, 1842: 145.

48. Phillips to Allen, March 30, 1842, Garrison Papers, Boston Public Library, cited by Sherwin, *Prophet of Liberty,* 131.

49. *Liberator,* June 17, 1842.

50. *Liberator,* June 24, 1842.

51. Speech at the L.N.R.A., reported in the Dublin *Morning Register,* May 23, reprinted in the *Liberator,* June 24, 1842.

52. It was not the first time O'Connell had encountered conflicts among the antislavery forces. At the World Anti-Slavery Convention in London in 1840, Garrison and the other radicals sat in the gallery in protest at the exclusion of female delegates. O'Connell, while sympathizing with the Garrisonians, did not take a stand. (See his letter to Lucretia Mott, O'Connell *Correspondence* VI, letter 2,721: 338–40.)

53. *Liberator,* October 7, 1842. The reference to property came in response to charges that the abolitionists had countenanced the stealing of horses by slaves in the act of running away. See Garrison's editorial in the *Liberator,* April 14, 1843, and the letter to O'Connell from Gerrit Smith in the *Liberator,* April 28, 1843.

54. *Pilot,* July 2, reprinted in the *Liberator,* August 5, 1842.

55. Phillips to Webb, June 29, 1842. Garrison Papers, Boston Public Library. The Beggarman reference was to the sarcastic title bestowed upon him by British opponents after he accepted a lifetime annuity awarded him by the Irish people in gratitude for his services.

56. Garrison *Letters* III, July 2, 1842: 92–3.

57. O'Connell deplored the riot, and asked why the Catholic clergy in the city had not used their influence to prevent it. At the same time, he renewed his criticism of those abolitionists who proposed "the abolition of Sunday and the setting aside of all clerical authority in matters of religion." (Speech at the L.N.R.A., reprinted in the *Liberator,* April 14, 1843, from the Dublin *Morning Registrar,* October 19, 1842.)

58. As Riach points out, the abolitionists were not without the capacity to exert pressure. Many of the Irish abolitionists were Protestants, whom O'Connell wished to keep in the L.N.R.A. in order to dispel charges that it was a sectarian organization. See "Ireland and the Campaign," esp. 190–1.

59. Philadelphia *Public Ledger,* February 28, March 12, April 16, May 7, 23, June 24, August 22, October 31, 1842, and January 13, 1843.

60. See the *Liberator* of June 16, 1843, for the text of the letter.

61. *The Irish Patriot,* 24–27.

62. The following account is based on Potter, *To the Golden Door,* T. A. Jackson, *Ireland, Her Own* (London, 1947), and Robert Kee, *That Most Distressful Country* (London, 1976).

63. Frederick Engels, "Letter from London," Marx-Engels *Collected Works* (New York, 1975) III: 391.

64. Critical discussions of O'Connell are James Connolly, *Labour in Irish History* (New York, 1921), especially Ch. 12, "A Chapter of Horrors: Daniel O'Connell and the Working Class" and T. A. Jackson, *Ireland Her Own,* Part III. Both of these studies take their lead from Engels' 1843 letter.

65. Potter, *To the Golden Door,* 399.

66. Riach, "Daniel O'Connell," 17; Philadelphia *Public Ledger,* July 6, 1843.

67. *Liberator,* July 7, 1843.

68. Philadelphia *Public Ledger,* June 28, 1843.

69. *Liberator,* July 21, 1843. O'Connell had made a speech to the L.N.R.A. commending Tyler, and later moved a resolution to that effect. See the *Liberator,* April 28 and May 12, 1843.

70. *Public Ledger,* September 26 and November 4, 1843.

71. Philadelphia *Public Ledger,* August 23, 1842.

72. *Public Ledger,* June 28, September 9 and 27, 1843. It will be recalled that Diamond was among the Philadelphians who had written to O'Connell in 1838. Binns was the brother of John Binns, another of O'Connell's 1838 correspondents.

73. Membership was granted on payment of $1. Whoever paid $5 or enrolled five members was named a Repeal Volunteer. See the *Public Ledger,* August 14 and 16, September 27, 1843. The *Public Ledger* of September 28, 1843 contained a list of contributors as of July 9, identified by county of origin and amount. This was important because contributors' names were enrolled in a book at L.N.R.A. headquarters in Dublin.

74. The *Public Ledger* of September 26 and 28, October 14, and November 11, 1843, carried reports of financial remittances from the Friends of Ireland to the L.N.R.A. ranging from one hundred dollars to two hundred pounds sterling; some of this money may have been counted more than once. The *Public Ledger* of September 27, 1843 carried a report of a remittance of one hundred pounds sterling from the Repeal Association.

75. *Public Ledger,* November 10 and 11, 1843.

76. Report in the *National Anti-Slavery Standard,* carried in the *Liberator,* July 14, 1843.

77. It should be pointed out that, in spite of accusations to the contrary, the abolitionists never asked the Repeal Association to declare itself on the question of slavery. The statement to the Association from the Pennsylvania Anti-Slavery Society was a response to charges that had been made against it by various Repealers in the course of efforts to dissociate themselves from O'Connell. See the *Public Ledger,* July 7, 1842.

78. Riach, "Ireland and the Campaign," 199.

79. The full text of the Cincinnati Address was printed in the *Liberator,* November 17, 1843.

80. Speech of October 24, 1843, *Liberator,* November 24, 1843. Riach, "Daniel O'Connell," 13. Haughton came to Garrison's defense in a letter, published in the *Liberator* of October 24, and Garrison repled to O'Connell with another, published December 8, 1843.

81. Riach, "Ireland and the Campaign," 212.

82. A report, written by Garrison, appeared in the *Liberator* of November 24, 1843.

83. Riach, "Ireland and the Campaign," 214–5.

84. Riach, "Ireland and the Campaign," 219.

85. Riach, "Daniel O'Connell," 19.

86. Riach, "Ireland and the Campaign," 226.

87. Riach, "Ireland and the Campaign," 220; Philadelphia *Public Ledger,* June 14, 1845.

88. Seumas MacCall, *Irish Mitchel* (London, 1938), 326–52.

## II ❧ WHITE NEGROES AND SMOKED IRISH

1. On two occasions officials with judiciary authority in Ireland declared that "The law does not suppose any such person to exist as an Irish Roman Catholic." It is impossible not to note the similarity of that summary with Judge Taney's famous dictum in the Dred Scott case a century later: "The Negro has no rights a white man is bound to respect." Descriptions of the Penal Laws can be found in the standard histories of Ireland. The list given here is based on Seumas MacManus, *The Story of the Irish Race* (New York, 1921), 454–460.

2. Kee, *Most Distressful Country*, 19.

3. Allen, *Invention of the White Race*, 27–52, 112–114. Another study analyzing racial oppression as a distinct type of rule is Stanley B. Greenburg, *Race and State in Capitalist Development* (New Haven, 1980), which focuses on four places where it evolved as the pillar of class rule: the U.S., South Africa, Ireland, and Israel. Greenburg, however, makes no terminological distinction between racial and "ethnic" domination.

4. W. E. H. Lecky, *History of Ireland in the Eighteenth Century*, 8 vols., (New York, 1878–1890) vol. II, 182, cited by Kee, *Most Distressful Country*, 18.

5. Jackson, *Ireland Her Own*, 100–01.

6. The effects of this set-up in the Irish countryside are depicted in Maria Edgeworth's novel, *Castle Rackrent* (1800).

7. The transformations of the Irish economy from Cromwell's time to the Famine are well summarized in Richard Williams, *Hierarchical Structures and Social Value* (New York, 1990), esp. chapters 9 and 10.

8. Allen, *Invention*, 92.

9. Kirby Miller, *Emigrants and Exiles: Ireland and the Irish Exodus to North America* (New York, 1985), 193.

10. *Emigrants and Exiles*, 194, 197, 198.

11. *Emigrants and Exiles*, 194, 195, 200.

12. *Emigrants and Exiles*, 297. For the imposition of English in Ireland, see Robert McCrum, William Cran, and Robert MacNeil, *The Story of English* (New York, 1986), 171–72.

13. J. Thomas Scharf and Thompson Westcott, *History of Philadelphia, 1609–1884*, 3 vols., (Philadelphia, 1884), vol. 2, 1392.

14. *Emigrants and Exiles*, 318.

15. Carl Wittke, *The Irish in America* (New York, 1956), vi, vii.

16. The Irish case suggests that ethnicity, like race, is a synthetic product. The writer's maternal grandfather, born in 1886 in Galicia under Hapsburg rule, was either "Austrian," "Polish," or "Jewish," depending on the context.

17. *Negro Population of the United States, 1790–1918* (Washington D.C., 1918), 221; *7th Census* (1850), 157, 178–9.

18. Benjamin T. Sewall, *Sorrow's Circuit, or Five Years Experience in the Bedford Steet Mission* (Philadelphia, 1859), 188.

19. Historical Society of Pennsylvania.

20. David P. Thelen and Leslie H. Fishel, Jr. "Reconstruction in the North: *The World* Looks at New York's Negroes, March 16, 1867," *New York History* 49: 4 (October 1968), 405–40. This was apparently true in Canada as well. According to Samuel Gridley Howe, "marriages, or open cohabitation, between black men and white women, were not uncommon. The marriages were mostly with Irish, or other foreign women." (*Report to the Freedmen's Inquiry Commission from Western Canada* [1864; New York, 1969]), 29.

21. James Oliver Horton and Lois E. Horton, *Black Bostonians* (New York, 1979), 21–23.

22. Rhode Island Black Heritage Museum, Providence.

23. Earl F. Niehaus, *The Irish in New Orleans 1800–1860* (Baton Rouge, 1965), 54.

24. Allen Steinberg, *The Transformation of Criminal Justice: Philadelphia, 1800–1880* (Chapel Hill, 1989), 51.

25. Emma Lapsansky, "South Street Philadelphia, 1762–1854: 'A Haven for those Low in the World,'" (Ph.D. dissertation, University of Pennsylvania, 1975), 190.

26. The Congress raised problems that courts were wrestling with well into the twentieth century. For a recounting of some of the legal history, and a discussion of the "not yet white ethnic," see "Whiteness and Ethnicity in the History of 'White Ethnics' in the United States," in David R. Roediger, *Towards the Abolition of Whiteness: Essays on Race, Politics, and Working Class History* (New York, 1994), 181–98, and Noel Ignatiev, "Immigrants and Whites," *Konch* 1 (Winter 1990): 36–39, reprinted in *Race Traitor* 2 (Summer 1993): 60–67.

27. Dale T. Knobel, *Paddy and the Republic: Ethnicity and Nationality in Antebellum America* (Middletown, Conn., 1986), 178.

28. Frances Kemble, *Journal of a Residence on a Georgia Plantation* (New York, 1863), 105.

29. Quoted from the (New York) *Irish-American*, January 6, 1850, in Florence E. Gibson, *The Attitudes of the New York Irish Toward State and National Affairs, 1848–1892* (New York, 1951), 15.

30. See Alexander Saxton, *The Rise and Fall of the White Republic: Class Politics and Mass Culture in Nineteenth-Century America* (New York, 1990), chapter 7; David Roediger, *The Wages of Whiteness: Race and the Making of the*

*American Working Class* (New York, 1991), chapter 6; and Eric Lott, *Love and Theft: Blackface Minstrelsy and the American Working Class* (New York, 1993).

31. Douglass is quoted in Lott, *Love and Theft*, 15. The contest was the subject of a 1991 off-Broadway musical, *Juba,* book and lyrics by Wendy Lamb.

32. Widely regarded as the first modern prison, the Walnut Street Jail has been the subject of numerous studies. Among standard institutional histories are Harry Elmer Barnes, *The Evolution of Penology in Pennsylvania* (Montclair, N.J., 1927) and Negley F. Teeters, *The Cradle of the Penitentiary* (Philadelphia, 1955). An insightful study, which devotes considerable attention to the Walnut Street Jail, is Michael Meranze, "Public Punishments, Reformative Incarceration, and Authority in Philadelphia, 1750–1835," (Ph.D. dissertation, University of California, Berkeley, 1987). From 1794 to the closing of the Prison in 1835 the Board of Inspectors met biweekly and, when necessary, more frequently. The minutes of the Board's meetings are contained in six volumes, currently stored in the City Archives, located on North Broad Street in Philadelphia, as Record Group 38.1.

33. Minutes of the Board of Inspectors, April 1, 1816.

34. Minutes of the Board of Inspectors, February 1, 1819; February 15, 1819.

35. Minutes of the Board of Inspectors, December 27, 1824.

36. Minutes of the Board of Inspectors, December 31, 1824.

37. Minutes of the Board of Inspectors, April 26, 1830.

38. Minutes of the Board of Inspectors, March 28, 1820.

39. Scharf and Westcott, *History*. Their account of the 1820 insurrection is in two places: vol. I: 602, and vol. III: 183–31.

40. *History* III: 1831.

41. Philadelphia *Sunday Dispatch*, November 27, 1859. Scharf and Westcott, who based their account of the insurrection on the *Dispatch* story, omit this detail.

42. Roberts Vaux, *Notices of the Original, and Successive Efforts, to Improve the Discipline of the Prison at Philadelphia* (Philadelphia, 1826), 70–4.

43. Vaux and Caleb Cresson, writing in 1816, estimated a return rate of one-fourth among those sentenced to Walnut Street. Source: Cresson and Vaux to William Allen, October 19, 1816, in Pennsylvania Prison Society, Minutes, 1810–1832. According to James Mease, *Observations on the Penitentiary System and Penal Code of Pennsylvania with Suggestions for Their Improvement* (Philadelphia, 1828), of a total of 2,824 persons convicted from 1810 through 1819, 472, or 16.7 percent, had been convicted previously in Pennsylvania. There is a discrepancy between Mease's total figure, for which he cites no authority, and the figure of 3,064 derived from Vaux's *Notices*. The *Report on Punishments and Prison Discipline* by the Commissioners on the Penal Code (Philadelphia, 1828) states that in 1825, 270 of 358 convicts and in 1826, 221 of 296, were first offenders.

44. Beginning in 1817, Vaux gives a breakdown of prisoners by sex.

45. *Census for 1820* (Washington D.C., 1821).

46. The one-third division is based on figures for occupational stratification of the City. In 1820, 55 percent of white, male heads of households were minor proprietors; 12.5 percent were skilled, nine percent were in semiskilled and service trades, and seven per cent were unskilled and menial. Adding the last three categories plus the poorest tenth among the minor proprietors gives the one-third figure used for calculation. For African-Americans, of course, the stratification was quite different: among male heads of household in 1811, seventy-five percent were in service and unskilled trades; in 1838 the corresponding figure was seventy-nine percent. (Source: Tom W. Smith, "The Dawn of the Urban-Industrial Age: The Social Structure of Philadelphia, 1790–1830," Ph.D. dissertation, University of Chicago, 1980.) As we shall see, nearly all of the prisoners were drawn from these strata.

47. This estimate is conservative, because it excludes all those in the jail other than convicted felons. In addition to the convicts there were the debtors, vagrants, persons awaiting trial, and runaways in the adjacent Prune Street Apartment. All authorities agree that the total number of inmates was equal to several times the number of actual convicted felons sentenced there. One observer stated that "in Philadelphia...more than two thousand five hundred are annually committed [to prison]; of whom not one-fourth are found to be guilty." (Edward Livingston, Letter to Vaux, *On the Advantages of the Pennsylvania System of Prison Discipline* (Philadelphia, 1828),14. Although the non-felons were not held there as long as the convicts, they were intimately connected with the life of the prison and undoubtedly infected by the contagion of revolt.

48. A survey of 520 convict men in prison on January 1, 1826 showed only five with clerical occupations, including one doctor and one lawyer; the remainder were all members of the proletarian class: eighty-four farmers (probably farm laborers), eighty-two laborers, and a mixture of sailors, weavers, shoemakers, carpenters, smiths, and waiters. (Convict Description Docket, PCA Record Group 38.41.) Batsheva Spiegel Epstein, in her study of a sample of 1,068 persons sentenced to the prison between 1795 and 1829, reports forty-four percent artisans. She assigns everyone who claimed a trade to the artisan class. As she notes, the prison authorities may have followed the same practice, recording as a craftsman someone who worked as a helper. Furthermore, only about half the cases in her sample had information about occupation. ("Patterns of sentencing and their implementation in Philadelphia City and County, 1795–1829," Ph.D. dissertation, University of Pennsylvania, 1981.)

49. Vaux gives the race of males committed for the years 1818 to 1824, excluding 1819.

50. Pennsylvania Prison Society, Acting Committee, Minutes, January 8, 1821. Document reprinted in *Report on the Penitentiary system made to the Senate of Pennsylvania* (Philadelphia, 1821). (HSP)

51. U.S. Census, 1820.

52. Convict Description Docket, PCA Record Group 38.41. This was an old story: of 837 convicted and sent to the jail between 1787 and 1795, 456 were white foreigners, of whom 323 were Irish. (Eighty-seven of the 124 Negroes were of foreign birth.) (Rochefoucault-Liancourt, *On the Prisons of Philadelphia by an European* [Philadelphia, 1796]). A Philadelphia editor observed in 1797 that "the *Irish Emigrants* and the *French Negroes* suffered "the most afflictive and accumulated distress" in the City. (John K. Alexander, *Render Them Submissive: Responses to Poverty in Philadelphia, 1760–1800* (Amherst, Mass., 1980), 79. Of a sample of convicts sentenced to the prison from 1794 to 1829, fifteen percent of those for whom the country of origin was recorded were from Ireland. (Epstein, "Patterns," 97).

53. Minutes of the Board of Inspectors, May 11, 1818.

54. Minutes of the Board of Inspectors, March 15 and March 29, 1819.

55. Minutes of the Board of Inspectors, August 2, 1819.

56. Minutes of the Board of Inspectors, December 27, 1824 and January 10, 1825.

57. Minutes of the Board of Inspectors, October 31, 1825.

58. Minutes of the Board of Inspectors, March 5, 1827.

59. PCA, Record Group 38.41 (P326). It is not certain that McIlhenny was of Irish descent; the "Mc" could be Scottish. In the 1826 list, the five other foreign-born prisoners whose surnames began with Mc were from Ireland.

60. PCA, Record Group 38.36 (P62a), folio 100.

61. Philadelphia *Sunday Dispatch*, November 20, 1859.

62. Philadelphia *Sunday Dispatch,* November 20, 1859.

63. Mease (*Observations*, 34) says that one out of sixteen Negroes was committed to prison in the year ending October 1, 1818, compared to one out of sixty whites. His proportion, calculated on a different base, is consistent with the figures given by Vaux.

64. Minutes of the Board of Inspectors, May 19, 1795. There is a mistake in arithmetic here, but it is not mine.

65. Minutes of the Board of Inspectors, June 16, 1797.

66. Caleb Lownes, *An Account of the Alteration and Present State of the Penal Laws of Pennsylvania, Containing also an Account of the Gaol and Penitentiary House of Philadelphia and the Interior Management Thereof* (Boston, 1799), 80–81.

67. Robert J. Turnbull, *A Visit to the Philadelphia Prison* (Philadelphia, 1796), 28.

68. *History*, vol. 2, 1830.

69. Minutes of the Board of Inspectors, June 9, 1812. "Only...during the

night." And what did the "boys" do at night?

70. Minutes of the Board of Inspectors, January 9, 1804, January 4 and March 14, 1808 and February 14, 1820.

71. Minutes of the Board of Inspectors, February, 14, 1820.

72. Minutes of the Acting Committee of the Prison Society, Vol 2, Part A, January 10, 1820 (HSP).

73. Minutes of the Board of Inspectors, February 24, 1823 and March 15, 1830.

74. Minutes of the Acting Committee of the Prison Society, January 10, 1814: "73 men are confined to the east wing, 47 of whom are Negroes." (HSP)

75. *A True and Correct Account of the Prison of the City and County of Philadelphia* (Philadelphia, 1820).

76. Pennnsylvania Prison Society, Acting Committee, Minutes, January 8, 1821. Document reprinted in *Report on the Penitentiary system made to the Senate of Pennsylvania* (Philadelphia, 1821).

77. Boston Prison Discipline Society, *Fifth Annual Report*, 1830, 33, cited by Teeters, *Cradle*, 107.

78. Minutes of the Board of Inspectors, August 2, 1819.

79. Minutes of the Acting Committee of the Prison Society, April 10, 1820 (HSP).

80. The facts of Branagan's life are taken from his own account, which he first published in *The Penitential Tyrant* (New York, 1807) and later reprinted with minor changes in *A Beam of Celestial Light* (Philadelphia, 1813) and *The Guardian Genius of the Federal Union* (New York, 1839). He refers to the beggars of Dublin in *Avenia* (Philadelphia, 1805). Most of his writings are at the Historical Society of Pennsylvania.

81. *Guardian Genius*, 18.

82. *Preliminary Essay* (Philadelphia, 1804), 182.

83. *Guardian Genius*, 20.

84. .\venia, 15–16. The "Columbian strain" refers, as Branagan's notes make clear, to renewed American participation in the slave trade.

85. That is the opinion of Lewis Leary, expressed in "Thomas Branagan: Republican Rhetoric and Romanticism in America," *Pennsylvania Magazine of History and Biography* 77:3 (July 1953): 332–52.

86. Gary Nash, *Forging Freedom: The Formation of Philadelphia's Black Community, 1720–1840* (Cambridge, Mass., 1988), 176. Nash cites the *New York Evening Post*, July 10 and 12, 1804 for the reference.

87. There is some discrepancy regarding the sequence in which Branagan's books were written. In the text of his article Leary lists in order *A Preliminary Essay* (1804), *Avenia*, *Penitential Tyrant*, and *Serious Remonstrances* (all 1805).

He says *PT* appeared in time for the 1805 Missouri debate over the status of new states admitted to the Union; I have no idea what he is referring to. However, his footnotes cite the 1807 edition. Nash gives the same order, but does not mention *PT*. He correctly criticizes Leary for casting Branagan as a consistent friend of abolitionism, although he mistakenly says that Leary omitted mention of *SR*. (Leary spends a page on it; had he been unaware of it, his error would be less serious.) Branagan himself, in his 1839 memoir, listed in order *PE*, *Avenia*, *SR*, and then a new edition of *PT*, 300 pages, published "before the all-important Missouri question was decided in Congress...and at the very time the British parliament were making arrangements for the abolition of slavery in their colonies." He could have been referring to the abolition of the slave trade in the British colonies, which took place in 1807. Nash is apparently unaware of the 1839 memoir. The Historical Society possesses only the 1807 "enlarged" edition, which contains a twelve-page diatribe on Dessalines, and I have been unable to locate the first edition. The discrepancy matters only to those seeking to identify the moment of Branagan's turn.

88. *A Glimpse of the Beauties of Eternal Truth* (Philadelphia, 1817), 4–5, in Leary.

89. Shelley Fisher Fishkin, *Was Huck Black?: Mark Twain and African-American Voices* (New York, 1993).

90. *Mark Twain's Letters to Publisher, 1867–1894*, Hamlin Hill, ed. (Berkeley, 1967), 174.

## III ◆ THE TRANSUBSTANTIATION OF AN IRISH REVOLUTIONARY

1. *The Correspondence of Daniel O'Connell* (Dublin, 1972) VI, letter 2,499: 128–30.

2. John Binns, *Recollections*, (Philadelphia, 1854) 14–23.

3. *Recollections*, 24–28.

4. *Recollections*, 52–3.

5. That label is, of course, ideological, excluding as it does earlier organizations of slaves, transported felons, and convicts. For a history of the London Corresponding Society, see E. P. Thompson, *The Making of the English Working Class* (New York, 1963).

6. *Recollections*, 41–2, 45.

7. *Recollections*, 55–6. Although the Society disclaimed responsibility for the incident, one member boasted to Binns that he had climbed on the carriage and attempted to assault the King.

8. *Recollections*, 66.

9. *White-Jacket*, ch. 36.

10. Thompson, *Making*, 166–70.

11. *Recollections*, 76.

12. Thompson, *Making*, 171.

13. *Recollections*, 85–9, 90, 93, 101–07, 133, 140.

14. *Recollections*, 143–5, 150.

15. *Recollections*, 157.

16. *Recollections*, 164.

17. Edward C. Carter II, "A 'Wild Irishman' Under Every Federalist's Bed: Naturalization in Philadelphia, 1789–1806," *Pennsylvania Magazine of History and Biography* XCIV: 3 (July, 1970): 331–46.

18. William Cobbett, *Detection of a Conspiracy formed by the United Irishmen, with the Evident Intention of Aiding the Tyrants of France in Subverting the Government of the United States* (Philadelphia, May 6, 1798). Cited in "A 'Wild Irishman'."

19. Carter notes that Cobbett's pamphlet was published before the Rising of '98, and three months before news of it appeared in the Philadelphia papers.

20. Carter, "A Wild Irishman." There is an error in the statistics given on p. 339: the figure 45% should read 65%.

21. Carter, "A Wild Irishman."

22. *Recollections*, 168–9.

23. Duane was U.S.-born, but had been taken to Ireland as a child, and grew up there. Binns and Duane had met in London in 1795. For information about Duane, see Kim Tousley Phillips, "William Duane, Revolutionary Editor" (Ph.D. dissertation, University of California, Berkeley, 1968). Jefferson had called the *Aurora* "our comfort in the gloomiest days" and "the rallying point for the Orthodox of the whole union." Charles Sellers, *The Market Revolution: Jacksonian America 1815–1846* (New York, 1991), 122.

24. *Recollections*, 170–1, 176–7, 196. There is a slight discrepancy in Binns's account. He gives the date of the *Argus*'s appearance as 1802, but internal evidence suggests it was 1803.

25. *Memoirs*, IV: 529 (February 20, 1820).

26. Jefferson to W. T. Barry, July 3, 1822, cited Phillips, "The Pennsylvania Origins," 500.

27. Quoted in Richard H. Brown, "The Missouri Crisis, Slavery, and the Politics of Jacksonianism," *South Atlantic Quarterly*, 65: 1 (Winter 1966): 55–72.

28. Edward S. Abdy, *Journal of a Residence and Tour in the United States of North America, from April, 1833, to October, 1834* (London, 1835) II: 9.

29. Marx and Engels, *The Civil War in the United States* (New York, 1961), 280–1.

30. Richard Hofstadter, *The American Political Tradition* (New York, 1974), 114.

31. Any of several Philadelphia figures might have served as the chronicler's Stephen Dedalus. Like Binns, William Duane supported the London Corresponding Society; in the U.S. he defended the Fries rebels, took part in a 1796 protest against the Alien Laws, organized a largely Irish militia with Jacobin sympathies, and was tried for sedition in 1799. Unlike Binns, he sided with the shoemakers in 1806, denouncing the tyranny that made them "a breed of white slaves." In 1814, he confessed that he thought slavery "congenial" to the African temperament. More radical than Binns, he spearheaded the Jackson campaign in 1822 and remained a Jackson loyalist; however, he died before the O'Connell affair took place. Another candidate was James Reynolds, the United Irish physician, author of the first utopian socialist tract written in America; but he, too, died before the stew of Irish-American attitudes toward slavery reached boil. An account of various figures is Richard Twomey, *Jacobins and Jeffersonians: Anglo-American Radicalism in the United States 1790–1820* (New York, 1989).

32. *Jacobins and Jeffersonians*, 179.

33. *Memoirs of John Quincy Adams*, ed. Charles Francis Adams. 12 vols. (Philadelphia, 1875) V: 112 (May 12, 1820). Adams mistakenly identifies Binns as an Englishman.

34. *Recollections*, 206.

35. Philip S. Klein, *Pennsylvania Politics 1817–1832: A Game Without Rules* (Philadelphia, 1940), 100.

36. *Report of the Committee Appointed by the House of Representatives to Inquire into the Conduct of the Governor*, quoted in Klein, *Pennsylvania Politics*, 104–5.

37. *Recollections*, 251–2.

38. Steinberg, *Transformation of Criminal Justice*, 17, 40.

39. *Recollections*, 254–5. In his memoirs Binns insisted that he did not use the aldermanic position to enrich himself. Steinberg upholds Binns's claim, calling him "a model of the honest, responsible alderman, a servant of the public interest in the eighteenth-century tradition of the elite magistrate—a man of means or talent administering laws disinterestedly, identified wholly with the law and the corporation of the city." *Transformation*, 40.

40. Steinberg, *Transformation*, 40.

41. *Recollections*, 245–6.

42. *Recollections*, 253, 255.

43. McCormick, *Party Formation*, 134, 147.

44. Steinberg, *Transformation*, 17.

45. M. Lisle to George Bryan, January 23, 1823. Bryan Papers, Historical Society of Pennsylvania. Cited in Klein, *Pennsylvania Politics*, 53.

46. *Jacobins and Jeffersonians,* 101; *Recollections*, 97–98, 279.

47. *An Oration Commemmorative of the Birth-Day of American Independence, Delivered before the Democratic Societies of Philadelphia on the 4th of July, 1810* (Philadelphia, 1810), cited in *Jacobins and Jeffersonians*, 95.

48. *Jacobins and Jeffersonians*, 202, 163.

49. *Democratic Press,* January 13, 1813.

50. *Democratic Press*, December 22, 1819. The article was written by Tench Coxe, a New School leader, merchant and manufacturer, who wrote frequently for the paper and regularly assumed editorial charge when Binns was on the road. The article concluded with the customary disclaimer, "I am no friend to slavery; I wish from my soul it were abolished."

51. *Recollections*, 74.

52. *Hazard's Register*, September 1834, 200–203.

53. *Recollections*, 322–25.

54. *Recollections*, 207.

55. Lee Benson, *The Concept of Jacksonian Democracy* (New York, 1969), 165–80, 317–28. What was true of New York was true of Philadelphia. See Peter B. Sheridan, "The Immigrant in Philadelphia, 1827–1860: The Contemporary Published Report," (Ph.D. dissertation, Georgetown University, 1957), 215–18.

56. *Freeman's Journal*, April 10, 1805, cited in Francis V. Cabeen, "The Society of the Sons of St. Tammany of Philadelphia," *Pennsylvania Magazine of History and Biography*, XXVII (1903): 45.

57. Philadelphia *Bulletin*, June 29, 1847. Amy Bridges writes that "Nativist-labor complaints about immigrant labor 'competition' need to be understood" not as "the competition of those who will do one's own job, but [as] the competition of a labor force whose presence allows a reorganization of work." See *A City in the Republic: Antebellum New York and the Origins of Machine Politics* (Cambridge, Mass., 1984), 96.

58. *Affairs of Party: The Political Culture of Northern Democrats in the Mid-Nineteenth Century* (Ithaca, N.Y., 1983).

59. Nicholas B. Wainwright, ed. "Diary of Samuel Breck," *Pennsylvania Magazine* 102: 4 (October 1978): 505. Breck reports this fact in recounting a conversation he had with James Forten, whom he met on the street one day. Forten's career illuminates the meaning of race in America. The wealthiest black man in the city, he owned a sail-making enterprise, employed some twenty or thirty laborers, black and white, and was on good terms with conservative white leaders. He reported to Breck that he had directed the votes of fifteen of his white employees—surely a testimony to his power—yet he himself could not vote. To my knowledge, Forten was the last Afro-American entrepreneur (before Reginald Davis of Beatrice Foods) whose investments did not depend on a segregated market or whose capital did not originate from some specialized "Negro" field like entertainment or catering.

60. Edward R. Turner, *The Negro in Pennsylvania* (New York, 1911), 185–93.

61. *Report of the Debates and Proceedings of the Convention for the Revision of the Constitution of the State of New York*, 1846, 1,018. Cited in Kerby Miller, unpublished manuscript.

62. The following chronicle of Walsh's career is based on Robert Ernst, "The One and Only Mike Walsh," *New York Historical Society Quarterly* 36: 1 (January 1952): 42–65, and Sean Wilentz, *Chants Democratic: New York City and the Rise of the American Working Class, 1788–1850* (New York, 1984).

63. For Wilkes, see Saxton, *Rise and Fall*, ch. 9.

64. The antirent movement was headed by another Irishman, Thomas Devyr, and was anathema to Van Buren.

65. The Fourierists, also known as Associationists, were followers of the Frenchman Francois Charles Marie Fourier (1772–1837), who advocated producers' cooperatives as the alternative to private capitalist ownership. Brook Farm, in West Roxbury, Massachusetts, was a Fourierist colony; it was fictionalized in Hawthorne's *The Blithedale Romance* 1852.

66. Orig. pub. *Boston Quarterly Review*, reprinted in Leon Stein and Philip Taft, eds., *Religion, Reform, and Revolution: Labor Panaceas in the Nineteenth Century* (New York, 1969).

67. John R. Commons and Associates, *A Documentary History of American Industrial Society*, vol. 7 (New York, 1958) 356, 361, 362.

68. *A Documentary History*, 217, 218, 219. The abolitionist position was essentially that adopted by Marx when he wrote his often quoted words in the chapter on the working day, "In the United States of North America, every independent movement of the workers was paralysed so long as slavery disfigured a part of the Republic. Labour cannot emancipate itself in the white skin where in the black it is branded. But out of the death of slavery a new life at once arose. The first fruit of the Civil War was the eight hours' agitation...." But that was not the view of his U.S. followers, either then or earlier.

69. Calvin Colton, who wrote a plea for *The Rights of Labor* (New York, 1846) in which he put forward a labor theory of value, stated that "when the rights of labor are spoken of in this work, the labor of slaves does not come into consideration, any more than that of horses." He immediately added the customary disclaimer of any wish "to disparage a slave as a human being." Stein and Taft, *Religion, Reform, and Revolution*. Luther spoke of his travels in the South in *Address on the Origins of Avarice* (Boston, 1834). For information on his life, see Carl Gersuny, "Seth Luther—The Road from Chepachet," *Rhode Island History* 33 (May 1974): 47–55, Louis Hartz, "Seth Luther: Story of a Working-Class Rebel," *New England Quarterly* 13: 3 (September 1940): 401–18, and Edward Pessen, *Most Uncommon Jacksonians* (Albany, 1967), passim.

70. See Albert J. Cottrol, *The Afro-Yankees: Providence's Black Community in the Antebellum Era* (Westport, Conn., 1982), 53–57, 154–55.

71. *Liberator*, August 26, 1842.

72. *Liberator*, October 29, 1841.

73. *Liberator*, January 14, 1842.

74. *Liberator*, August 7, 1842.

75. A modern history of the Dorr Rebellion is a book of that title by Marvin E. Gettleman (New York, 1973), which presents a brief for the Dorrites. Robert J. Cottrol, in *Afro-Yankees*, manages to provide a more balanced picture in just a few pages.

76. *Afro-Yankees*, 77. Rhode Island was the only state where black people, having lost the right to vote, regained it prior to the Civil War. They were able to make use of it over the next two decades, particularly in Providence, where they sometimes constituted the balance of power in closely contested elections. An 1859 effort of black Rhode Islanders to desegregate the public schools became a factor in national politics. See Lawrence Grossman, "George T. Downing and Desegregation of Rhode Island Public Schools, 1855–1866," in *Rhode Island History* 36: 4 (November 1977) and James L. Huston, "The Threat of Radicalism: Seward's Candidacy and the Rhode Island Gubernatorial Election of 1860," *Rhode Island History* 41: 3 (August 1982).

77. Sidney G. Fisher, *A Philadelphia Perspective: The Diary of Sidney George Fisher Covering the Years 1834–1871*, ed. Nicholas B. Wainwright (Philadelphia, 1967), 162.

78. Melville prophesied doom, in *Mardi* (1849) and above all in *Moby Dick* (1851). For an interpretation of *Moby Dick* as Melville's comment on contemporary politics, see Alan Heimert, "*Moby Dick* and American Political Symbolism," *American Quarterly* XV (Winter 1963): 498–534. For the reaction by leading figures of the time to the crisis brought about by the Mexican War, and an elaboration of the parallels between the European and American "1848," see Michael Paul Rogin, *Subversive Genealogy: The Politics and Art of Herman Melville* (Berkeley, 1979), esp. ch. 4. Some have dated the breakup of the Jacksonian coalition to 1844, when Van Buren was denied the Democratic nomination for president because of his opposition to the immediate annexation of Texas as a slave state. See *Diary of Gideon Welles* (New York, 1960), vol. II, 387, cited in Eric Foner, *Free Soil, Free Labor, Free Men: The Ideology of the Republican Party Before the Civil War* (New York, 1970), 151.

79. *Congressional Globe*, 29th Congress, 1st Session, Appendix, 317.

80. For a discussion of the relation of Free-Soilism (and later Republicanism) to abolition, see Albert Fried, *John Brown's Journey: Notes and Reflections on His America and Mine* (New York, 1978), 171–207.

81. Brooklyn *Daily Eagle*, May 6, 1858. Whitman had earlier declared his admiration for Calhoun, illustrating perfectly the continuity between proslavery and free-soil sentiments. See Lorenzo D. Turner, "Walt Whitman and the Negro," *Chicago Jewish Forum* 15 (Fall 1956). The Free-Soil movement was so committed to excluding Afro-Americans from the territories that it failed even to appreciate their importance to its own project. For example, Free-Soilers

rejected Frederick Douglass's advice that the settlement of a few hundred free black families in Kansas would build a "wall of fire" against slavery. The Civil War would reveal who was more realistic, the "practical" men who sought to restrict slavery without enlisting the Negro in the battle, or the abolitionists.

82. *Providence Journal*, November 6, 1848, cited in *Afro-Yankees*, 88.

83. Wittke, *The Irish in America*, 62; George Potter, *To the Golden Door*, 533. Both writers furnish information about Irish-American farming settlements, and the efforts to promote them.

84. Cited in Cynthia J. Shelton, *The Mills of Manayunk: Industrialization and Social Conflict in the Philadelphia Region, 1787–1837* (Baltimore, 1986), 98.

85. On the colonization project and Hughes's opposition, see Wittke, *The Irish in America*, 67–70 and Potter, *To the Golden Door*, 540–47.

86. The Free-Soil movement also had its inner tensions: many of the Republican Party capitalists who wished to exclude slavery from the Western territories had no interest in seeing their wage slaves leave in droves to become farmers, thereby driving up the costs of labor in the east. See Fred A. Shannon, "The Homestead Act and the Labor Surplus," *American Historical Review* 41 (1936): 637–651, reprinted in Vernon Carstensen, ed. *The Public Lands: Studies in the History of the Public Domain* (Madison, Wisc., 1963), 297–313. It would be possible to write a history of class struggle over free land, often assuming the form of quarrels over the "Indian question," going back to Governor Berkeley of Virginia and including John Quincy Adams and the National Republicans. For a suggestive treatment, see Alexander Saxton, *Rise and Fall*, ch. 1.

87. Clarence H. Danhof, "Farm-Making Costs and the 'Safety Valve': 1850–1860," *Journal of Political Economy*, vol. 49 (1941): 317–59, reprinted in Carstensen, *The Public Lands*, Ficklin was overly optimistic; by 1890, the federal government had distributed more than four times as much land to the railroads as it gave to farming settlers. See Shannon, "The Homestead Act," 298, 303.

88. New York *Evening Day Book*, January 26, 1860, cited by Kerby Miller, unpub. ms.

89. *Metropolitan Record*, January 26, 1863, cited by Miller.

90. Charles Fanning, ed., *The Exiles of Erin: Nineteenth-Century Irish-American Fiction* (Notre Dame, Ind., 1987), 146.

91. Cited by Kerby Miller, unpub. ms.

92. The best account and analysis of the riots is Iver Bernstein, *The New York City Draft Riots: Their Significance for American Society and Politcs in the Age of the Civil War* (New York, 1990).

## IV ❧ THEY SWUNG THEIR PICKS

1. John McElgun, *Annie Reilly: or, The Fortunes of an Irish Girl in New York*.

*A Tale Founded on Fact* (New York, 1873) in Fanning, ed., *The Exiles of Erin.*

2. H. B. C. Pollard, *The Secret Societies of Ireland: Their Rise and Progress* (London, 1922), 38. Pollard, who was on the staff of the chief of police of Ireland, provides valuable information from the policeman's point of view. Modern histories are Michael Beames, *Peasants and Power: The Whiteboy Movements and Their Control in Pre-Famine Ireland* (New York, 1983) and T. Desmond Williams, ed., *Secret Societies in Ireland* (New York, 1973), a collection including "The Ribbonmen" by Joseph Lee, who provides statistics for eruptions of Ribbonism and argues that the main agrarian conflicts occurred not between landlords and farmers but between laborers and cottiers on one side and farmers on the other, suggesting the market orientation of agriculture and the affinity between Ribbonism and trade unionism.

3. William Forbes Adams, *Ireland and Irish Emigration to the New World from 1815 to the Famine* (New Haven, 1932), 178, cited by Jean Hurley, "The Irish Immigrant in the Early Labor Movement 1820–1862" (Master's Thesis, Columbia University, 1959), 22. The most complete study of the canal is Walter S. Sanderlin, *The Great National Project: A History of the Chesapeake and Ohio Canal* (Baltimore, 1946). Peter Way's book, *Common Labour: Workers and the Digging of North American Canals 1780–1860* (Cambridge, England, 1993) is the definitive work on canal labor; I came across it after having completed the research for this study, and have in several places noted where it elaborates on points I am making.

4. Richard B. Morris, "Andrew Jackson, Strikebreaker," *American Historical Review* vol. 55, no. 1 (October 1949): 54–68.

5. *Niles Weekly Register*, November 29 and December 20, 1834, January 31, 1835, cited by Hurley, "The Irish Immigrant," 24–25.

6. Morris, "Andrew Jackson;" Sanderlin, *The Great National Project*, 117–22; Hurley, "The Irish Immigrant," 28.

7. W. David Baird, "Violence Along the Chesapeake and Ohio Canal: 1839," *Maryland Historical Magazine*, vol. 66, no. 2 (Summer 1971): 121–34; Sanderlin, *The Great National Project*, 122.

8. John R. Commons and Associates, *History of Labour in the United States* (New York, 1966), I: 416.

9. William A. Sullivan, *The Industrial Worker in Pennsylvania 1800–1840* (Harrisburg, 1955), 152.

10. Commons, *History of Labour*, I: 416–17.

11. *New York Tribune*, July 15, 1841; *Boston Pilot*, August 27, September 3, 1842, cited by Hurley, "The Irish Immigrant," 30–32.

12. Hurley, "The Irish Immigrant," 29.

13. Way lists fifty-seven strikes on U.S. and Canadian canals, plus ninety-three incidents of riot, faction fighting, and civil unrest, between 1827 and 1853.

*Common Labour*, 287–95.

14. Way reports that south of Maryland "slave labor was the norm...throughout the period of canal construction," and that slaves and "white" laborers were both employed on the James River canal in the 1840s and 1850s (*Common Labour*, 88, 192). Sanderlin reports that stockholders on the C&O rejected purchasing slaves to work on the canal, but that did not prevent individual contractors from using them (*The Great National Project*, 116). For a discussion of strikes among slaves, see George P. Rawick, *From Sundown to Sunup: The Making of the Black Community* (Westport, Conn., 1972), chapter 6.

15. "The origins [in Ireland] of county feuds are unclear," writes Way, "but they may have resulted from conflict between agricultural workers of one county and transient blackleg labourers from another who competed for limited harvest jobs." Referring to the feud between Corkonians and those known as Fardowners (from the west coast province of Connaught), he writes, "This particular feud had not been heard of in Ireland, however, but was something new, bred on canals where workers, the majority of whom came from these two regions, were placed in direct competition for jobs" *Common Labour*, 193–94).

16. Paul A. Gilje, *The Road to Mobocracy: Popular Disorder in New York City, 1763–1834* (Chapel Hill, 1987), 137.

17. Robert Ernst, *Immigrant Life in New York City 1825–1863* (New York, 1949), 106, 107.

18. The foregoing argument draws on David Roediger, *Wages of Whiteness: Race and the Making of the American Working Class* (London and New York, 1991), chapter 2.

19. *African Repository* IV (June 1828), 118. Under the caste system, no black person could be free even in the limited sense most whites were. "The most miserable of bone-gatherers—the most oppressed of weavers, thank their God that they are not *slaves*. The one can gather bones, when he pleases, and go where he pleases to do it. The other can *strike*, and at least remind the despot that he is a *man*—and neither can be slaughtered with rifles nor torn to pieces with bloodhounds." ("E. H. C.," "Life in Philadelphia. By a Philadelphian," *Baltimore Saturday Visitor*, March 22, 1846, reprinted in *Herald of Freedom* [Concord, N.H.], April 24, 1846.) While "E. H. C." was right in one sense, the effects of racial caste were so severe that it is doubtful whether the social distance between the free (black) bone-gatherer and the slave was greater than that between the bone-gatherer and the (white) weaver.

20. W. E. B. Du Bois, *Black Reconstruction in America: An Essay Toward a History of the Part Which Black Folk Played in the Attempt to Reconstruct Democracy in America, 1860–1880* (New York, 1935), 13.

21. In the South, where hiring out of slaves was a common practice, the slaveholders opposed white labor's attempts to erect barriers to the employment of slaves in skilled occupations. Because the color bar never established

two totally separate labor markets, any improvement in the wages of one sector of the labor force would tend to generate upward wage pressure from other sectors. Hence the slaveholders had an interest in depressing the wages of white labor as well as black, which explains why their sympathy for Northern white labor did not go beyond using its plight to argue the superiority of chattel over wage slavery as a system appropriate for all labor. See George Fitzhugh, *Cannibals All, or Slaves Without Masters* (Cambridge, Mass., 1960). Like the slaveholders, the abolitionists recognized the connection between slavery and the condition of the free laborer.

22. John Finch, *Notes of Travel in the United States,* (London, 1844), John R. Commons and Associates, *A Documentary History of American Industrial Society* (New York, 1958) VII: 60.

23. See for example, Leon F. Litwack, *North of Slavery: The Negro in the Free States, 1790–1860* (Chicago, 1961), 153–186.

24. See, for example, C. L. R. James, *The Black Jacobins: Toussaint L'Ouverture and the San Domingo Revolution* (New York, 1963).

25. Racial slavery means "not simply that some whites own black slaves, but that no whites are so owned; not simply that whites are by definition non-slaves, but that the poor and laboring non-slave-holding whites are by racial definition enslavers of black labor." (Theodore William Allen, "Class Struggle and the Origin of Racial Slavery: The Invention of the White Race," *Radical America* 9: 3 [May–June, 1975]). In 1830, 3,777 Negroes owned slaves (Lorenzo J. Greene and Carter G. Woodson *The Negro Wage Earner* [New York 1930], 11). The denial of citizenship rights to these men of property underscores the racial character of the society.

26. Turner, *The Negro in Pennsylvania*, 41.

27. Nash, *Forging Freedom*, 38. See also Ira Berlin, "The Revolution in Black Life," in Alfred F. Young, ed., *The American Revolution* (DeKalb, Ill., 1976), 349–82.

28. Du Bois estimated that "between 1790 and 1820 a very large portion, and perhaps most, of the artisans of Philadelphia were Negroes. "*The Philadelphia Negro: A Social Study* (New York, 1967), 33. That is an astonishing assertion, given that during those years black people made up about one-tenth of the city's population. Du Bois cites no source for his estimate, which is difficult to reconcile with figures from city directories. According to Gary Nash (*Forging Freedom*, 149) the proportions of black males who were artisans was 2.2 percent in 1795, 5 percent in 1811, and 6.8 percent in 1816. The problem is that the city directories recorded the occupations only of male heads of households; hence Nash's figures represent only a small portion of the city's black male population, about a third in 1795 and less in the latter two years, and do not include those who were still slaves or were living in dependent relations with former owners. The historian is advised to be cautious in rejecting any statement of fact made by Du Bois.

29. Tom W. Smith, "The Dawn of the Urban-Industrial Age", 172–73.

30. Nash, *Forging Freedom*, 144–45, and passim.

31. Theodore Hershberg, "Free Blacks in Antebellum Philadelphia: A Study of Ex-Slaves, Freeborn, and Socioeconomic Decline," *Journal of Social History* 5: 2 (Winter 1971–72): 183–209.

32. *Register of Trades of the Colored People in the City of Philadelphia and Districts* (Philadelphia, 1838), 1–8; *The Present State and Condition of the Free People of Color of the City of Philadelphia and Adjoining Districts* (Philadelphia, 1838), 10; *A Statistical Inquiry into the Condition of the People of colour of the city and districts of Philadelphia* (Philadelphia, 1849), 18.

33. Benjamin C. Bacon, *Statistics of the Colored People of Philadelphia* (Philadelphia, 1856), 15.

34. *Proceedings of the Ohio Anti-Slavery Convention* (Cincinnati, 1835), 19. Cited in William L. Katz, ed. *Eyewitness: The Negro in American History* (New York, 1967), 156.

35. "Letters to Anti-Slavery Workers and Agencies," *Journal of Negro History*, vol. 10 (July 1925): 408–419.

36. *Hazard's Register* IX: 361.

37. *Pennsylvanian*, January 10–15, 1845, cited by Charles H. Wesley, *Negro Labor in the United States 1850–1925: A Study in American Economic History,* 79.

38. Speech of Frederick Douglass, *Niles Register* XLVI: 441, cited in *Negro Labor*, 78.

39. For the South Carolina conspiracy, see *The Trial Record of Denmark Vesey* (Boston, 1970). Still the most comprehensive study of the movement of wage laborers in the Jacksonian Period is by John R. Commons and Associates.

40. John Ferral (sometimes spelled Farrell), prominent 1830s Philadelphia unionist and president of the National Trades' Union, was an Irish-born hand loom weaver, probably of Dissenting stock. Thomas Hogan of Philadelphia was elected vice-president at the first convention of the National Trades' Union in New York in 1834. Robert Flanagan and John Donnell were officers of the Philadelphia Black and White Smiths.

41. Seth Luther, *An Address delivered before the Mechanics and Working-men of the City of Brooklyn on the Celebration of the Sixtieth Anniversary of American Independence* (Brooklyn, 1836), 18–20; letter of John Ferral to Luther, June 22, 1835, Commons, *Documentary History* 6: 41.

42. *Boston Courier*, June 4, 1835, Commons, *History of Labour* I: 417.

43. *Niles Register*, XLVIII (June 6, 1835): 235, quoted in Sullivan, *The Industrial Worker*, 153.

44. *Pennsylvanian*, June 3, 4, 1835.

45. *Saturday Evening Post*, June 10, 1835, cited by Sullivan, *The Industrial*

*Worker*, 135.

46. Letter to Seth Luther, Commons, *Documentary History* VI: 41.

47. *Pennsylvanian*, June 6, 1835, Sullivan, *The Industrial Worker*, 136–37.

48. *United States Gazette*, June 3, 1835; *Pennsylvanian*, June 22, 1835, *The Industrial Worker*, 137.

49. *The Industrial Worker*, 137.

50. *The Industrial Worker*, 155.

51. Bruce Laurie, *Working People of Philadelphia 1800–1850* (Philadelphia, 1980), 91.

52. Letter to Seth Luther, Commons, *Documentary History* VI: 42.

53. Commons, *History of Labour* I: 392–93. The six-to-six workday included an hour for breakfast and an hour for dinner.

54. *Mechanic's Free Press*, November 29, 1828.

55. *Pennsylvanian*, July 26, 1834.

56. Commons, *Documentary History* VI, 254.

57. Philip S. Foner, *History of the Labor Movement in the United States* (New York, 1947) I, 112.

58. Commons, *History of Labour* I, 377–78.

59. *The Industrial Worker*, 154–55.

60. *United States Gazette*, August 21, 1834.

61. Edward Magdol, *The Antislavery Rank and File* (Westport, Conn., 1986). John C. Calhoun admitted that only five percent of the people in the North approved of slavery. See Kraditor, *Means and Ends*, 195.

62. "American labor simply refused, in the main, to envisage black labor as a part of its problem. Right up to the edge of the war, it was talking about the emancipation of white labor and the organization of stronger unions without saying a word, or apparently giving a thought, to four million black slaves." (Du Bois, *Black Reconstruction in America*, 29.)

63. *Mechanic's Free Press*, September 11, 1830. The paper was not above racial stereotyping, as for instance in a report of "Jonathan, a gentleman of sable hue," caught sleeping in the street by the watchman, who "proceeded to try the consistency of Jonathan's head with his rattle," which broke, "the head being rather harder...." (*Mechanic's Free Press*, November 8, 1828.)

64. *Address to the Workingmen of New England* (Boston, 1833).

65. *National Trades' Union*, March 12, 1836, cited by Lorman Ratner, *Powder Keg: Northern Opposition to the Antislavery Movement 1831–1840* (New York, 1968), 20–21.

66. *National Laborer*, September 13, 1836, Foner, *History*, I, 268.

67. *National Laborer*, September 17, 1836, Foner, *History*, 273.

68. Luther, *Address to Mechanics and Workingmen*.

69. *Congressional Globe*, 25th Congress, 3rd Session, Appendix, 237–241.

70. *Workingman's Advocate*, November 21, 1835, cited by Ratner, *Powder Keg*, 63.

71. Foner, *History*, I, 272. The verse is an example of how white labor activists appropriated the language of abolition for their own purposes. As David Roediger points out, they commonly railed against "white slavery" and "wage slavery," not as an expression of solidarity with the slave but as "a call to arms to end the inappropriate oppression of whites." See Roediger, *Wages of Whiteness*, 68; also Barry Goldberg, "Slavery, Race, and the Languages of Class: 'Wage Slaves' and White 'Niggers'," *New Politics* 11 (Summer 1991): 64–83.

72. What would proletarian abolitionism have looked like? It would have treated slavery like low wages, long hours, or any other grievance, as something to take action against. For starters, it would have called upon free workers to refuse to work with slaves or handle slave-grown cotton. Instead of pursuing that course, white workers tried to kill or maim slaves, refused to work alongside free Negroes, and boycotted the products of "colored labor." The difference, to take a line from Mark Twain, is like that between the lightning and the lightning-bug. "White-labor apologists" (the term is Theodore Allen's) have sought to establish the antislavery record of the (white) labor movement. The classic works of this school are Herman Schluter, *Lincoln, Labor and Slavery* (New York, 1913) and Bernard Mandel, *Labor: Free and Slave* (New York, 1955); a recent example is Herbert Shapiro, "Labor and Antislavery: Reflections on the Literature," *Nature, Society, and Thought*, vol. 2, no. 4 (October 1989). Melville's words are from *The Confidence-Man*, chapter 21.

73. Sterling D. Spero and Abram L. Harris, *The Black Worker* (New York, 1969), pp. 3–16.

74. Frederick Law Olmsted, *The Cotton Kingdom* (New York, 1861) I, 276.

75. Niehaus, *The Irish in New Orleans*, 44–47.

76. *The Irish in New Orleans*, 76.

77. *Statistical Inquiry*, 17, 18.

78. *Colored American*, July 28, 1838, cited in Edward Pessen, *Jacksonian America: Society, Personality and Politics* (Homewood, Ill., 1978), 43.

79. U.S. Census Manuscripts, 1855, Ernst, *Immigrant Life*, 69.

80. *Daily Sun*, November 10, 1849, cited by Bruce Laurie, *Working People*, 157.

81. Hershberg, "Free Blacks," 192.

82. *A Statistical Inquiry*, 18. As Greene and Woodson note, "Foreigners immigrating into this country went freely into all menial work except washing and

ironing, in which it seems that they could not compete with Negro women."
(*The Negro Wage Earner*, 3.)

83. *The Liberator*, March 16, 1860, cited in Philip S. Foner and Ronald L. Lewis, eds. *The Black Worker: A Documentary History from Colonial Times to the Present* (Philadelphia, 1978), I, 164.

84. Cited by Kerby Miller, unpub. ms., 41

85. Frederick Douglass, *Life and Times of Frederick Douglass; Written by Himself* (London, 1962), 298–99.

86. According to Carl Wittke, the term "Irish nigger" was commonly used to describe the lowliest sections of the Irish laboring class. (*The Irish in America*, 34.) Jonathan A. Gluckstein comments that "designating Irish immigrant canal or construction workers as 'white negroes' was a common means of dramatizing their exploitative working conditions..." (*Concepts of Free Labor in Antebellum America* [New Haven, 1991], 340.)

87. As the National [Black] Convention of 1848 in Cleveland declared, "such [menial] employments have been so long and universally filled by colored men, as to become a badge of degradation, in that it has established the conviction that colored men are only fit for such employments."

88. See Wesley, *Negro Labor*, chapter 1; Robert William Fogel and Stanley L. Engerman, *Time on the Cross: The Economics of American Negro Slavery* (Boston, 1974), 38–43; Roger Shugg, *Origins of Class Struggle in Louisiana* (L.S.U. Press, 1939), 88–92; Robert S. Starobin, *Industrial Slavery in the Old South* (London, 1970), passim.

89. Hasia Diner provides an example of this cultivated amnesia. She writes, "Much of the Irish hostility against blacks in...the antebellum North...sprang from the fear that black women might challenge the Irish monopoly in domestic service." (*Erin's Daughters in America: Irish Immigrant Women in the Nineteenth Century* [Baltimore, 1983], 92.) There is only one other, equally nonspecific, reference to black women in the book.

90. *Negro Labor*, 77.

91. Shelton, *The Mills of Manayunk*, 54, 55, 90.

92. Philip Scranton, *Propietary Capitalism: The textile manufacture at Philadelphia 1800–1855* (Philadelphia, 1983), 257. Scranton attributed the preponderance of Irish in unskilled jobs in part to their greater youth.

93. For the first four decades of the nineteenth century, Philadelphia was more important than Boston as a port of arrival for immigrants from Britain. Shelton argues that, in contrast to New England, where mill owners recruited from a relatively scarce labor pool in the rural hinterland, the abundance in Philadelphia of immigrant skilled labor retarded the introduction of the power-loom (and also explains why Manayunk manufacturers had no need for the paternalism that was a well-known feature of the Lowell mills). According to

Shelton, several factors in the 1820s overcame the resistance to new methods, but the labor force continued to be drawn from the same regions as before. See *The Mills of Manayunk*, chapters 2 and 3.

94. For documented descriptions, see *The Mills of Manayunk*, chapter 3.

95. The literature on the formation of the industrial labor force in the antebellum period rarely addresses the relation between the labor market and race, and even the studies of the Irish immigrant generally take for granted the presence of Irish and the absence of black workers in the new industries. One study I found suggestive is Ezra Mendelsohn, *Class Struggle in the Pale: The Formative Years of the Jewish Workers' Movement in Tsarist Russia* (Cambridge, 1970), 19–23, which examines the question, "Why were Jews not employed at the mechanized factories?"

96. On race discrimination in Southern textile mills, see Broadus Mitchell, *The Rise of Cotton Mills in the South* (Baltimore, 1921).

97. Hershberg, "Free Blacks," 191

98. From time to time, arguments were made that the Negro was at least equal, if not superior, to others for factory work. Thomas P. Jones, an Englishman who had lived in the South, delivered an address at the Franklin Institute in Philadelphia in 1827, in which he declared people of African descent "peculiarly suited" to manufacture, because "only a small degree of intelligence is necessary to the acquisition of the utmost skill in the performance of an individual operation" and because they had the propensity to imitate and enjoyed being confined to one simple operation. Robert Dale Owen, in an 1848 address before a mercantile audience in Cincinnati, noted that "the operations now performed by factory workers are chiefly of a simple and mechanical kind demanding no special exertion of intellect...a Southern slave of ordinary intelligence can readily be taught to perform them." (Cited in Gluckstein, 415, 159) The political economist Francis Bowen argued that because of "the rude labor" to which they had been accustomed, "Foreigners generally, and the Irish in particular, cannot be employed at all" in the factory, "except in that small proportion to the total number of hands which will make it possible to restrict them to the lower or less difficult tasks." (Quoted by Stephan Thernstrom, *Poverty and Progress* [New York, 1978], 101.) Of course the white factory laborers—who had a direct interest in ascertaining the truth of the Negro's capacity—had no illusions on that score, as witnessed by their unwilligness to leave the matter to free and open competition.

99. "[T]he white workmen...were by training better workmen on the average than Negroes; they were stronger numerically and the result was that every new industrial enterprise started in the city took white workmen. Soon the white workmen were strong enough to go a step further than this and practically prohibit Negroes from entering trades under any circumstances....Thus partially by taking advantage of race prejudice, partially by greater economic efficiency and partially by the endeavor to maintain and raise wages, white

workmen have...monopolized the new industrial opportunities...." (Du Bois, *The Philadelphia Negro*, 126.)

100. "The factory contributed to, indeed enhanced, the economic and social marginalization of blacks in nineteenth-century America. Instead of finding employment in the newer industrial sector of the economy, blacks were generally relegated to older occupations....This exclusion from the increasingly important industrial sector of the economy meant exclusion from many of the dynamic forces that were shaping nineteenth-century American society....Exclusion from the factory had important economic and occupational effects, but it may have had even more important social consequences." (Cottrol, *The Afro-Yankees*, 151–52.)

101. Speaking of the period after 1850, Herbert Hill writes, "European immigrants made [use] of labor unions to become assimilated and develop as a privileged section of the working class." ("Race, Ethnicity and Organized Labor: The Opposition to Affirmative Action," *New Politics*, vol. 1, no. 2 [Winter 1987]: 31–82.) "By 1900 Irish immigrants or their descendants held the presidencies of over 50 of the 110 unions in the AFL." (Stephan Thernstrom, ed., *Harvard Encyclopedia of American Ethnic Groups*, [Cambridge, Mass., 1980], 538). For the period since the Civil War, see also David Montgomery, "The Irish and the American Labor Movement," in David Noel Doyle and Owen D. Edwards, *America and Ireland, 1776–1976* [Westport, Conn., 1980], 205–18.

102. Hurley, "The Irish Immigrant," 121, 122; Amy Bridges, *A City in the Republic: Antebellum New York and the Origins of Machine Politics*, (Ithaca, 1987), 99, 100, 183.

103. Hurley, "The Irish Immigrant," 95.

104. *Irish American*, November 20, 1852, cited by Ernst, *Immigrant Life*, 73.

105. U.S. Census Manuscripts, 1855. [Ernst 66, 214–17]

106. Oscar Handlin, *Boston's Immigrants* (New York, 1967), 252, 253.

107. Dennis Clark *Erin Heir's: Irish Bonds of Community* (Lexington, Kentucky, 1991), 54.

108. Bruce Laurie, George Alter, Theodore Hershberg, "Immigrants and Industry: The Philadelphia Experience, 1850–1880," Theodore Hershberg, ed., *Philadelphia: Work, Space, Family, and Group Experience in the Nineteenth Century* (New York, 1981), 109–11.

109. *Emigrants and Exiles*, 318.

110. *Emigrants and Exiles*, 319.

111. Frank J. Webb, *The Garies and Their Friends* (London, 1857, repr. New York, 1969), 297–98. Philip S. Lapsansky makes the point that *The Garies* "is not an antislavery novel, rather it is an anti-racist work, and the first novel to deal with race relations and colorphobia in the urban north." Although the novel was published in England shortly after it was written, with a preface by Harriet

Beecher Stowe, its first American edition was not until 1969, perhaps because its author was Afro-American, perhaps because, as Lapsansky notes, "most antislavery Americans of the time were not prepared to confront the issues of northern racism and colorphobia raised in the novel." (*Annual Report of the Library Company of Philadelphia* [Philadelphia, 1990], 28, 29.)

112. Anna Dickinson, *What Answer?* (New York, 1868), 11, 60, 299.

113. *Life and Times* (London, 1962), 210–11.

114. M. Ray Della, Jr., "The Problems of Negro Labor in the 1850's," *Maryland Historical Magazine*, vol. 66, no. 1 (Spring 1971): 14–32.

115. Alban P. Man, Jr., "Labor Competition and the New York Draft Riots of 1863," *Journal of Negro History* (vol. 36, no. 4,): 375–401; Wittke 126; Basil Leo Lee, *Discontent in New York City, 1861–1865* (Washington, 1943) 139–41; *Liberator*, August 8, 1862; New York *Tribune*, August 6, 1862; Williston H. Lofton, "Northern Labor and the Negro," *Journal of Negro History*, vol. 34, no. 3, 251–273; *Douglass' Monthly* (September 1863).

116. James D. Burn, *Three Years Among the Working Classes in the United States During the War* (London, 1865), xiv.

117. *Herald*, March 31, April 16, 1853; Foner, *The Black Worker*, 190.

118. "Although trade-unions exerted a minor influence on antebellum workers, they occasionally voiced labor's principal demands, aspirations, and prejudices." Litwack, *North of Slavery*, 159.

119. Bernstein, *New York City Draft Riots*, 120; *Tribune*, November 6, 1850, January 23, 1855, August 1, 1862; April 14, 1863; Albon P. Man, "Labor Competition"; Ernst, *Immigrant Life*, 108.

120. Bruce Laurie, *Working People*, 157–58.

121. David Brody, "Workers and Work in America," in James B. Gardner and George Rollie Adams, eds., *Ordinary People and Everyday Life: Perspectives on the New Social History* (Nashville, Tenn., 1983), 147. The story in Philadelphia, like that in New Orleans and some other ports, was more complicated than in New York. In those places, for a variety of reasons, the Irish were not strong enough to push black workers entirely off the docks, and were forced to accept some variant of job sharing, which to them was simply another tactic of white-interest unionism. See Eric Arnesen, *Waterfront Workers of New Orleans: Race, Class and Politics* (New York, 1991), which mistakenly labels the resultant armed truce "inter-racial solidarity."

## V ❧ THE TUMULTUOUS REPUBLIC

1. The *Pennsylvania Magazine of History and Biography* vol. 74, no. 3 (July 1955) contains an article by Roger Butterfield providing a summary of Lippard's life and a bibliography of his works. David S. Reynolds has written a

book about Lippard, and published a collection of Lippard's writings. He also discusses his work in *Beneath the American Renaissance: The Subversive Imagination in the Age of Emerson and Melville* (Cambridge, Mass., 1989), as does Richard Slotkin in *The Fatal Environment: The Myth of the Frontier in the Age of Industrialization, 1800–1890* (Middletown, Conn., 1985.) Lippard shared the common white labor-radical stance of pretending sympathy for the black slave while at the same time stressing the greater wrong done the white wage worker. In one of his novels he writes, "In the South, they drive stalwart Negroes to the cotton fields, and bid them labor, but they feed and clothe them well; nay in some cases the ebony-faced African is treated with the same kindness as the Planter's own child." (*The Nazarene* [Philadelphia, 1845], 166.)

2. For documentation of specifically racial events in Philadelphia during the period, see John M. Werner, *Reaping the Bloody Harvest: Race Riots in the United States During the Age of Jackson, 1824–1849* (New York, 1986), chapter 5. The following account draws on John M. Runcie, "'Hunting the Nigs' in Philadelphia: the Race Riot of 1834," *Pennsylvania History*, 39: 2 (April 1972): 187–218, and Philadelphia newspapers of the period, some of whose accounts were reprinted in *Hazard's Register* XIV (1834): 126–28. Antiblack riots in Philadelphia did not begin in 1834: Gary Nash cites examples back to 1815 (*Forging Freedom*, 213, 225, 227).

3. *United States Gazette*, August 14, 1834; *Hazard's Register*, August 23, 1834, 127.

4. See *National Gazette and Literary Register*, July 15, July 17, 1834; *Pennsylvania Inquirer and Daily Courier*, July 9, July 12, July 14, July 15, July 16, 1834; *Pennsylvanian*, July 9, July 11, July 14, July 15, 1834; *Pennsylvania Gazette and Universal Daily Advertiser*, July 12, July 14, 1834; *United States Gazette*, July 7, July 14, 1834. A treatment of the New York Riot is Linda K. Kerber, "Abolitionists and Amalgamators: the New York City Race Riots of 1834," *New York History* 48: 1 (January 1967): 28–39.

5. *United States Gazette*, August 21, 1834. In all likelihood the attackers included some of the men who, it will be recalled, became the heroes of the general strike six months later.

6. For the text of the report, see *Hazard's Register* XIV (1834): 200–203.

7. *Pennsylvania Gazette and Universal Daily Advertiser*, August 19, 1834; Edward S. Abdy, *Journal of a Residence and Tour in the United States of North America* (London 1835) vol. III, 325. Abdy had earlier recorded about the Boston Irish that "nearly all of them, who have resided there any length of time, are more bitter and severe against the blacks than the native whites themselves. It seems as if the disease were more virulent when taken by inoculation than in the natural way." (*Journal* I, 159.)

8. Emma Jones Lapsansky, "'Since They Got Those Separate Churches': Afro-Americans and Racism in Jacksonian Philadelphia," *American Quarterly* 32: 1 (Spring 1980): 54–78.

9. Annual Reports of the Union Benevolent Association, 1836–38, cited by Runcie, "Hunting the Nigs," 203.

10. *The Bank Director's Son* (Philadelphia, 1851), 13.

11. George Rogers Taylor, ed. "'Philadelphia in Slices,' by George G. Foster," *Pennsylvania Magazine of History and Biography* 93: 1 (January 1969): 23–72.

12. Emma Jones Lapsansky, "South Street Philadelphia, 1762–1854: 'A Haven for Those Low in the World,'" (Ph.D. dissertation, University of Pennsylvania, 1975), 133–5.

13. Lapsansky, "South Street," 226.

14. Benjamin Sewell, *Sorrow's Circuit, or Five Years' Experience in the Bedford Street Mission* (Philadelphia, 1859); and *The Homeless Heir; or Life in Bedford Street: A Mystery of Philadelphia*, by John, The Outcast (Philadelphia, 1856).

15. Dale Light, "Class, Ethnicity and the Urban Ecology in the Nineteenth-Century City: Philadelphia Irish 1840–1890" (Ph.D. dissertation, University of Pennsylvania, 1984), 29, 36.

16. Lapsansky, "South Street," 146.

17. Runcie, "Hunting the Nigs," 204.

18. I have been led to this view in part by reflecting on recent events in Howard Beach and Bensonhurst, New York City.

19. Michael Feldberg, *The Turbulent Era: Riot and Disorder in Jacksonian America* (New York, 1980), 4–5; David Grimsted, "Rioting in Its Jacksonian Setting," *American Historical Review* 77: 2 (April 1972): 361–97. There is a voluminous theoretical and documentary literature on rioting in Jacksonian America, much of it stimulated by events of the 1960s.

20. Karl Polanyi, *The Great Transformation* (Boston, 1957), 186.

21. Francis Grund, *The Americans in Their Moral, Social and Political Relations* (Boston, 1837), 180, cited in David Grimstead, "Rioting," 364–65. I do not claim that Madison *et al* or their successors were consciously applying Machiavelli's theories; it would take someone more familiar than I with the main currents of American thought to demonstrate that hypothesis. Perhaps they just stumbled by luck into a workable system.

22. Many before me have commented on the tendency of public officials to wink at certain kinds of mob violence: for example, Paul Gilje writes, "Magistrates expected the lower classes to blow off a little steam now and then. Indeed, rowdy behavior might even be seen as a form of social insurance." (*The Road to Mobocracy: Popular Disorder in New York City, 1763–1834* [Chapel Hill, 1987], 235.) Gilje's failure, and that of others, to note that permission to riot was granted only to those of the white skin suggests how deeply engraved psychologically the color line remains. (His assertion, immediately following the passage quoted above, "By August 1834, this belief no longer held," is not true for Philadelphia.) Here in the text I use the masculine pronoun generically; though barred by law from voting and by custom from rioting, white women

belonged to a community that did those things, and their membership in it determined their place more than the sex discrimination they suffered. They may not have rioted, but neither did their acts trigger any riots, except in one type of case, to be noted in the next chapter.

23. Michael Feldberg, *The Philadelphia Riots of 1844: A Study of Ethnic Conflict* (Westport, Conn., 1975), 10.

24. Scharf and Westcott, *History of Philadelphia,* III: 1779; David R. Johnson, *Policing the Urban Underworld: the Impact of Crime on the Development of the American Police, 1800–1887* (Philadelphia, 1979), 18, 21; John C. Schneider, "Community and Order in Philadelphia, 1838–1834," *Maryland Historian* 5: 1 (Spring 1974): 15–26.

25. *United States Gazette*, August 15, 1834.

26. *Pennsylvanian*, July 15, 1835.

27. *Hazard's Register* XVI (August 1835): 138–40. See also 163–65 and 188–89 in the same volume.

28. The following account is drawn largely from Werner, *Reaping the Bloody Harvest*, 188–200.

29. August Pleasonton diary, May 17, 1838. Historical Society of Pennsylvania.

30. Pleasonton diary, May 19, 1838.

31. Feldberg writes, "Of the thirteen persons arrested in the riot, all had Irish-sounding names and working class occupations." He admits this may say more about who was arrested than about who took part. See *Turbulent Era*, 51. Since the publication of Leonard L. Richards' *"Gentlemen of Property and Standing": Anti-Abolition Mobs in Jacksonian America* (London, 1970), it has become commonplace to attribute the burning of Pennsylvania Hall to those at the upper end of the income scale, yet *in this case* Richards offers no evidence to support his hypothesis. Julie Winch distinguishes between those who burned the Hall and those who attacked the Presbyterian Church and the orphanage on the two days following. See *Philadelphia's Black Elite: Activism, Accommodation and the Struggle for Autonomy, 1787–1848* (Philadelphia, 1988), 148, ftn. 210.

32. Pleasonton diary, June 8, 9, 10, 11, 12, 15, 1838.

33. Letter from Robert Smyth to his brother, William Smyth, County Antrim, courtesy Kerby Miller. The letter reads further: "The negroes were walking in a temperance procession with their banners displaying what we did not like.... There was from one to two thousand colored people in the procession about twelve o'clock a.m., and about 2 o'clock p.m. there was not the face of a single colored person to be seen in either our city or county. There was estimated about 5,000 whites in the mob and the massacre was dreadful....The white mob burned the first night property belonging to the colored people to the amount of 25,000 dollars consisting of their hall and one of their churches, which I think

was a shame to molest the temple of the Lord, though it belonged to those of high color."

34. *Liberator*, September 2, 1842.

35. *Journal of Commerce*, August 2, 1842, reprinted *Liberator*, August 12, 1842.

36. *Liberator*, August 12, 1842; Anthony Bimba, *The Molly Maguires* (New York, 1932), 39. These rioters from Pottsville may have been the fathers or grandfathers of some of labor's most famous martyrs.

37. *Journal of Commerce*, reprinted *Liberator*, August 26, 1842.

38. *Public Ledger*, reprinted *Liberator*, August 26, 1842.

39. Leonard P. Curry, *The Free Black in Urban America, 1800–1850* (Chicago, 1987), 107.

40. Werner, *Reaping the Bloody Harvest*, 223.

41. Feldberg, *Turbulent Era*, 39.

42. Steinberg, *Transformation of Criminal Justice*, 138.

43. *American and Gazette*, n.d.; *Daily Times*, November 22, 1849.

44. "The number of casualties in a Jacksonian riot... was a function of the resistance that crowds encountered while pursuing their aims....When rioters met resistance and a return of force,...they were far more likely to grow angered, employ deadly weapons, and seek the blood of their victims." (Feldberg, *Turbulent Era*, 49–50.)

45. See chapter 49 of the Third Book of the *Discourses*, the very last chapter, where Machiavelli explains that the admission of too many foreigners to the privileges of Roman citizenship destabilized the Republic. Again, I am not suggesting that the Founders consciously designed a republic ruled by the color line; but by the Jacksonian period every public official of a Northern city must have known that the one thing guaranteed to bring about his downfall would be to use cannon against white race rioters, or allow black people to arm in self-defense. The repression of the New York Draft Riots marked the beginning of a break with history, and Melville's poem hailing that repression ("The House-top") is unique in American literature.

46. *United States Gazette*, August 20, 1834.

47. Pleasonton diary, May 20, 1838.

48. Cecil Woodham-Smith, *The Great Hunger* (New York, 1962), 411–12.

49. MacManus, *The Story of the Irish Race*, 605.

50. Potter, *To the Golden Door*, 152.

51. Julie Winch, "Philadelphia and the Other Underground Railroad," *Pennsylvania Magazine of History and Biography* 111 (January 1987): 3–25.

52. Roi Ottley and William J. Weatherby, *The Negro in New York: An Informal Social History* (New York, 1969), 80–81.

53. Kate E. R. Pickard, *The Kidnapped and the Ransomed* (Syracuse, 1856), 246.

54. Scharf and Westcott, *History* I, 617.

55. C. Peter Ripley, ed. *The Black Abolitionist Papers, Volume III, the United States 1830–1846* (Chapel Hill, 1991), 38

56. William H. Siebert, *The Underground Railroad from Slavery to Freedom* (New York, 1898), 346; *8th Census of the U.S.*, 1860, xv–xvi, 338.

57. *Hazard's Register* XI (May 1833): 331–32; (June 1, 1833): 337–48.

58. *Hazard's Register* XIV (1834): 200–203.

59. Earl R. Turner, *The Negro in Pennsylvania*, 179, ftn. 181.

60. *Hazard's Register* IX: 77.

61. Gary Nash, *Forging Freedom*, 212. For the participation of black people (on both sides) of the American War of Independence, see Benjamin Quarles, *The Negro in the American Revolution* (Chapel Hill, 1961).

62. Peter B. Sheridan, "The Immigrant in Philadelphia, 1827–1860: The Contemporary Published Report" (Ph.D. dissertation, Georgetown University, 1957), 81–82; *Hazard's Register* IV: 3 (July 18, 1829): 45.

63. Scharf and Westcott, *History* I: 615; *United States Gazette*, 1825 (cited by Klein, *Pennsylvania Politics*, 34); *Mechanic's Free Press*, May 17, 1828.

64. Reminiscences of John Farrar, manuscript HSP.

65. Charles Godfrey Leland, *Memoirs* (New York, 1893), 216–217; Elizabeth M. Geffen, "Violence in Philadelphia in the 1840s and 1850s," *Pennsylvania History* 36: 4 (October 1969): 380–410. Virtually everyone who writes about working-class Philadelphia during the period makes mention of the fire companies. General accounts are Frank H. Schell, "Old Volunteer Fire Laddies, the Famous, Fast, Faithful, Fistic, Fire Fighters of Bygone Days," (unpub. manuscript in Frank H. Schell Papers, Historical Society of Pennsylvania) and Andrew H. Neilly, "The Violent Volunteers" (Ph.D. dissertation, University of Pennsylvania 1959). *Hazard's Register* IV: 18 (October 31, 1829), 285, lists forty-four companies in the city.

66. Scharf and Westcott, *History* III: 1906–07.

67. George Rogers Taylor, "Philadelphia in Slices"; Geffen, "Violence." David R. Johnson, *Policing the Urban Underworld* includes an appendix with an alphabetized list of fifty-two gangs, with the dates they appeared in the *Public Ledger*.

68. Steinberg, *Transformation*, 146.

69. *Life and Adventures of Charles Anderson Chester, the Notorious Leader of the Philadelphia "Killers"* (Philadelphia, 1850), 27–28. Lippard later reworked this novelette and published it under the title *The Bank Director's Son*.

## VI ❧ FROM PROTESTANT ASCENDANCY TO WHITE REPUBLIC

1. The standard work on the Philadelphia elite is E. Digby Baltzell,

*Philadelphia Gentlemen* (Glencoe, Ill., 1958).

2. The classic treatment of nativism is Ray Allen Billington, *The Protestant Crusade 1800–1860: A Study of the Origins of American Nativism* (New York, 1938); a good work, with an annotated bibliography, is Tyler Anbinder, *Nativism and Slavery: The Northern Know Nothings and the Politics of the 1850s* (New York, 1992).

3. George Lippard, *The Nazarene, or The Last of the Washingtons: A Revelation of Philadelphia, New York, and Washington, in the Year 1844* (Philadelphia, 1846), 166–168.

4. Frederick Engels, *The Condition of the Working-Class in England in 1844*, Marx-Engels *Collected Works*, 4:433–34.

5. Sam Bass Warner, Jr., *The Private City: Philadelphia in Three Periods of Its Growth* (Philadelphia, 1968), 144.

6. For the 1844 riots, see Michael Feldberg, *The Philadelphia Riots of 1844: A Study of Ethnic Conflict* (Westport, Conn., 1975); David Montgomery, "The Shuttle and the Cross: Weavers and Artisans in the Kensington Riots of 1844," *Journal of Social History* vol. 5, no. 4 (Summer 1972), 411–46; John Hancock Lee, *Origin and Progress of the American Party in Politics* (Philadelphia, 1855).

7. Scharf and Westcott, *History of Philadelphia* I, 623, call it "the first disturbance in the city or county in which race prejudice was manifested."

8. Feldberg, *The Philadelphia Riots*, 106. The account of the Kensington and Southwark riots relies on this work.

9. Both Sam Bass Warner in *The Private City* and Feldberg in *The Philadelphia Riots of 1844* view the 1844 riots as crucial moments. Warner identifies 1844 as the beginning of ethnic politics, and Feldberg provides an excellent account of the struggles between elite conservatives and modernizing industrialists over the new methods of policing.

10. *Public Ledger*, July 19, 1844; *Spirit of the Times*, July 9, 1844, both cited by Geffen, "Violence in Philadelphia."

11. Lee, *Origin and Progress*, 78, says one Irishman was killed.

12. August 15, 1843, cited in John C. Schneider, "Community and Order in Philadelphia, 1838–1848," *Maryland Historian*, vol. 5, no. 1 (Spring 1974), 15–26.

13. "Philadelphia Riots," facsimile, HSP.

14. Geffen, "Violence in Philadelphia."

15. *Public Ledger*, October 18, 1845, cited in David R. Johnson, *Policing the Urban Underworld* (Philadelphia, 1979), 29.

16. Steinberg, *Transformation*, 147.

17. Sidney George Fisher, *A Philadelphia Perspective: The Diary of Sidney George Fisher, 1834–1871*, Nicholas B. Wainwright, ed., (Philadelphia, 1967), 226.

18. The following account draws on Warner, *The Private City*, 210–12, and

Howard O. Sprogle, *Philadelphia Police Past and Present* (Philadelphia, 1887), 90–93.

19. Geffen, "Violence in Philadelphia."

20. *Public Ledger*, November 17, 1849, cited in Johnson, *Policing*, 32.

21. Warner, *The Private City*, 153–55.

22. The best account of consolidation and its relation to the development of the police is Steinberg, *Transformation*, 119–95.

23. Steinberg, *Transformation*, 171.

24. "Native Americanism," *Brownson's Quarterly Review* II (January 1845): 80–97, cited in Ira M. Leonard and Robert D. Parmet, *American Nativism, 1830–1860* (New York, 1971), 130.

25. "The Shuttle and The Cross," 421, 426. Montgomery's argument is ingenious and has been widely accepted, but it does not explain why working-class nativism reached its peak *after* the economic recovery had begun.

26. Fisher Diary, 177, 167.

27. Steinberg, *Transformation*, 151.

28. *Public Ledger*, November 12, 1853.

29. The only biography of McMullen is Harry C. Silcox, *Philadelphia Politics from the Bottom Up: The Life of Irishman William McMullen, 1824–1901* (Philadelphia, 1989), on which the following account draws.

30. Silcox, *Philadelphia Politics*, 36.

31. Letter, William McMullen to Samuel J. Randall, April 26 1875; May 24, 1876; July 23, 1879; December 30, 1880, Samuel J. Randall Collection, Special Collections, Van Pelt Library, University of Pennsylvania, cited in Silcox, *Philadelphia Politics*, ftn. 154.

32. The only full-length history is Robert Ryal Miller, *Shamrock and Sword: The Saint Patrick's Battalion in the U.S.-Mexican War* (Norman, Oklahoma, 1989).

33. Cited in William G. Bean, "An Aspect of Know Nothingism," *South Atlantic Quarterly* vol. 23, no. 4 (October 1924): 321. Bean and Anbinder, *Nativism and Slavery*, have most fully explored the link between Know Nothingism and anti-slavery. It should be noted, however, that however much the Whig Free Soil Republican opponents of slavery expansion allied themselves with nativist prejudices, the abolitionists themselves never sank to that level, even in their worst moments of exasperation. On the heels of the nativist riots in Philadelphia, Garrison had written, "The immediate cause of these frightful outbreaks is unquestionably to be attributed to the formation of the Native American Party—a party which should be discountenanced by every friend of human brotherhood....It was in Louisiana, among slaveholders, that this native party originated. They were fearful that the warm appeals of Daniel O'Connell and Father Mathew to the Irish in this country...would be heartily responded to by them....But the Irish have disregarded the noble entreaties of their coun-

trymen at home..., and 'verily, they have their reward.'" (*Liberator*, July 12, 1844.) Ten years later, on August 11, 1854, the *Liberator* published a letter from a Maine correspondent who wrote, "passage to the United States seems to produce the same effect upon the exile of Erin as the eating of the forbidden fruit did upon Adam and Eve. In the morning, they were pure, loving, and innocent; in the evening, guilty—excusing their fault with the plea of expecting advantage to follow faithfulness."

34. Anbinder, *Nativism and Slavery*, 54.

35. *Public Ledger*, June 15, 1855, cited David R. Johnson, *Policing the Urban Underworld*, 38.

36. Leonard and Parmet, *American Nativism*, 129–30.

37. Silcox, *Philadelphia Politics*, 49.

38. Sprogle, *Philadelphia Police*, 108, and David R. Johnson, "Crime Patterns in Philadelphia, 1840–1870" in Davis and Haller, *Peoples of Philadelphia*, 102.

39. Feldberg asserts (*Philadelphia Riots*, 190) that "riots declined in Philadelphia after 1854 because one group of potential rioters was usually wearing the uniform of a policeman." In fact, after 1856 both groups were simultaneously uniformed, and one group of their potential victims was not.

40. Grant's innovation, which has been called the invention of modern warfare, was anticipated by some of the campaigns in the wars of the French Revolution.

41. See Noel Ignatiev, "'The American Blindspot': Reconstruction According to Eric Foner and W. E. B. Du Bois," *Labour/Le Travail* 31 (Spring 1993): 243–51 for an elaboration of this point.

42. I am here appropriating Disraeli's famous intervention in the Darwinian debate.

43. The phrase is from the diary of businessman George W. Fahnestock, March 5, 1863, cited by Russell F. Weigley, "A Peaceful City": Public Order in Philadelphia from Consolidation Through the Civil War," Allen F. Davis and Mark H. Haller, eds. *The Peoples of Philadelphia: A History of Ethnic Groups and Lower-Class Life, 1790–1940* (Philadelphia, 1973), 166. For the attitudes of Philadelphia Democrats during the War, see also Fisher Diary, 431, 439, 451.

44. Weigley, "A Peaceful City," 164–65.

45. Fisher Diary, 439.

46. Weigley, "A Peaceful City," 165, 167–68.

47. For the city during the War see Weigley, "A Peaceful City," 155–173, and William Dusinberre, *Civil War Issues in Philadelphia, 1856–1865* (Philadelphia, 1965).

48. George Morgan, *The City of Firsts* (Philadelphia, 1926), 165.

49. See Philip Foner, "The Battle to End Discrimination Against Negroes on Philadelphia Street Cars," *Pennsylvania History* 40 (1973): 261–90.

50. Silcox, *Philadelphia Politics*, 70.

51. Geffen, "Violence in Philadelphia," 408.

52. Silcox, *Philadelphia Politics*, 71–72.

53. Steinberg, *Transformation*, 206.

54. Du Bois, *The Philadelphia Negro*, 372.

55. Sidney G. Fisher noted that universal suffrage was supported by Republicans (whom he considered conservative) and opposed by Democrats, "each contradicting thus the principles of its own party for the sake of partizan [*sic*] success, the Republicans, because they hope to gain the Negro vote in the South and elsewhere in the next elections, the Democrats, because if they advocated Negro suffrage they would lose the Irish vote." (Fisher Diary, 492)

56. Jonathan Weaver to Randall, September 29, 1870; D.I. Driscoll to Randall, June 8, 1870. Randall Collection, HSP, cited Silcox, *Philadelphia Politics*, 75.

57. *Bulletin*, October 12, 1870, cited *Philadelphia Politics*, 74.

58. *Press*, October 13, 1870, cited *Philadelphia Politics*, 75.

59. Steinberg, *Transformation*, 207.

60. Silcox, *Philadelphia Politics*, ch. 4.

61. Unlike other major U.S. cities which had corrupt, reactionary, Democratic boss rule, Philadelphia enjoyed for decades corrupt, reactionary, Republican boss rule, until it was ousted in 1950 by Democratic reformers headed by Richardson Dilworth and Joseph Clark. I believe that further research would show that the roots of this distinctiveness lay in the ability of the city's Republican Party to work out a satisfactory arrangement with the Irish after the white-supremacist riot of 1871.

62. Silcox, *Philadelphia Politics*, 96–97.

63. Silcox, *Philadelphia Politics*, 101, 85, 90–92. Silcox devotes a chapter to the relationship between the two. The Randall Collection at the University of Pennsylvania contains, among other things, 181 letters written by McMullen to Randall from 1864–1890, which cover local politics in detail, patronage matters, and personal and family affairs.

64. W. E. B. Du Bois, *Black Reconstruction in America*, 347.

65. C. Vann Woodward, *Reunion and Reaction* (second edition, revised: New York, 1956), 6. Although Woodward does much to enrich the historian's knowledge of the specific way in which the bargain was struck, his account does not invalidate that summary. The Compromise of 1877 was itself largely symbolic, because by that time the North had already turned its back on the Southern black voter; but that was by no means clear at the time.

66. Woodward, *Reunion and Reaction*, 194.

67. For a recounting of the methods that were used to conduct "free elections" in the South, see Du Bois, *Black Reconstruction*, ch. 16.

68. The combination of force and fraud to overthrow the Reconstruction regimes was famously known as the "Mississippi Plan," after the locale where it was first successfully implemented.

69. Silcox, *Philadelphia Politics*, 115.

70. Silcox, *Philadelphia Politics*, 147.

71. Silcox, *Philadelphia Politics*, 115–19.

72. *North American*, April 1, 1901, cited Silcox, *Philadelphia Politics*, 14.

## AFTERWORD

1. "Ideology and Race in American History," J. Morgan Kousser and James M. McPherson, *Region, Race and Reconstruction* (New York, 1982), 143–177.

2. The closest thing to them are the writings of Mathew Carey, especially *Essays on the Public Charities of Philadelphia* (Philadelphia, 1830).

3. First published in 1941 as volume L of the Harvard Historical Studies, revised and published in 1958 by Harvard University Press. The edition I have was published in 1976 in New York by Atheneum.

4. *Boston's Immigrants*, 133.

5. Carl Wittke, *The Irish in America*; Potter, *To the Golden Door*; Carl Ernst, *Immigrant Life in New York City*.

6. *The Irish in Philadelphia* (Philadelphia, 1973); *Erin's Heirs* (Lexington, Ky., 1991).

7. Dale T. Knobel, *Paddy and the Republic* (Middletown, Conn., 1986).

8. Old Left labor historians, notwithstanding valuable work they did on Afro-American history, never allowed the race question to interfere with their celebration of what they called the labor movement. For examples see Anthony Bimba, *The History of the American Working Class* (New York, 1927), Richard O. Boyer and Herbert M. Morais, *Labor's Untold Story* (New York, 1955), or the work of Philip S. Foner. The criticisms of Gutman's work I make here are not intended to invalidate his contributions to the field of Afro-American history, e.g., *The Black Family in Slavery and Freedom* (New York, 1976); the problem I am addressing is his failure to locate slavery and freedom in their proper place in the history of the working class in America.

9. Gutman's essay was first published in *The Negro and the American Labor Movement*, ed. Julius Jacobson (New York, 1970), and later republished in Herbert G. Gutman, *Work, Culture, and Society in Industrializing America* (New York, 1977).

10. Sterling D. Spero and Abram L. Harris (New York, 1969).

11. *The Black Worker*, 352–53; 374, 375. Gutman states falsely in his preface (viii) that the UMW escaped Spero's and Harris's censure.

12. *International Journal of Politics, Culture and Society*, 2: 2 (Winter 1988):

132–200. The next issue carried a number of replies to Hill, and the one follow-ing it a rejoinder by Hill. See also Herbert Hill, "Race, Ethnicity and Organized Labor: The Opposition to Affirmative Action," *New Politics* 1: 2 (Winter 1987) and the exchanges in the following issue for a discussion of related questions. Hill was not the first to dissent from the white-centric view of the working class: there is a critical tradition among Afro-American historians and publicists going back to Du Bois, Garvey, and Charles H. Wesley. But he was the first to devote major attention to the canonical text of the Gutman school. For other criticisms of the New Labor History on this score, see Lawrence T. McDonnell, "'You Are Too Sentimental': Problems and Suggestions for a New Labor History," *Journal of Social History* 17 (Summer 1984): 629–54. and Michael Kazin, "Marxism and the Search for a Synthesis of U.S. Labor History," *Labor History* 28: 4 (Fall 1987): 497–514. One need not agree with Kazin about the uselessness of the class struggle interpretation as a tool of historical analysis to appreciate his criticisms of the Gutman school.

13. *International Journal of Politics, Culture and Society* 2: 3 (Spring 1989): 369.

14. *International Journal of Politics, Culture and Society* 2: 3 (Spring 1989): 364. I would have preferred that Shulman refer to "white workers" rather than to the "white working class"; a racially defined working *class* is an oxymoron.

15. Bruce Levine, Stephen Brier, David Brundage, Edward Countryman, Dorothy Fennell, Marcus Rediker, Joshua Brown (Visual Editor), *Who Built America? Working People and the Nation's Economy, Politics, Culture, and Society, Volume I: From Conquest and Colonization Through Reconstruction and the Great Uprising of 1877.* The American Social History Project, under the direction of Herbert G. Gutman (New York, 1989). My comments are directed toward this vol-ume only, and especially to Parts Two and Three; there is also a second volume.

16. *Who Built America* I, 415.

17. *Black Reconstruction in America* (New York, 1935), 727.

18. Saxton's earlier work, *The Indispensable Enemy: Labor and the Anti-Chinese Movement in California* (Berkeley, 1971) was a path-breaking challenge to white labor mythology.

19. John Henry was the steel-driving man, subject of "the noblest American ballad of them all," in the words of Pete Seeger, *American Favorite Ballads* (New York, 1961), 82.

20. The quoted words are from E. P. Thompson, "The Making of a Ruling Class," *Dissent* (Summer 1993): 380.

# INDEX

abolitionism, 13, 134–36, 178, 180, 194
n.77, 213 n.72, 224 n.33; and O'Connell,
8–9, 14, 19–21, 23, 26–29; and Irish
Repeal, 10–14, 17–19, 22–23, 26–31;
and white labor, 99, 106–108
Act of Union, 6, 37
Adams, John Quincy, 72, 75, 84, 190 n.37;
quoted, 67, 70
*Address on the Right of Free Suffrage,* 82
*Address to the Working Men of New
England,* quoted, 81
*African Repository,* quoted, 111
Afro-Americans, 40–42, 47, 54–57, 97, 106,
142–43, 178, 179, 180, 196 n.20, 215
n.98, 217 n.121; exclusion from occu-
pations, 100–102, 109–13, 115, 117–19,
216 n.100. *See also* slavery
Alien and Sedition Acts of 1798, 65
Allen, Richard, 9, 14, 19, 22
Allen, Theodore W., 35; *The Invention of
the White Race,* 187–88; quoted, 37
American Anti-Slavery Society, 8, 26
American Republican Club, 149
American Republican Party, 158

Binney, Horace, 152
Binns, John, 62–67, 70–75, 126, 138, 188
n.8; quoted, 62–63, 65, 72, 75
Binns, Joseph, 27
Birdsall, Fitzwilliam, 69
Birney, James G., 9, 189 n.30
Boston *Catholic Diary,* quoted, 13
Boston *Pilot,* 10, 13–14, 21; quoted, 24, 26
Bradburn, George, 17, 22; quoted, 11
Brady, Thomas, quoted, 21
Branagan, Thomas, 51–57; quoted, 52, 53,
54, 55, 56, 57, 142
Brotherhood of the Union, 124

Brown, John, 184
Brownson, Orestes, quoted, 79, 158, 163
Buchanan, James, 16
Buckalew, Charles R., 167
Burns, Anthony, 17, 162

Cadwalader, George, 152
Calhoun, John C., 69, 72, 79, 84
California House Riot, 155–56
Cameron, Simon, 167
Camp William Penn, 167–68
Cassidy, Lewis, 166
Catholic Emancipation, 6, 14, 25
Catto, Octavius, 168, 171
Child, Lydia Maria, 165
citizenship, 41, 65–66, 76
Civil Rights and Force Bills, 173
Civil War, 85, 87–88, 164, 166, 184
Clark, Hugh, 149
Clay, Henry, 72
Collins, John A., 9, 13
*Colored American,* quoted, 109–10
Commons, John R., quoted, 104
Compromise of 1877, 173, 174
Connecticut Colonization Society, 97
Conrad, Robert T., 160, 162
Cooper, Thomas, 66
Crawford, William, 72, 75
Cropper, James, 7

Democratic Party, 67–69, 72, 75, 79,
157–58, 160, 161–63, 167, 169, 170, 172,
173, 174, 181; and nativism, 69, 87, 76;
and slavery, 69, 97, 165–66; and Irish,
75–77, 85, 87, 148, 166; "Peace
Democrats," 165, 166
Diamond, Alex, 27
Dissenters, 35, 36, 38

Donohoe, Patrick, 14
Doran, Joseph M., 27, 138
Dorr, Thomas, 82–84
Douglass, Frederick, 11, 82, 102, 107, 164, 206 n.81; quoted, 111, 165
Duane, William, 66, 142, 202 n.23, 203 n.31
Du Bois, W. E. B., 185, 188, 210 n.28; quoted, 173, 184, 215 n.99
Duffy, John, 171

Emancipation Proclamation, 164
Engels, Frederick, quoted, 25
Evans, George Henry, 78, 79; quoted, 80, 108

Federalist Party, 67, 70, 71, 75, 76; and Irish, 65–66
Female Anti-Slavery Society, 134
Ferral, John, 150; quoted, 104, 105
Ficklin, Orlando B., quoted 87
Fields, Barbara J., 178, 187
Finch, John, quoted 97–98, 99
Fifteenth Amendment, 170
Fisher, Sidney George, quoted, 84, 159, 165–66
Flying Horses Riot, 74, 125–28, 132–33, 139, 141; role of Irish,127, 130, 136
Foner, Philip S., 120
Forten, James, 102, 126, 204 n.59
Fourierism, 78, 205 n.65
Fox, Daniel, 168, 170, 171
Free Soil Movement, 79–80, 85–87, 207 n.86
French Revolution, 63
Friends of Ireland and of Repeal, 27
Friends of Ireland Society, 15
Fuller, James C., 9, 11, 19

Garrison, William Lloyd, 10, 12, 20–21, 28, 29, 31; quoted, 9,11, 14, 16–17, 22–23, 30, 82
Gas Ring, 177
Grattan, Henry, 36, 62
Greeley, Horace, 16
Grund, Francis, quoted, 132
Gunn, Lewis G., quoted, 107
Gutman, Herbert, 180–182, 184

Haiti, 56
Hammond, James H., 69
Handlin, Oscar, *Boston's Immigrants,* 179
Hardy, Thomas, 63
Haughton, James, 9, 23
Hayes, Rutherford B., 173, 174
Henry, Alexander, 163, 167
Hibernian Anti-Slavery Society, 9
Hill, Herbert, 182–83
Hughes, Bishop John J., 77, 86, 153; quoted, 12

Ingersoll, Charles Jared, 148
Ireland, land tenancy in, 34, 35, 36, 37
Ireland, emigration from, 37–40, 45, 55
Irish Address, 6, 17–19, 21–23, 29, 30; quoted, 9–10
Irish Americans, 40–42, 47, 86–87, 88, 89, 99, 109, 116–17, 127–30, 136–38, 140, 150–53, 155, 162, 163–64, 166, 178, 179, 180, 187, 196 n.20; and slavery, 7–14, 16–19, 21–23, 27–31, 162, 166; immigration of, 37–40, 41, 65; as workers, 38–40, 92–96, 97–99, 102–06, 109–13, 115–17, 119–21, 217 n.121; as whites, 59, 69, 70, 96, 111–112, 164; and Democratic Party, 75–77, 85, 87

Jackson, Andrew, 67, 70, 72, 167
Jacksonian Democracy, 68–69, 74, 85, 185
James, C. L. R., 179
James, John W., 15, 16, 18
Jefferson, Thomas, 67–68
Johnson, Frank, 145
Johnson, Richard M., 16, 27, 30

Kansas, debate over slavery, 79
Kelley, Abby, 82, 189 n.20
Keyser, John, 159
Keystone Club, 161, 166–67
"Killers," 144, 155, 160–62
Kneass, Horn R., 163
Know Nothing Party, 157, 162, 167, 224 n.33
Kramer, Samuel, 163

labor, 93–94, 95–96, 97–99, 100, 103–106, 109–110, 117, 126, 137, 150–51, 166; wage labor and slavery, 20, 68–69,

78–81, 85, 96–97, 99, 106–109, 209 n.21, 217 n.1; Irish-American, 38–40, 92–96, 97–99, 102–06, 109–13, 115–17, 119–21; black artisans, 100–02; and race, 111–12, 115–16, 183–86, 215 n.98, 215 n.99, 216 n.100; textile workers, 113–15, 150. *See also* slavery

Law and Order Party, 82–83

Leeds, William, 175

Levin, Lewis, 163

*Liberator,* 9, 11, 17, 22

Lincoln, Abraham, 164, 165, 166, 167

Lippard, George, 156; quoted, 124, 128, 144, 149, 217 n.1

London Corresponding Society, 63–65

Longshoremen's United Benevolent Society, 120

Loyal National Repeal Association, 7, 14, 19, 23, 27

Luther, Seth, 81–84, 103, 107, 108; quoted, 81

Marx, Karl, quoted, 68–69, 205 n.68

Mathew, Father Theobald, 188 n.13

McCall, Peter, 154

McClellan, Gen. George, 167

McCormick, Richard P, quoted, 73

McGee, Thomas D'Arcy, 86

McIlhenny, William, 44, 46–47

McManes, James, 175

McMichael, Morton, 163, 168

McMullen, William, 160–163, 167–176; quoted, 160

Mechanics' Union of Trade Associations, 102–03

Melville, Herman, 108, 190 n.37, 206 n.78, 221 n.45

Mexican War, 84, 142, 161

militias, 142, 145; role in riots, 132–33, 136, 156

Miller, J. P., 11

Miller, Kerby, 39, *Emmigrants and Exiles,* 179, 180

minstrelsy, 42

Missouri Compromise, 67, 74, 162

Mitchel, John, 31

Montgomery, David, quoted, 158

Mooney, Thomas, 20

Moore, Ely, 108

Moyamensing Hose Company, 155, 161–63, 167–71

"Mulhoolyism," 172

Nanny Goat Riot, 151

Nat Turner's Rebellion, 184

*Nation,* 31

*National Laborer,* 108

National Trades' Unions, 107

nativism, 73, 106, 148–49, 150–54, 157, 158, 159, 160, 162, 164, 224 n.33; and Democratic Party, 76; and Irish, 148–49, 150–53, 155, 157

New Labor History, 180–84, 185

New York *Aurora,* 77–78

New York City Draft Riot, 88, 121

New York *Evening Day Book,* quoted, 87

New York *Herald,* 12

New York *Metropolitan Record,* quoted, 88

New York Trades' Unions, 108

New York Working Men's Party, 80

Northumberland *Republican Argus,* 67

O'Connell, Daniel, 6–9, 11–14, 16–31, 62, 74–75, 99, 107, 174; quoted, 7, 23–24, 57

Otis, Harrison Gray, 65–66

Owen, Robert, 80

Painter, Nell Irvin, quoted, 182

"Pardoning Power," 132, 138–39

Parsons, Judge, quoted, 138

Peel, Sir Robert, 24

Penal Codes, 34–35, 36, 195 n.1

Pennsylvania Anti-Slavery Society, 23, 100, 134, 194 n.77

Pennsylvania Hall Riot, 134–36, 138–39, 154

*Pennsylvanian,* 141

People's Party, 167

Philadelphia, 127–30, 155, 226 n.61; civil disorders, 125–27, 133–39, 150–56, 157–60, 164; nativism in, 148–49, 158–59; police force, 154, 156, 159–60, 163–64; consolidation, 156–57; election fraud, 160–62, 163, 169–70; and civil

war, 165
Philadelphia *Aurora,* 66–67, 70
Philadelphia *Bulletin,* 155, 170
Philadelphia *Democratic Press,* 70–74
Philadelphia general strike of 1835, 81, 103–4, 157; role of Irish, 103, 105–6
Philadelphia *Mechanics' Free Press,* 86, 141, 105, 107
Philadelphia *Native American,* 151
Philadelphia *Press,* 170
Philadelphia *Public Ledger,* 135, 139, 152, 159–60
Philadelphia Trades' Union, 105–6
Phillips, Ann, 9
Phillips, Wendell, 9–11, 17–19, 22, 165; quoted, 21
Pickens, Francis W., quoted, 69
Pierce, Franklin, 79
Pleasonton, Col. August James, 134–136; quoted, 134
Polanyi, Karl, quoted, 131
politics; Federalists vs. Republicans, 65–66, 67; slaveholders and Democratic Party, 69; party politics in Pennsylvania, 72–73; Philadelphia elections, 157–58, 160, 161–63, 165, 169–71; civil war, 166–67; Compromise of 1877, 174
Polk, James K., 75
Priestly, Dr. Joseph, 66
Protestant Ascendancy, 35, 37
Purvis, Robert, 27, 141

*Quaker City, The,* 124
Quakers, 148
Quincy, Edmund, 10

race, 35, 37, 173, 178, 185–87, 209 n.19; and Irish, 59, 69, 70, 96, 111–12, 164; "White Republic", 89, 96, 159, 164, 175; and labor, 96–97, 111–12, 164; and slavery, 96–97, 99–02, 164, 210 n.25
race riots, *see* California House Riot; Flying Horses Riot; Pennsylvania Hall Riot; Philadelphia, civil disorders; Temperance March Riot
Randall, Samuel J., 170–74, 176
Reconstruction, 164, 173, 184

Redeemer governments, 173, 174, 175
Registry Act, 169–70
Remond, Charles Lenox, 9, 11
Repeal, 6–7, 18, 24, 28–29; and abolition of slavery, 10–14, 16–19, 21–23, 26–31, 99; repeal societies, 15, 23, 99, in Boston, 17, 30, in New Orleans, 18, 31, in Philadelphia, 18, 23, 26–28, 31, 138, in Louisiana, 19, in Albany, New York, 19, in Mobile, Alabama, 21, in Natchez, Tennessee, 26, in Charlestown, South Carolina, 26, 29, in Baltimore, Maryland, 26, in Cincinnati, Ohio, 28, 29, 99, in Savannah, Georgia, 29, in Portsmouth, Virginia, 31, in Norfolk, Virginia, 31
Republican Party, 69, 70, 72, 75, 76, 87, 158, 167, 169, 170, 172, 173, 174, 226 n.61; and Irish, 65–66, 76, 85; and slavery, 67, 165–166
Reynolds, James, 203 n.31
Rhode Island Suffrage Association, 82–83
Riots of 1844 (nativist), 150–154, 157–60, 164
Roediger, David, *The Wages of Whiteness,* 185, 213 n.71; quoted, 186
Rogers, Nathaniel P., 17
Rowan, Archibald Hamilton, 62
Ruggles, Samuel, 163

Saint Patrick Battalion, 161
Saxton, Alexander, 96; *The Rise and Fall of the White Republic,* 185
Scotch-Irish, 39
Sewall, Samuel, quoted, 65
Seward, William, 16
Shapley, Rufus E., *Solid for Mulhooley,* 172
Shiffler, George, 151, 160
Shulman, Steven, 182
Silcox, Harry C., 170, 172; quoted, 174, 175
slavery, 26, 68, 69, 97, 140–41, 164, 184–85; and Irish-Americans, 7–14, 16–19, 21–23, 27–31, 69, 162, 166; and wage labor 20, 68–69, 78–81, 85, 99–02, 106–09, 173, 209 n.21, 217 n.1; and race, 96–97, 100, 164, 210 n.25
*Slavery in the United States* (Paulding), 107

Smith, Gerrit, 21, 29
Society of United Englishmen, 64
Society of United Irishmen, 36, 64–65, 75
Sojourner Truth, 165
Spartan Association, 77–79, 83
Spirit of the Times, quoted, 152
Still, William, 168
Stevenson, Andrew, 188 n.9
Stokely, William S., 170
Stokes, William, 18, 28; quoted, 26–27
streetcar desegregation, 168
Subterranean, 77; quoted, 78
suffrage, 76, 77, 82–83, 134, 165, 173; in Rhode Island, 82–83
Sumner, Charles, 162
Swift, Mayor John, 106, 135; quoted, 157
Swift, Jonathan, A Modest Proposal, 36

Tammany Society, 75, 77–78
Tandy, James Napper, 62
Tappan, Lewis, 21, 29
temperance, 23, 136–38, 149
Temperance March Riot, 136–138
ten-hour day, 103–07
Texas, annexation of, 26, 29, 57, 62, 78, 85
textile industry, 112, 113–15, 150
Thoreau, Henry, Walden, quoted, 85
Tilden, Samuel J., 173, 174
Tone, Theobold Wolfe, 36
"trinity" houses, 128, 131
"tumultuous republic," 131, 159
Twain, Mark, 145; The Adventures of Huckleberry Finn, 57–59, 184; quoted 58–59, 184
Tyler, John, 30, 78
Tyler, Robert, 16, 27, 29; quoted, 16

underground railroad, 140, 184
unions, 92, 93, 102, 103, 111, 115, 116, 120

United Mine Workers, 181–82
United States Gazette, 153

Van Buren, Martin, 67–68, 79, 85
Vaux, Richard, 148, 162–63, 176
volunteer fire companies, 143–44, 153, 155, 169

Walker, David, Appeal, 184
Walnut Street Jail, 42–51; labor in, 42–44; insurrections in, 44, 46, 51
Walsh, Mike, 77–79, 84; quoted, 78–79
Watmough, John, 163
Webb, Frank J., The Garies and Their Friends, 118, 156
Webb, Richard Davis, 9, 14
Wesley, Charles H., quoted, 112
Whig Party, 67, 75, 148, 157–58, 160, 185; and nativism, 159, 162
"White Republic," 89, 96, 159, 164, 175
Whitman, Walt, 77; quoted, 85–86, 206 n.81
Who Built America, 184
Wilentz, Sean, 77, 182, Chants Democratic, 183
Wilkes, George, 77
Williams, Richard, Hierarchical Structures and Social Value, quoted, 186
Wilmot, David, quoted, 85
Woodward, C. Vann, quoted, 173
Working Man's Advocate, 78, 80, 108
Working Man's Association of England, 107
Working Men's Parties, 102, 105, 106
World Anti-Slavery Convention, 9
Wright, Elizur, quoted, 8
Wright, Fanny, 80
Wright, Isaac H., quoted, 18

Young Ireland, 31